THE TRUE AND COMPLETE STORY OF
'MACHINE GUN'
JACK McGURN

AMANDA J. PARR

THE TRUE AND COMPLETE STORY OF
'MACHINE GUN'
JACK MCGURN

Matador
9 De Montfort Mews
Leicester LE1 7FW, UK
Tel: (+44) 116 255 9311 / 9312
Email: books@troubador.co.uk
Web: www.troubador.co.uk/matador

ISBN 1 905237-13-8

Cover illustration: © Getty Images

Typeset in 11pt Plantin Light by Troubador Publishing Ltd, Leicester, UK
Printed in the UK by The Cromwell Press Ltd, Trowbridge, Wilts, UK

Matador is an imprint of Troubador Publishing Ltd

To my wonderful husband Graham, for all your love and understanding, and for your unquestioning belief in me.

and

In loving memory of Kirsten

CONTENTS

ACKNOWLEDGEMENTS

I would like to express my sincere gratitude to the following people and agencies, all of whom have provided invaluable information throughout the course of my research: without them, this book would have gone no further than the confines of my mind.

Thank you to all the staff at the Chicago Historical Society, the National Archives and Records Administration (NARA) in the Northeast Region, Washington D.C, Great Lakes Region and Maryland. A special thank you goes to the staff of the Freedom of Information – Privacy Acts Section at the FBI, for the veritable mine of priceless information, and to the Office of the Secretary of State of Illinois and The Illinois State Archives. Thank you also to the Office of the Clerk of the Circuit Court of Cook County, the staff of California State Archives and the National Archives Bureau of Prisons' Records. The Illinois Regional Archives Depository and the International Association for the Study of Organized Crime were of immense help to me and to them, I extend my sincerest thanks.

I would like to say thank you also to the Historical Newspaper Archives in New Jersey, for their help in sourcing media accounts of the day.

I must also express my gratitude to Mario Gomes at www.alcapone-museum.com who was immensely helpful, not least in introducing me to John Binder. John's fabulous photo collection was the source for many of the photographs for this book.

A special thank you goes to Eddy Podevijn, proprietor of Wapenhandel Podevijn in Zottegem, Belgium. His passion for firearms afforded me the rare opportunity to fire a 1928 Thompson submachine gun, which enabled me to fulfil a dream, and gave a tangible reality to the legend.

I also wish to say thank you – in fact 'thank you' does not seem to be a strong enough phrase – to my wonderful husband Graham, who has been a constant and unshakeable source of love and support, and who believed in me when it was difficult to believe in myself. I could never have done it without you.

PREFACE

On the surface, the life of 'Machine Gun' Jack McGurn is a straight forward account of the archetypal good-boy-gone-bad, a man who harboured a latent, yet vicious criminality just waiting to explode. Beneath the surface however, lies a myriad of Chinese Whispers, tales that have been told and retold throughout the generations, and no matter how inadvertently, have been twisted and altered with each retelling. The result is a myth filled narrative which, whilst thoroughly entertaining, does not do justice to the compelling reality.

Jack McGurn, or Vincenzo Gibaldi to give him his birth name, was not an inherently evil man, nor was he predisposed to violence, or any other criminality for that matter. Indeed, an unremarkable boy, born to equally unremarkable Sicilian parents is perhaps the best description of how his life began. Yet it is precisely that description which first piqued my curiosity and set me on a five year long journey to find the truth about the life of one of the Chicago Outfit's most enigmatic men.

In the early 1900's, Little Italy on Chicago's Near West Side, could hardly be described as a healthy environment in which to raise a family. Poverty, compounded by the overwhelming xenophobic nature of society, created a daily struggle not to survive, but to simply exist. Those raised in this bold and so called brave 'New World' found themselves without standing in both the old and new social structures, resulting in adolescent and even pre-pubescent boys joining or forming gangs merely to find a sense of belonging. It is here therefore, where the life of Jack McGurn should first set out on the well trodden road that leads first to petty crime, before moving on to violence and eventually murder…but it does not. So how exactly does a boy who reaches the age of eighteen without committing a single criminal act – no matter how petty – evolve into one of mob history's most prolific and notorious hit men?

The answer lies in a volatile combination of the fickle cruelty of fate and the traditional and ancient codes of the Sicilian upbringing: viewing your family as an extension of your own self and having the strength of character to avenge any wrong committed against it. So when, at the tender age of eighteen, McGurn's father was brutally murdered by Black Hand extortionists, his anguished sense of loss was tempered by an innate desire for vengeance. So it is here where Jack McGurn makes his first and somewhat spectacular foray into society's underworld, absorbing the rudimentary education of gangland and steeling himself for the murders he must commit. None of us can ever truly predict the consequences of the choices we make, and Jack McGurn was certainly no different. Never could he have foreseen that the acts he carried out in the pursuit of vengeance and his quest for justice would bring him to the attention – and into the affections – of the most notorious kingpin of organized crime: Al Capone.

McGurn's involvement with Capone's Outfit effectively continued the sense of tradition and history, for Capone's mob was the latest – and indeed the most organized – in a long line of criminal gangs to emerge on the streets of Chicago. From before the Great Chicago Fire of 1871, organized crime had been prevalent in the city, yet where those who had gone before had merely inhabited the streets of the 'Windy City' Capone controlled them. Chicago was at his beck and call, with no corner of the city left free from his tentacles of influence. At the height of his power Capone carried everyone – from the Mayor of Chicago, police captains and judges, to the bell-boys at his luxurious hotel residence – around in his pockets like loose change, and used his power to exploit society's ubiquitously puissant blend of fear and greed. However, by Capone's own admission, it was Jack McGurn, having risen through the ranks of the Outfit and into the crime czar's affections, who was central to that power.

McGurn was treated more as a right hand man or favourite son, much to the envious chagrin of many other high ranking Outfit members. Capone displayed total faith in McGurn's ability as both a bodyguard and a hit man, a faith he repaid in full when he personally saved Capone's life during a bodacious assassination attempt. McGurn's position as an untouchable member of Capone's Outfit was duly secured when he successfully masterminded and executed the most infamous mass murder in the history of gangland: The St. Valentine's Day Massacre.

During the research for this book, I was afforded access to many previously unreleased files, sources of information which proved invaluable when attempting to piece together the fractured and often fragmented world of Jack McGurn. Close examination of the records provided a precious insight into the mind of a man who at the very least could be described as colourful, yet for whom paradoxical is a more apt superlative. For Jack McGurn was not only a man who appeared able to make a distinction between killing and murder, a man whose actions left an indelible impression on criminal history, but he was also a man of incredible tenderness. He was a charmer, a loving husband and doting father, a public benefactor and ruthless killer, a man who delighted in showing everyone around him a good time, but in whom it was in your best interests not to cross swords with.

When I first began the writing of this book, I had in mind to tell each event as it happened, to seek to make sense of the immense volume of information and misinformation, to lay to rest the mythical inaccuracies and, most importantly, to allow you to see the colourful era of prohibition through the eyes of a man who was listed in the top three of America's Public Enemies. Now that the book is finished, I hope that I have achieved the two things which I set out to achieve – to keep you entertained, and to tell you what I believe to be the true and complete story of 'Machine Gun' Jack McGurn.

CHAPTER ONE

THAT TODDLING TOWN

CHICAGO – perhaps the most famous city of America's Midwest – notable for its Jazz and Blues bars, the Sears Tower, the Tribune Tower, the infinite number of State Street restaurants, not to mention the records of the *'godfather of swing'* Frank Sinatra, which have long since assured the city's status of immortality. Chicago is a city that captures the imagination, a city where one can tread in the footsteps of some of history's most famous – and infamous – figures. There is something in the air here, a certain *je ne sais pas* that holds the ability to create magic between people. However, notwithstanding the touristy romanticisms and historical attractions, the *'Windy City'* has become inextricably synonymous with that roaring period in history known as prohibition. In fact, whilst almost eighty years have passed since the sound of machine gun fire died on the city's streets, the infamy and legend of the era remains very much alive; so much so that for the vast majority, the name Chicago conjures up the image of one man – Al Capone.

This fact is certainly true of Hollywood, which has ensured that this irrepressible icon of the 1920's, is never far from the silver screen. Movies such as *'Little Caesar,' 'The Untouchables'* and *'Public Enemy'* have glamorized this criminal genius of his time to such an extent that the audience now invariably regards him as little more than a loveable rogue. Another infamous movie *'Scarface,'* made in 1932, was also purported to portray the life of Capone. The writer however denied this, stating that it was merely a depiction of the gangster life in general rather than a portrayal of an individual. Nevertheless, the movie touched a nerve in America's governmental hierarchy and was banned until after WWII. Yet contrary to popular opinion, Al Capone was not the only, nor was he the first gangster in Chicago. There were others before him and whilst they were, in their own way just as powerful, they were nowhere near as infamous.

★ ★ ★

It was the Potawatomi Indians who laid claim to being the original inhabitants of what the world has come to know as Chicago. Indeed, the very name Chicago is rather a bastardization of the Indian term of *'Checagou,'* literally translated as *'bad smell'* on account of the skunk cabbage that clogged the quagmires feeding into the Chicago River. The Potawatomi held the area as their own until 1670, when, following initial explorations by Jacques Marquette and Louis Joliet, a French trader by the name of Pierre Moreau, erected a cabin as a stopover point for traders on the area where the Chicago River drains into Lake Michigan. Nevertheless, the area remained in the charge of the Indians; indeed over a century would pass before the Potawatomi would see the first permanent settler – a Haitian-American by the name of Jean Baptiste Point de Sable.

Arriving in 1778, Point de Sable is now the man whom historians credit as being the founder of modern Chicago. Between 1778, and 1779, he set up and managed a trading post on the site of Pierre Moreau's stopover point, before accepting a commission by the British Lieutenant Governor Patrick Sinclair to manage the Governor's estate near Detroit, known as *'The Pinery.'* It was to be a post he would hold until around 1785, when he moved back to Chicago to set up home on the site of the present Tribune Tower. From here he farmed and traded, and despite being illiterate, he proved himself to be an excellent farm manager. Before long, his humble farm had been transformed into a sizeable estate. Although the exact point in time is unclear, it is known that he fell in love with and married a Potawatomi Indian girl by the name of Catherine and with whom he had two children – a son named Jean Baptiste Jr. and a daughter named Suzanne. However, in spite of his burgeoning family and prosperous estate, Point de Sable remained a mere tenant, as the region continued to be owned by the indigenous tribe.

Then in 1794, came the *'Battle of Fallen Timbers,'* a war between the Potawatomi and an army led by General Anthony 'Mad Anthony' Wayne. It was the General who would emerge as the victor, claiming as his prize a six square mile tract of Indian land. In 1803, Fort Dearborn was built on the site and in the blink of an eye, the first all white settlement emerged... and the Potawatomi was consigned to history.

The year 1848, brought with it the completion of the Illinois-Michigan Canal, a waterway conjoining the Illinois River with the Chicago River's southernmost tributary. It would prove to be a massive breakthrough with regards to the development of Chicago, for it provided the farmers of the Midwest with access to the eastern markets, a field which had previously been completely out of reach. The newly constructed waterway also provided access – via the Mississippi River – to the as yet untouched cities of New Orleans and St. Louis. It appeared that the emergence of Fort Dearborn had induced Chicago into a proliferation that was almost unstop-pable, for in a mere forty-five years the humble settlement had exploded into the largest city in Illinois, with a population in excess of one-hundred thousand.

During the 1860's, the Chicago Harbour on the Chicago River became *the* major Midwest trading post. More than thirteen-thousand ships a year docked at the harbour, loading and unloading their cargoes of grain, fruits and other foodstuffs. Passenger ships too would often dock at the harbour, only they would unload a cargo of a very different kind: immigrants. These immigrants, originating from Germany, Italy, Sicily, Poland, Russia and Ireland, as well as from numerous other countries, all shared one thing in common: they were all following a dream, the dream of creating a new life in a new world. Whilst it is true that the vast majority of immigrants landed first at New York's Ellis Island, it is also true that their arrival brought with it the realization that their new life was not about to be all that easily created. Many discovered a great prejudice amongst the American people, a preju-dice which although directed at all immigrants, seemed to be primarily aimed at the Italians and Sicilians, whom they regarded as lazy and stupid. It was a belief which was fed by the social studies of the day, with the vast majority painting such a picture that if one did not know any better, one would think that all Italian people were not too dissimilar to Neanderthal man. Even the educated sociologists of the day were generally less impartial than the average citizen. Century Magazine for example, carried a regular column written by an eminent student of sociology named Edward

Alsworth Ross. In one such column he portrayed the Italian and Sicilian immigrants as uncultivated, vulgar and loutish, continuing his contemptuous onslaught with the charge that such people lacked the power to take rational care of themselves and that they were, in his opinion, specimens of mankind far too unintelligent to survive. He went on to inform his readers that these people were better off in their own country, after all, *'they like it there in the squalor filled slums.'* One supposes that Ross never stopped to consider that *'these people'* obviously like it so much in the slums and the squalor that they were fully prepared to risk everything, including their lives, in order to improve their existence by the smallest fraction. The result of this media fuelled perception was that employment was hardly plentiful, after all, who would wish to employ persons from a *'second class race?'*

To combat this ever present problem, many immigrants travelled on to Chicago where, in contrast to New York, narrow-minded bigotry was nowhere near as inbuilt. One of the reasons for this may have been the fact that the city's founding father, Jean Baptiste Point de Sable, was himself a foreigner and whose children were borne of an Indian mother; therefore one could argue that the subsequent generations of native Chicagoans had the mixed blood of their descendants coursing through their veins. Another reason could have been the fact that at that point in time, Chicago was undergoing yet more major development – a kind of metamorphosis – from a rural hick town built on reeking bogs and wetlands, to a thriving industrial city. The Union Stockyards were being created, as was the city's vast passenger railroad system and all of this work required labour, plenty of it and the cheaper the better. The immigrants were only too happy to fill this gap in the market and so on they travelled, still searching for the dream.

The sheer number of immigrants who arrived in Chicago was most easily demonstrable by the seemingly unstoppable population boom. By 1870, the one-hundred thousand strong population had more than tripled to over three-hundred thousand, a third of whom were Italian and Sicilian. Each immigrant group established their own intrinsic area; the Italians and Sicilians inevitably clung together to form two major Latinate quarters which came to be known unimaginatively as Little Italy and Little Sicily, whilst the Germans, Poles, Jews, Blacks and Irish each developed their own racial quarters. A new Chicago was forming, the economy was booming and the transplanted Europeans were on their way to realizing their dream. Life was good.

Then at 9.45pm on October 8, 1871, disaster struck. At 137 DeKoven Street in the barn of Mrs. Catherine O'Leary, a cow accidentally knocked over a lantern causing a small fire. The incident should have ended as quickly as it had begun however, that year had seen an unusually dry summer – there had been not so much as a hint of rain for fifteen weeks – and these conditions, combined with the wooden construction of the vast majority of the city, turned Chicago into a tinder box. Fire soon engulfed the city, its intense heat and ferocity strong enough to allow it to jump the Chicago River not once, but twice. As if the fire itself was not enough to contend with, the flames set the tar works alight, plunging the city into a dense and toxic fog. Even the Chicago Tribune building could not escape the inferno. The Great Fire of Chicago raged out of control for twenty-five hours. When the fire was finally extinguished, it left destruction comparable only to the Great Fire of London in its wake. More than three-hundred people lost their lives, seventeen-thousand, four-hundred and fifty homes were destroyed and ninety-thousand people were rendered homeless. The city estimated that there was in total, around $150,000,000 worth of damage. The somewhat cruel irony was the fact that the source of the Great Fire, namely the O'Leary house, was one of the few buildings to remain in tact; though the barn itself was almost completely destroyed, the actual homestead was virtually untouched by the flames.

In Greek mythology, the Phoenix was a beautiful bird which consumed itself by fire only to rise anew from its ashes. In the dark aftermath that followed the Great Fire, the people of Chicago found their strength and vowed that in the days, weeks, months and even years to come, they would make Chicago rise, like the mythological Phoenix from the ashes of its devastation. The most troubling question was however, what do you do with the rubble from over seventeen-thousand homes?

The answer was to rebuild the city on top of the rubble, thus raising the level of the city by around six feet. Even today, one can still see the effects of this remarkable piece of civil engineering in the form of houses, untouched by the fire, which now have their entrances six feet *below* street level. However, one of the major consequences of raising the city was the emergence of subterranean passageways, which came to be exploited by muggers, thieves and pickpockets who would use them to evade detection. This allegedly gave rise to the term *underworld* as a description for an organized criminal fraternity that exists within society and yet operates below that society's rules. This villainous group inevitably came to need a leader, someone who could coordinate the forces to maximize profit. Step forward Michael Cassius McDonald, a man who would become the inaugural crime czar of Chicago's underworld.

Rather like the modern day Mafia bosses, McDonald ensured that no matter what business venture the young ruffians operated, a percentage of their take was kicked back to him. He did not care much as to what kind of business the hoods engaged in. Whether it was through mugging, burglary or fencing stolen goods, as long as McDonald got his cut he was happy. In return for the kickbacks, his *employees* were guaranteed protection from virtually anyone wishing to clip their criminal wings.

Eventually McDonald gravitated away from the ruffians and went on to own a saloon situated at the intersection of Clark Street and Monroe named *'The Store.'* This was a bar, gambling house and brothel all rolled into one. Placing all three of society's major vices under one roof proved unsurprisingly successful and The Store soon became the largest place of its kind in downtown Chicago. Hardly an unintelligent man, McDonald soon realized the potential of the alliance of crime and compliant politicians and before long, many of the city's upstanding political figures were boosting their income at the expense of McDonald. Over time the alliance became so successful that the McDonald backed Mayor of Chicago, Carter Harrison, served four consecutive terms in office from 1897, to 1903, ousting Mayor Medill who was campaigning on the *'Republican Reform Bill.'* Mayor Medill had vowed to rid Chicago of vice, liquor and crime, an obvious disaster for McDonald should he succeed, and so the crime czar had used all his political capital to nip the problem in the bud. Notwithstanding this fact, saloons and politics were not the only interests that McDonald had. His other great love was sports, in particular boxing and as the years went by and his wealth and power increased, he eventually provided the backing for John L. Sullivan to make his bid for the Heavyweight World Championship in 1892. Whilst this partnership between gangster and boxer was certainly high profile, it was hardly the first and most definitely would not be the last.

Very little else is known of Michael Cassius McDonald, other than he died of natural causes in 1907, and left by all accounts, a somewhat sizeable fortune. McDonald was eventually succeeded by James 'Big Jim' O'Leary, the son of Catherine O'Leary, the owner of the cow which caused the Great Fire. It appears somewhat ironic that the mother of the then most powerful man in the Chicago underworld had once indirectly destroyed the city almost to the point of no return. It could be argued that over time gangsters would continue to destroy the city, though admittedly not by fire.

Like every major city, Chicago had its vice districts – Satan's Mile, the Willows and the Sands – to name but a few. Whilst these areas openly and brazenly existed, it was an area named the Levee which became the most prominent and would continue to be so, even throughout the reign of Al Capone. The Levee covered the blocks between Clark Street and Wabash Avenue and from Eighteenth to Twenty-Second Streets, taking up the downtown area and the Near South Side. If viewed from above, it was essentially a square, a square of vice rather like the red light district in the Amsterdam of today. The bordellos located in the Levee were designated by a red lantern which was hung over the door, this supposedly being how the 'red light district' came to be so called. Political control in the Levee was at that time in the hands of two of the most incorrigibly corrupt politicians ever to set foot in Chicago. They were Michael 'Hinky Dink' Kenna and 'Bathhouse' John Coughlin.

Michael Kenna, whose nickname was Midwest slang meaning 'tiny' or 'frail,' began his working career as a newspaper boy. To look at the man, it was easy to see how his nickname came to be acquired; barely five feet one inch tall and with a slight build and thin, wispy moustache, Kenna was the image of ill health. This perception was however, completely fallacious and Kenna soon moved on to own and run a saloon called the 'Working Man's Exchange.' The Exchange was a two floor property – the first floor housing the saloon itself, whilst the second floor was home to all manner of waifs and strays – from 'cardsharps' or professional gamblers, to tramps, vagrants and down-on-their-luck entrepreneurs. These people did not pay rent and, when Kenna ventured into politics the reason became crystalline, for these unfortunates, shunned by society, provided the sure votes that could win or deny a certain politician his seat.

John Coughlin began his working life as a rubber or masseur in the Palmer House Baths, working his way up to eventually owning his own bathhouse, hence the nickname. At six feet two inches and blessed with the build of a professional wrestler, Coughlin was the proverbial gentle giant. Despite his immense size, it could be said that Coughlin was given over to rather effeminate tendencies; indeed he came to be renowned for his aesthetically atypical and often outrageous dress sense.

It was during this era that the term *'racket'* reportedly came into use. It stemmed from a practice common amongst corrupt businessmen, whereby a benefit fund would be set up by the businessman in question and on behalf of some deserving cause or other. A benefit dinner or ball would then be arranged, with a set price for tickets and the proceeds going to the stipulated cause. Of course, all the monies somehow ended up in the coffers of the organizers, supposedly unbeknown to the partygoers. These events often became rowdy, so much so that they came to be known as *'rackets'* on account of the level of noise. Today the word *'racket'* has become widely used in the context of describing an illegal business, indeed the New Oxford Dictionary dictates that the meaning of the word racket is *'a way of making money etc, by dubious or illegal means.'* However, it also goes on to state that a racket can be nothing more mendacious than a *'game'* or *'a line of business.'* Yet when one researches the word *'racketeer'* it is clearly stated that is a *'person who operates a dishonest scheme.'* The United States Code, Title 18, elaborates on this, stating that *'racketeering activity' means (A) any act or threat involving murder, kidnapping, gambling, arson, robbery, bribery, extortion, dealing in an obscene matter or dealing in a controlled substance or listed chemical (as defined in section 102 of the Controlled Substances Act) which is chargeable under State Law and punishable by imprisonment of more than one year.'*

Taking the lead from Michael McDonald, O'Leary, Kenna and Coughlin, or *'The Lords of the Levee'* as they came to be known, continued with the partnership of organized crime and politics. O'Leary handed overall control of the Levee, both political and criminal, to Kenna and Coughlin in return for a kickback of the sizeable profits. Between them, Kenna and Coughlin ran a protection racket in the Levee, providing political and legal protection to all those plying their trade within the district, for a fee of course. With the proceeds of this racket, a Defence Fund was created and two lawyers kept on a retainer to ensure that, should any of the inhabitants of the Levee be arrested, legal representation would always be on hand, twenty-four hours a day, seven days a week. Handing over control of the Levee proved to be a major coup for O'Leary. The Levee was flourishing, with now more than two hundred houses of ill repute operating within its domain. *'The Little Green House'* and *'The Bucket of Blood'* were just two of the colourful names of the bordellos housed within its borders. However, the areas social center was most definitely *'Friedburg's Dance Hall'* and whilst it may not have been the largest address in the vicinity, it was certainly the most raucous. Standing on Twenty-Second Street, Friedburg's Dance Hall housed a saloon with dancing and gambling and a separate section on the first floor for 'other activities.' The Levee was on a roll; there seemed to be an endless supply of money flowing into the coffers and business in general was on the up and up. Things were going well... for a while.

Public opinion is like a wild animal; it can turn against you at any time and usually without warning. Protests by the religious sections of the community were pricking the city's conscience, culminating in the Church Federation of Chicago, which comprised over 600 churches located throughout the Chicago area, pressuring the Mayor of Chicago to investigate vice conditions within the city. They claimed that tales of forced prostitution abounded, and whilst it was clear that many of the girls employed within the vice trade were acting of their own free will, a study by the Federal Government learned that two-hundred and seventy-eight girls under the age of fifteen had been rescued from the Levee, having been drugged, kidnapped and forced into the prostitution trade. The result of this study was the creation of the Mann Act. Named after its author – a congressman, James Robert Mann – the act made the transportation of women across state lines for immoral purposes a Federal offence. Before long, the pressure became too great and by the end of 1904, every vice area in Chicago had been closed for good, or so it seemed.

Another social problem in Chicago was not going to be so easily solved, primarily because it concerned just a single section of the community, namely the Italians and Sicilians. In Italian, this problem was known as *'La*

Mano Nera,' which translates as *'The Black Hand.'* The Black Hand was not, as is commonly believed, an organized criminal body. Rather, it was a group of freelance extortionists who sought to exact tribute from wealthy Italian or Sicilian businessmen. Their modus operandi was simple. The intended victim would be sent a polite, yet formulaic letter which stated that the anonymous sender knew the recipient to be a kind and reasonable man and as such, also knew that he would not mind making a standard contribution to the sender's equally anonymous cause. In case the recipient failed to appreciate the veiled threat, the letter was signed with either an inky black handprint or another sinister symbol, such as skull and crossbones.

In spite of the letters' polite articulation, The Black Hand was not averse to resorting to more menacing threats should the original letter be ignored. Throughout Chicago's Little Italy and Little Sicily, Black Hand murders, bombings and kidnappings could hardly be considered an uncommon occurrence. In Little Italy, the crossroads of Milton Street and Oak Street became chillingly known as *'Death Corner'* due to the vast number of Black Hand murders which took place there. In the fifteen months between January 1910, and March 1911, there were thirty-eight Black Hand related murders, all of which took place at Death Corner. Oak Street still remains to this day, however it appears that Milton Street has long since been consigned to the annals of history.

Little Italy's macabre sites did not end there, for there was also the hauntingly named *'Dead Man's Tree.'* This was a Poplar tree standing on Loomis Street and upon which The Black Hand took to posting the names of their next victims. This course of action generally created the desired effect of shattering the nerves of the proposed victim, thus making them an easier target. The acutely superstitious inhabitants of Little Italy believed that the souls of the dead hung upon Dead Man's Tree and haunted Death Corner and as such, avoided these areas like the plague. The Black Hand's victims were not however, restricted to the rich yet unobtrusive citizens. Occasionally, it was a more public figure which fell into *La Mano Nera's* sights.

One such figure was the renowned and respected opera singer, Enrico Caruso. In early 1913, the fabulous artist was performing at an engagement in New York. Following his appearance, a typical Black Hand threat was delivered to his dressing room. Caruso considered it senseless to inform the proper authorities – as did many prominent victims – and promptly paid the $2,000 demand. The Black Hand now considered Caruso fair game and the great tenor promptly received a supplicate, only this time there was a *'pay or die'* message attached. Rightly fearing for his life, Caruso notified the police who wasted no time in setting a trap. Upon their instructions, the operatic maestro paid the said amount, leaving it as arranged under the steps of the theater. When the extortionists came to collect their dough, the net closed in. It emerged that the two men who had been captured in the sting had no criminal record, nor had any links with organized crime indeed, they were completely unknown to any law enforcement agencies. This event serves as a perfect example as to just how freelance *La Mano Nera* actually was.

The vast majority of Italians had been brought up to be only too aware of *La Mano Nera*. Like the Mafia, its genesis was in Sicily though it had over time, transplanted itself into American society. However, unlike the Mafia, *La Mano Nera* would in time, fade into obscurity.

The year was now 1915, and James O'Leary was gone. It is not known how exactly 'Big Jim' met his end, though it is known that he was laid to rest in Chicago's Mount Olivet Cemetery, alongside his mother, father and sister. Ironically, it seemed that one 'Big Jim' had made way for another, with James 'Big Jim' Colosimo filling the void left by O'Leary. Colosimo too undertook a partnership with criminal stalwarts Kenna and Coughlin, a union which proved to be more powerful than anything that had gone before. With their backing, William Hale Thompson – perhaps the most crooked elected official in Chicago's already colourful history – was elected Mayor during that year's primary. Thompson was an advocate of the *'open town'* policy, whereby anything and everything was allowed. With the political climate securely under his control, Colosimo's empire flourished. He took to affecting a glamorous image, eventually wearing so many diamonds on his ample frame that people came to know him as *'Diamond Jim.'*

Colosimo opened a restaurant located at 2126 South Wabash Avenue, called the Colosimo Café. The restaurant emerged as *the* place to see and be seen. The stars of the era came to eat and perform there and before long the Colosimo Café was packed to the rafters each and every night. Today, whilst

South Wabash Avenue still remains, the building which once stood at 2126 can now sadly only be seen in historical books and photographs.

By mid 1920, Colosimo had discovered that his success had brought with it some unwelcome observers, namely the dreaded *La Mano Nera*. Initially he ignored the letters and their velvet threats however, when the threats became too menacing to ignore, Colosimo sent for his nephew in New York, a man named John Torrio. Upon his arrival, Torrio realized that the problem was worse than he had anticipated and informed his uncle that he would need help in resolving the matter, but that he would only use his own people. Colosimo gave Torrio the permission to import anyone he believed necessary in order to rid him of the parasitic menace. This Torrio did, sending a message to New York that he needed someone trustworthy and reliable to come to Chicago to work alongside him. A young man stepped into the fray, a man whom Torrio had known for a good many years now, someone who had run errands for him whilst he was still a young boy. This young man had good reason to leave New York, for at that time he was under investigation as the prime suspect in the murder of a small town hood named John Howard, who had been shot dead in a downtown bar. Torrio, knowing that he could trust the young man implicitly, gave his permission for him to make his way over to the Midwest. A few days later, the young man took his first steps on the streets of Chicago. His name was Al Capone.

All of this was of course only the beginning. Chicago, like a well crafted set was merely setting the stage for the epic saga which was to come. Corrupt as they were, 'Hinky Dink' Kenna and 'Bathhouse' Coughlin were merely cogs turning in the urban machine. Native Chicagoans would see new *'Lords of the Levee'* indeed they would see new *'Lords of Chicago.'* The play that was about to acted out would fascinate the public and engender a morbid enchantment with the gangster. Obsequies and gangster chic would lend an intense meaning and excitement to the times. It was a time like no other, a one off occurrence that possibly would never be repeated. This was a story which would live on in the memory of people for decades to come…if not forever.

CHAPTER TWO
COMING TO AMERICA

"Give me your tired, your poor,
Your huddled masses yearning to breathe free
The wretched refuse of your teeming shore
Send these, the homeless, tempest tossed to me
I lift my lamp beside the golden door"

So reads the last verse of the poem *'The New Colossus'* by American poet Emma Lazarus, which is inscribed at the foot of the Statue of Liberty. Given to America as a gift from France in 1884, and erected on October 28, 1886, *'Lady Liberty'* or the Statue of Liberty as she is more commonly known was, to many of the immigrants who landed on the shores of America, *the* most awe inspiring site in the world. Standing fifty meters high and holding aloft, in her right hand a torch, a symbol of freedom, her heavenly face declared that they had arrived – after many long and arduous days at sea – at their destination; that they had succeeded in their quest and had made it to the New World.

For a little over two and a half millennia, the island of Sicily – the largest island in the Mediterranean – has known violence and very little else. The people have waged a constant battle to remain true to their heritage, as they witnessed their beautiful homeland succumb to invasion after invasion. At one time or another, the Greeks, Phoenicians, Carthaginians, Romans, Barbarians, Moors (Arabs) and Normans, have all claimed Sicily as their dominion. Each invader brought with them their own unique form of destruction, crippling the economy, raping the landscape and each time leaving the people with less and less of themselves. Yet of all the invaders who came to the island, it was the Greeks who made the most indelible impression, not just upon the land, but on its history, its folklore and undoubtedly its people. In certain instances one finds that the Greek and Sicilian histories are almost inextricably linked; for example, Archimedes, the distinguished and esteemed Greek mathematician, was in fact born in Syracuse in 287BC. Indeed, Greek mythology overflows with accounts and references to Sicily, such as the Cyclops – the beleaguering pestilence of Odysseus – who is said to have inhabited Mount Etna, whilst the Straits of Messina that separate the Italian mainland from the island of Sicily, were sailed by the mythological Argonauts, immortalized in Don Chaffey's brilliant 1963, epic *'Jason and the Argonauts.'* Hercules is also said to have swam that same stretch of water, whilst the Arethusa spring that lies deep in the heart of Syracuse, is said to be the Greek nymph of the same name, who was changed into the spring by her lover Artemis, in order for her to escape the attentions of the river god, Alpheus. As we will later discover, even in relatively modern history, the links between the Greeks and the Sicilians are the ties that bind.

The Sicilian people, having finally become accustomed to the Greek way of life, then found themselves being invaded by the Romans. Upon arrival, the Romans introduced a prohibition on Christianity, a serious problem for a people for whom Christianity was the dominant religion. It was a decision which would engender the first major struggle of the Sicilian people, a struggle that would see many native citizens martyred in the quest purely to be in control of their own nation, religion and destiny. The Sicilian people eventually emerged victorious, when Emperor Constantine finally lifted the Christianity ban in 313AD. The Roman armies abandoned Sicily soon after, preferring to concentrate on the conquest of the as yet untouched Eastern lands, such as Constantinople. However, the Sicilians were not alone for long, as the island was once again forced to yield to the invading forces of the Barbarians, Vandals and Ostrogoths, though the reign of these would-be conquistadors was relatively short lived.

The curse of the invaders was exacerbated by the natural phenomenon that is Mount Etna. Throughout all the human struggles she continued to erupt, destroying anything and everything and constantly shaping the already battle scarred landscape to her own design. As a result of all these hardships, the Sicilian people grew in their resilience, soaking up every nuance of mankind and becoming knowledgeable of Mother Nature. Most importantly, they learned that it was better to remain silent lest any potential enemies discover your innermost thoughts. Indeed, over the centuries the Sicilians have developed their own, rather unique proverbs – words of wisdom which provide a window into the psyche of these Southern Mediterranean's. Proverbs such as *'Flies cannot fly into a closed mouth'* and *'Never trust your friend unless your friend is a mute or a dog,'* displays the Sicilian's preference for a code of silence. Another, *'Don't become a sheep unless you want to become a wolf's meal,'* seems to underline the desire purely to be themselves and to resist the obvious temptation to follow the will of their overlords, many of whom the people had seen trampled underfoot.

The Sicily of the late 1800's, found that the ordinary citizens were virtually being starved, with the vast majority of the essential foodstuffs being prioritized for their rulers. In rural areas, the feudal system headed by the fearsome *'gabellotti,'* saw to it that even those who were able to make their living through farming, were eventually ruined by the exorbitant land taxes that they were forced to pay. These hardships were aggravated by the fact that Sicily, along with its sister country Italy, was rapidly becoming *the* most overcrowded place in Europe, with the incessant increase in numbers serving to ensure that the already meager employment became ever more scarce.

One of the thousands of citizens feeling the pinch was a young man named Angelo Gibaldi. Also known as Tommaso, or Thomas, Angelo was born in 1885, in the southern coastal fishing village of Licata, and was a true Sicilian in every sense of the word. Throughout his childhood, fishing had been the family business and having helped his father on the boats since he was just old enough to walk, he was fully conversant with the rudiments of the trade and thus well equipped to take over the family business when the time came.

In 1903, when Angelo was eighteen years old, he married his childhood sweetheart, Giuseppa Verderame – also known as Josephine – two years his junior and from the neighbouring village of Gela. In October of the same year, Josephine discovered she was pregnant and, on July 2, 1904, gave birth to a healthy baby boy. Upon this, their first born son, they bestowed the somewhat appropriate name of Vincenzo, meaning *'conqueror.'*

Delighted as they were by the birth, the new parents knew that they were now faced with a colossal dilemma. Angelo realized that many things had changed since his father's time, when fishing provided a family with a more than adequate salary. He knew that today, there was no way he could possibly raise a family on a fisherman's income; he also knew that decisions had to be made and that they had to be made post haste. Following lengthy discussions with Josephine, Angelo saw what he had to do. There was little option but to make the journey that so many of his countrymen had already made, across the vast ocean to the land they called America. He was not however, prepared to risk the safety of his wife and child, and so a hard to bear yet sensible plan was formed. Angelo would leave for America alone, he would find work, set up a home and then and *only* then, would he send for Josephine and Vincenzo. (Research shows that Angelo was actually due to travel to America prior to the birth of Vincenzo, on November 2, 1903. His name appears on the manifest of the passenger ship, *Phoenicia*, where he states that he is married, but with no dependants. However, his name was then crossed off the list, meaning that for some reason, possibly that they had discovered that Josephine was pregnant with Vincenzo, he did not travel that day)

Vincenzo was just eight months old when Angelo left the small fishing village for good and set off to create a new life for himself and his family: his destination, America. Angelo could never have known whether his plan of starting again in a new and foreign country would work out, for whilst it was true that many of his countrymen – one and half million in fact since 1900, – had sought out a new life in America in the same way that he was about to do, forty percent had returned after having found it more difficult than they had imagined to start again. Notwithstanding this fact, many immigrants simply went to America to find work, with the intention of returning to their homeland after perhaps a few months, considerably richer than when they left. As many of the Italian and Sicilian immigrants were considered unskilled and had barely a basic education, a vast number of them only managed to obtain work of the hard, physical type, for which there was but minimal pay. Angelo was different, not just in the fact that he was travelling to America with the intention of remaining there, but also that he could read and write his own native language, a factor which gave him a considerable advantage over the vast majority of men, women and children that had set off from the ports of Naples and Palermo. English was of course another matter, but it seems only natural that he would be eager to learn, especially if it meant bringing the dream another step closer. Although Angelo was willing – if not compelled – to take the gamble, he was less inclined to put his family through the upheaval without first knowing whether it would be worth it. So, on February 22, 1905, Angelo set sail from Naples aboard the passenger ship *Napolitan Prince*, bound for America. He did not know, indeed he could not have known, that Josephine was pregnant for a second time. One wonders if he had known, whether history would have ultimately been written differently.

The *Napolitan Prince* – a two-thousand and nine-hundred gross ton vessel – was built in 1889, for the Portuguese company Mala Real Portugueza and was originally named the *Rei de Portugal*. In 1902, she was sold to the British Prince Line who renamed her as the Napolitan Prince. Travelling at a top speed of twelve knots, her voyage to America would last a total of seventeen days, time spent in opulence and comfort should you be wealthy enough to be one of just twenty-five first class passengers. For Angelo Gibaldi however, such wealth could be found only in the unadulterated confines of his dreams; indeed, it had taken months of scrimping and saving just to come up with the $24 needed for his third-class ticket.

It was hardly an exaggeration to say that the third-class or '*steerage*' passengers were afforded no luxury whatsoever on board the ships. Steerage conditions were crowded and unsanitary, with the passengers being treated more like cattle than people; many accounts claimed that the immigrants were jammed into the berths so tightly, that they barely had room to turn around. Before embarkation, the would-be passengers were asked a total of twenty-nine questions, including name, age, marital status, the reason for travel, whether they held a pre-paid ticket, whether they had any relatives already residing in the United States and if they were suffering from any disability or communicable disease. The manifest for the passengers and crew of the Napolitan Prince shows that in response to these questions, Angelo stated that he had a cousin – also named Angelo – residing in Brooklyn, with whom he intended to stay. Bizarrely however, the ship manifest also reveals that Angelo either claimed, or the presiding officer believed, that he was unable to read and write, yet various other documents deem this to be false.

The Napolitan Prince housed five steerage berths, all of which were located in the hold. On the day that Angelo Gibaldi began his epic voyage to the New World, each berth held its maximum capacity of three-hundred men, women and children. Here they were expected to sleep, live, bathe and eat, with access to the upper, more opulent decks, strictly prohibited. With so many souls sharing the same cramped space and with little or no ventilation, the heavy, dank air felt increasingly leached of its life giving oxygen. When it came to food, the general rule was that you got what you paid for and whilst the provisions were undoubtedly wholesome, they certainly bore little, if any resemblance to the menus offered to the more wealthy passengers. The other amenities were less than standard to say the least; just six toilets were available to the fifteen-hundred steerage passengers and only cold sea water was provided with which to bathe. A great many of the immigrants spent almost the entire voyage lying in their bunks suffering from seasickness, yet as a fisherman, it is unlikely that such a condition ever bothered Angelo. Naturally, with such a lack of regard for basic hygienic facilities, around two percent of passengers arriving at the shores of America were denied entry due to sickness, much of which had been contracted on board the ships. As a result, many shipping companies took to giving compulsory vaccinations and wash downs with disinfectant, to all steerage passengers before they were allowed to board. One can imagine – after enduring over two weeks at sea, in such harsh, contaminated conditions – the physical exhaustion and mental fatigue of the tempest tossed souls as they entered the port of New York and gazed for the first time, upon the serene face of Lady Liberty.

Designated as the first Federal Immigration Station by President Benjamin Harrison, Ellis Island opened its doors for the first time on New Years Day, 1890. Just a few hours later, a fifteen year old Irish girl by the name of Annie Moore, became the first of millions of immigrants to be processed there. Indeed, between 1890, and 1952, twelve million immigrants passed through its doors, many of whom discovered that their ordeal, rather than coming to an end, was in fact only just beginning.

A great many immigrants came to know Ellis Island as *'The Island of*

Tears,' a somewhat unforgiving name, yet one which was not altogether unjustified. Following their arrival at the pier, Angelo Gibaldi, together with the rest of the exhausted travellers were then transported by barge to the island's immense receiving halls…and it was here that the uncertainty and confusion set in. Inside the receiving halls the immigrants were ushered into orderly lines however, the immigration officers failed to appreciate the fact that many people were travelling as an entire family. Therefore, it was not uncommon to find that families had been separated into different lines, an action which merely added to the already overwhelming sense of displacement and trepidation. It was also claimed that many of the officers took to pushing and even beating the immigrants, should they fail to stay in line or if they became too vocal in expressing their consternation at being parted from their husbands or wives and children.

Finally, and after many hours of waiting in line surrounded by screaming children, tearful mothers and cantankerous officers, Angelo Gibaldi arrived at the processing desk. Here he was cross examined on his answers to the twenty-nine questions he had been asked prior to embarkation, seventeen days earlier. It was a nerve wracking time, for should he fail to answer any question correctly, or if he was deemed suspicious either in character or body language, he would be ushered aside and kept for further inspection. This process lead to a great many immigrants often being kept back and was perpetually confounded by the fact that, aside from those travelling from England or Ireland, the vast majority could not speak a word of English. Naturally, the immigration service did their best to provide interpreters, yet these knew only the basic language at the very least and were almost incapable of understanding the numerous dialects that spilled in a constant garble from the mouths of the fatigued and agitated migrants. Indeed, it is probable that the immigration service holds the key to solving a little mystery surrounding the spelling and pronunciation of Angelo Gibaldi's name. Whilst many records list his name as Angelo Gibaldi, an equal number list him as Angelo Gebardi. This can be explained by the fact that the immigration officers at Ellis Island, in a desperate attempt to work efficiently through the immense backlog of passengers, merely wrote down the migrants names phonetically. Therefore, when one imagines the name Gibaldi being pronounced in a heavy, southern Sicilian accent, it is easy to understand how, amongst all the noise and confusion, it could have been misheard as Gebardi.

Assuming he answered all his questions correctly, Angelo would then have been taken in front of a doctor who would perform a medical inspection that was so hurried, they became known as *'six second physicals.'* Anyone with even the slightest hint of infection or disease, was either sent back to their homeland or doused in disinfectant and kept in quarantine until the malady had been cured, which in some cases took up to six weeks. Today, it seems almost akin to the quarantine laws that certain countries bestow upon animals. Of course, all of this took a great deal of time; the records show that even if Angelo's papers were found to be in order and he himself to be in reasonably good health, the Ellis Island procedure would have taken between four and five hours.

The records are a little vague to say the least, when it comes to detailing whether Angelo Gibaldi's six second physical diagnosed any ailments, or whether he came ashore exhausted and homesick but otherwise in the best of health. The one fact that the records do tell us however, is that after going through the pantomime which was the immigration proceedings, he found himself in the vast, sprawling metropolis that is New York City. Once there, as he had previously stated, he intended to stay with his cousin, and so like the majority of the displaced souls of his homeland, Angelo gravitated towards an area now known as Little Italy. It is somewhat paradoxical that despite the fact that this peoples greatest desire was to build a better life, they were at the same time creating a world not too dissimilar from the one they had recently left. If it was possible to look into their minds, it may have been discovered that these immigrants wanted the best that this brave New World could offer – in terms of home comforts, wealth and opportunity – whilst at the same time wishing to feel as though they had never left their native land. Within their world however, there were no prejudices, the people stuck together and helped each other out. It was as the world used to be, when community spirit was not something which was discussed in past tense.

However, in the city outside their world, the prejudices encountered were immense, yet subtle in their own way. For example, the look that would be thrown at the stranger with the dark complexion who had just entered a store, or the way in which a man would protectively pull away his wife or girlfriend so that she may not have to suffer the indignity of brushing past one with an extraneous appearance. Certain individuals would even cross the street to avoid sharing the same stretch of pavement with such a penurious soul. Very few people would actually go so far as to say anything, but the perception and body language spoke louder than a thousand tongues. Unemployment and poverty amongst the immigrant community soared to disproportionate levels, with very few business owners wishing to employ a *'lazy, stupid, foreigner.'* The racism of the average citizen could be attributed to their feeling that they were being, for want of a better word, invaded; a feeling not too surprising, given the fact that by 1920, one in four people in New York was an immigrant. So suffocating was this everyday society, that New York gave one the feeling of entrapment and it was in part because of this, that Angelo decided to quit the *'Big Apple'* in order to try his luck in the *'Windy City,'* wherefrom stories of plentiful work abounded.

As a newly arrived immigrant with very little money, less than $10 by his own admission, it is likely that Angelo would have made the journey from New York to Chicago via river boat. Whilst this was certainly the cheapest form of travel, the journey of over fifteen-hundred miles along first the Hudson, then the Ohio, Illinois and finally the Chicago River would have been nonetheless arduous, taking approximately thirteen days. Undoubtedly, Angelo would have been immensely relieved when, at long last, the boat docked in the Chicago Harbour.

Upon leaving the Harbour, Angelo once again found himself in the world within a world of Chicago's Little Sicily. Although Chicago is certainly far removed from New York, some of the xenophobic prejudices remained and it was with more than a slight sense of disillusionment that Angelo once again found work to be somewhat limited. At the same time however, he realized that a great many of his countrymen and women were unable to read or write, whilst he was fully articulate in the written word. He also saw that like himself – once the homesickness set in – these people were desperate to keep in touch with the families and friends that they had left behind. Certainly not a dim-witted man, Angelo put these two facts together and before long, came up with a business of reading and writing letters for his friends, neighbours, in fact anyone who felt the need to contact their loved ones. As a business, there was obviously a fee for this service and although paltry by today's standards, the money nevertheless went towards his primary overhead: the $3 a week rent on a small tenement apartment located on South Sangamon Street in the heart of Little Sicily. Today, the figure of $3 a week is so inconsequential as to be hardly noticed, yet when one takes into account the fact that in 1905, the bulk of the populace earned on average between $10-$15 per week, at the very least the rent alone took up just under a third of their income. It is highly unlikely however, that Angelo was making anywhere near this level of income solely through the business of reading and writing letters. For this reason, he required a further salary, yet as we have already seen, employment amongst the immigrant community was limited to say the least. Still, Angelo was both patient and persistent, and was prepared to go to any lengths (including changing his surname to the more socially acceptable French family name DeMory) in order to bring his dream just that one step closer. Finally, after many days of asking, of affecting ignorance at the disdainful looks that were shot in his direction, and asking again, he eventually obtained employment in a small café on the outskirts of Little Sicily.

His new employer was a Greek man, with the rather colourful name of Fury Argolia. The Hellenic populace were generally just as frowned upon as the Italians and Sicilians, occasionally more so considering the fact that their complexions were often darker than those of their Latin counterparts and as such, completely unnatural to the *'white'* Americans. For this reason, the close relationship between those of Hellenic and Sicilian descent continued to be maintained. Fury owned a café located at 960 West Harrison Street, on the border between Little Sicily and Greek Town, a road which today forms part of the campus of the University of Illinois at Chicago. Angelo's duties were of the menial variety, such as the washing of dishes and the cleaning of the tables and floor. It could hardly be described as a glamorous occupation, but Angelo knew that if he were to be able to send for his family as he so desperately wished, it was a job he had to do. In addition, it was providing him with the funds that one day, he hoped, could be used to start a business of his own.

Back in Sicily, Josephine was now heavily pregnant with their second child, whilst Vincenzo was a healthy toddler of fourteen months. In Sicilian culture, family plays an important – if not *the* most important – role, with title of *'grandmother'* or *'grandfather'* being taken extremely seriously, in contrast to the more modern and somewhat flippant terms of endearment. As such, during Angelo's absence, both Josephine's and Angelo's parents saw to it that she, together with Vincenzo and their unborn grandchild, were financially and emotionally cared for. This indeed put a strain on the family coffers, especially as Josephine's parents still had her seven year old brother to care for. Every month however, Angelo would send whatever money he could afford back home, whilst any further gaps in the finances were filled by Josephine herself who, as a skilled seamstress, regularly took in piece-work for the garment factories in neighbouring Agrigento. Notwithstanding the financial hardships, Josephine missed Angelo terribly and longed for the day when they could be reunited; a longing so powerful, that it caused her heart to ache with an acute, physical pain for which – as anyone who has ever been in love will testify – there is no known cure.

Meanwhile, Angelo was still working at the café on West Harrison Street, spurred on each day by the dream of securing both his and his family's future, by one day owning his own business. He knew that the road towards this goal would be long and laborious, yet if he could by any means achieve it, then the trials and tribulations that had so far faced him on this journey, would pale into insignificance. Angelo knew of no one from his country who owned their own business in this New World, and he knew that for himself to do so would be a major step forward. It was this ideal which became his sole driving ambition. Every hour of every day – each minute that the café was open – Angelo was there, working like a dog and sweating like the proverbial pig. He made sure that he kept up the rent payments, but other than that, lived on the bare minimum. As meals were free to the employees during working hours, Angelo ate at the café. In the winter when he went home, he refused to heat the small tenement room any more than was absolutely necessary until eventually, he had saved what he believed to be enough money to support a young family. A letter – together with a pre-paid ticket – was immediately sent to Sicily, informing Josephine that she should begin making plans for the journey to the New World.

November 7, 1906, two months after receiving word that she could join her beloved husband, Josephine Gibaldi, along with her two sons – Vincenzo now two years old and Salvatore who at five months old, was still a babe in arms – and her now eight year old brother Francesco, boarded the passenger ship *The Gregory Morch*, destined for America. (The records concerning this voyage are a little confusing, indeed, it is almost impossible to find any records which substantiate the fact that The Gregory Morch actually existed. Upon closer examination however, it appears that the reason for this is that the ship, built in 1889, by the Fairfield Company Ltd. of Glasgow, was originally named the *S.S. Munchen*. However, on February 3, 1902, whilst on her way to the Suez Canal, she ran aground on Yap Caroline Islands. She was subsequently re-floated and sold to the Northern SS Company of Russia, who renamed her *The Gregory Morch*) It is also somewhat unclear as to why Josephine's brother was taken along on the voyage, yet it appears that the most likely explanation is also the simplest. Every parent undoubtedly wants the best for their children, to give them every chance of a head start in life and to afford them every opportunity that they themselves may have been denied in their own childhood. Josephine's parents were certainly no different, and having seen that their daughter's fledgling family stood every chance of succeeding in the New World, took the heart breaking decision to allow their youngest son to go along, in the hope that it may allow him to lead an improved and more prosperous life.

For Josephine and the children, the journey from Palermo to New York would last seventeen days, during which time they were subject to the same steerage conditions as endured by Angelo on board the Napolitan Prince. On the day of departure, The Gregory Morch held her maximum capacity of seventeen-hundred and sixty three steerage passengers, all of whom were cramped into six berths. For a mother travelling alone with three infants aged between eight years and five months, one can only imagine the sleepless, stench filled, emotional horror of the journey, especially with diseases such as Cholera and Diphtheria in plentiful supply. Indeed, it is appropriate at this point to mention the extraordinary strength of character that Josephine – who was herself just nineteen years of age – must have possessed in order to survive the voyage with both her health and sanity intact.

Surprisingly, the panacea to the tension of the voyage was Ellis Island, for it was generally known amongst the vast majority of the immigrants, that women arriving with a child or children under the age of twelve and bearing a pre-paid ticket, were almost exclusively allowed into the country with relatively few questions asked. The reason for this was the American government believed that if the women and children already had a family member residing in the country, they were then less likely to become a state burden. Indeed, so widespread was this knowledge that in one day, over one-thousand women and children arrived at the port of New York, each one of them bearing a pre-paid ticket.

After passing through the bewildering immigration procedure, Josephine, Vincenzo, Salvatore and Francesco boarded another vessel, this time bound for Chicago. A little under two weeks later, the exhausted travellers finally docked in the Chicago Harbour. In the wintertime, it is not difficult to comprehend how Chicago came to bear the nickname of the *'Windy City;'* a bitter chill wind that penetrates the body right to the bone, blows almost continually, whilst the freshly fallen snow cloaks the city in a pure white veil, giving it the look and feel of a magical winter wonderland.

The sheer joy that engulfed Angelo at the very moment that he was reconciled with his family, was almost inconceivable. They say that absence makes the heart grow fonder and without the aid of a diary, it is romantic to believe that this was certainly true for Angelo and Josephine, that they saw each other even more handsome and beautiful than when they parted. It would have certainly been an intensely emotional time, especially so since this was the first time Angelo had laid eyes on his new son, Salvatore. As for Vincenzo – who was a mere babe in arms the last time Angelo saw him – he now came ashore on his own two feet, a toddler striding out into a brave new world. As Angelo watched Vincenzo running towards him, taking his first, infant steps on American soil, neither he nor Josephine nor anyone for that matter, could have foreseen the incredible events that the future held in store for him…a future which fate itself had ensured was already written.

CHAPTER THREE
A NOBLE ART

Angelo and Josephine Gibaldi was an unusual Sicilian couple, in the sense that they had been married already for three years and yet only had two children. True, the couple had been apart for just over a year of those three, but in Sicilian terms that was hardly an excuse. Therefore, the couple was overjoyed when a year after being reunited in the United States and when Vincenzo was three years old, Josephine announced that she was carrying their third child, and at the end of 1907, another son, Francesco was born. Responding to the prejudices which the couple knew were commonplace in this society, they decided to try and protect their children by Americanizing their names. This is shown in the annual census of 1920, where Vincenzo has been altered to the more acceptable Hebrew equivalent of James, whilst Francesco and Salvatore have been mutated into Frank and Sam respectively. Angelo and Josephine would eventually go on to have four more children; Angeline being born in 1913, Antonio or Anthony in 1915, Calogero or Charles in 1917, and finally, in 1919, Josephine, named after her mother.

It was not long before the couple realized that the diminutive tenement apartment, although adequate for a man alone, was far too small for a burgeoning family. The obvious solution was to move to a larger dwelling and soon the perfect location was discovered. The house, located at 631 South Sangamon Street, was in essence only a few doors away from the tenement apartment, yet it could just as easily have been a world away. The sparsity of their previous dwelling was replaced by soft furnishings and although they were hardly expensive, they nevertheless went a long way in creating a much homelier atmosphere. By the time Vincenzo was old enough to attend school, Angelo was still in employment at Fury Argolia's café and it seemed that life was only getting better and better. This is not to say that they had all the luxuries and home comforts that they desired, but they did have far more than they had back in Sicily, which had been their sole desire all those months ago.

Without a doubt, Angelo looked upon Vincenzo very much in the same way as his own father had looked upon him – as the next in line as head of the family. He had high hopes for his eldest son and every day – just as he would with the other children – instilled in him the importance of good schooling and of a good education. So it was at the tender age of five that Vincenzo was enrolled in Reese Elementary School, a place where he would come face to face with the prejudices that up until now, he had only heard his mother and father speak about.

The schools of 1909, were, to the native children, dreadfully Draconian. To the Italian and Sicilian children however, it was dystopia, the idea that the Latin immigrants were lazy and stupid, having invariably carried through into the education system. Indeed, in many cases, it was fair to say that these children were purposely held back, although quite the reason why is far from clear. One theory is that the American people had been bestowed with that exquisite quality that is all too prevalent in human nature, namely, that they do not take kindly to being proved wrong. Imagine the scene should it be discovered that these *'dago's'* or *'wops,'* these stupid *eye-talians* were not so stupid after all. A further problem which befell the schools of the early twentieth century was the age of the teachers employed within them. It was not uncommon to find an eighteen year old, inexperienced girl, in charge of a class of pupils who were perhaps only eight or ten years her junior. As a result, a great many children dispensed with their education almost as soon as it had begun, either of their own free will or otherwise. For Vincenzo however, it was not quite so drastic, and he succeeded in prolonging his education up until the age of fourteen, which under the circumstances was highly remarkable, if not commendable.

Schools are often regarded as a place of safety, yet oddly enough it was at school where Vincenzo was first exposed to violence. There were everyday fights in the playground between pupils, which even by today's standards, can barely be described as uncommon, yet there was also violence in the classrooms between pupils and teachers. The youthful inexperience of the teachers meant that life had not yet equipped them with the vital skills needed to peaceably control a classroom of rowdy children, a factor which often manifested itself in regular beatings of the youngsters. For their part, the pupils generally fought fire with fire and responded with equal aggression. Cocooned in this volatile world, Vincenzo was forced to make a choice – either take the beatings as a normal, everyday occurrence or learn how to fight. He chose the latter, and in doing so, discovered that he actually liked the brutal physicality of the fight. It was therefore quite apt that after leaving school at the tender age of fourteen, Vincenzo became involved in a pursuit in which he would become notably adept, namely the noble art of boxing.

Many young boys have a great deal of energy building up inside them, an energy which, in a large amount of cases, can turn out to be the catalyst that sends its host on a collision course that almost without exception, has but one outcome – crime and inevitably violence. Even in the cities of today, street gangs are anything but uncommon and in the Chicago of 1918, it was certainly no different. Being in a gang made an adolescent boy feel that he belonged, that he was special, even powerful. For most however, that was as far as the perks went and it was downhill all the way from there, as petty crimes slowly developed into those of a more serious nature. Vincenzo was one of the prodigious exceptions. Without a doubt he had the energy, indeed the anger, which inevitably stems from unrealized or unrec- ognized potential, yet he found that he was hardly enamored by the prospect of becoming a gang member; in any case he had, by this time, already witnessed first hand what fate usually befell those guys. In mid 1918, Vincenzo was presented with his answer, when a family friend intro- duced him to a local boxing club.

The club was organized by a man named James Sawyer, who was also the proprietor of The Sawyer Biscuit Factory, a baked goods packing factory situated in an area of downtown Chicago known as the Loop. Years later in an FBI statement, James Sawyer would state that he immediately saw potential in Vincenzo and that the young man did not disappoint. He proved himself to be a conscientious student, avidly learning the principles of boxing as well as excelling in its training. Vincenzo was inspired by the glamorous, professional fighters of the day, not least of which was Jack Dempsey, a man who would soon become the young boy's hero. As the months went by and his strength and stamina increased, James Sawyer took

Vincenzo aside and intimated that in time, Vincenzo himself could be one of the greats in his natural weight class of Welterweight. Indeed, Sawyer could see that Vincenzo was more than adequately suited to that particular division. At five feet seven inches, his adolescent body was developing into a trim one-hundred and forty-seven pounds and it was clear that he possessed an inordinate amount of strength for his size. After witnessing this strength, not to mention the honesty and determination that literally overflowed from this young man, James Sawyer decided to offer him a job as a delivery packer at his factory. This employment, in addition to giving him the respectability which comes from earning an honest living, would also serve to increase his strength and build his muscle tone, requiring as it did the physical loading and unloading of heavy crates from the backs of the delivery trucks. Vincenzo knew that there were far worse jobs to be had and when he was told that his starting pay would be $10 a week, he did not have to think twice.

On July 4, 1919 – two days after Vincenzo's fifteenth birthday – his interest in boxing became an all consuming passion: for that was the day when Jack 'The Manassa Mauler' Dempsey won the Heavyweight World Title from Jess Willard in Toledo, Ohio. The fight was the first ever to be broadcast over the wireless and listening to the action in his father's parlour, Vincenzo's imagination was enraptured. Willard was the undeniable favorite, however when the fight began, it was difficult to see why. 'The Manassa Mauler' was in a class of his own and knocked his opponent down an astonishing *seven* times in the first round alone. By the third round it was all but over, as the valiant yet hopelessly outgunned Willard, could take no more. Vincenzo told himself that he was prepared to put in the hours of gruelling hard work that his training demanded, in order to achieve the level of proficiency that Dempsey was at right at that moment. When he discovered that Dempsey gained his extreme strength and stamina through carrying and delivering huge bags of ice, Vincenzo threw himself into his work at the factory, often taking on extra shifts as part of his training. He had the heart, he had the style, he had the determination and yet, despite all of this, he could never make the big time, for there was one minor detail which stood in his way – his name.

The xenophobic nature of society meant that anyone with a Christian name or surname ending in a vowel was immediately segregated into a lower social class, whether they displayed acute talent or not. As a result, many immigrants chose to change their names – either by Americanizing them as Vincenzo's family had done – or indeed, altering them completely. Vincenzo was of the latter and decided that if he were to flourish in his chosen vocation, he had to have an easily remembered, yet completely un-Italian name. Following hours of mulling over the problem, he eventually came up with an appellation which resounded with Irish tones, Irish being far more socially acceptable than Italian; although, with his naturally wavy, ebony hair and soulfully deep brown eyes, he looked every inch a Sicilian. From this point forth however, he would be known as *Jack McGurn* – except of course to his family and friends, who would always refer to him as Vincenzo or James. As his amount of competitive fights increased, he was awarded a nickname and eventually came to be recognized as 'Battling' Jack McGurn. Throughout all the hard work, he harboured the dream of one day turning professional, yet that cruel prankster more commonly known as fate, had not yet shown its full hand.

CHAPTER FOUR

A NOBLE EXPERIMENT

Six months after the battle between Dempsey and Willard, another fight was set to be contested, one which would take infinitely longer than a mere eleven minutes to resolve. On January 17, 1920, the Eighteenth Amendment to the Constitution of the United States – also known as the Volstead Act or National Prohibition Act – came into effect. As from midnight, the *'sale, manufacture and transportation of intoxicating liquors'* was prohibited by Federal Law. Described by Herbert Hoover as a *'noble experiment,'* it essentially made criminals out of what, until that day, had been law abiding citizens.

The idea of prohibition was first brought to the fore by members of the Anti Saloon League – formed in 1893 – and the Women's Christian Temperance Union. The WCTU charged that women were in effect becoming *'drinking widows,'* as their husbands spent all of their time – and money – in local saloons. They believed that if alcohol were to be banned, the saloons would close their doors for good, their husbands would spend more time at home and peace and tranquility would reign across the country. With the wisdom of hindsight, it is easy to see what a spectacular failure such an act would be destined to become. The Anti Saloon League chimed in with its own declaration that the prohibition of alcohol would cut crime and corruption, improve public health and reduce the tax burden by curbing the level of prison inmates and hospital patients. Despite many vigorous protests, the Anti Saloon League and the WCTU soon succeeded in the enactment of local prohibition laws and before long, the prohibition campaign was adopted into the political agenda.

By 1916, a Minnesota congressman by the name of Andrew A. Volstead – a staunch supporter of the Anti Saloon League and the Women's Christian Temperance Union – had drafted the Eighteenth Amendment to the constitution and brought it before Congress for its first debate. Under the codes of the constitution, thirty-six of the then forty-eight states of America, had to ratify the amendment in order for it to become law. The momentum gained by the WCTU and the Anti Saloon League was now at almost an unstoppable level and in 1917, when the amendment came before the Senate, it was passed by a landslide majority after just thirteen hours of debate. A few months later, the amendment was accepted by the House of Representatives and, by January 1918, the state of Ohio became the thirty-sixth state to vote in favour of adopting Volstead's proposal. With the law passed, the National Prohibition Act was officially written into the constitution on January 16, 1919, and was set to become law one year later, at the stroke of midnight on January 17, 1920.

Fate, together with its perverse alter ego irony has, at various stages throughout history, played its own unique pranks upon the unsuspecting people of the world. Time is its closest ally; decisions are its playthings, whimsically wielded and manipulated according to its mood. Thus, when the United States Congress decreed that the National Prohibition Act would officially come into effect on January 17, 1920, they were not acting of their own free will, but upon the mischievous will of fate. For that day was the twenty-first birthday of Al Capone, a man who would become the personification of prohibition and who, upon the very day of the law's enactment would be legally allowed to drink.

As previously stated, prohibition was from the outset, destined to be a ubiquitous failure. As Eve had so infamously demonstrated in the Garden of Eden, it is human nature to crave that which is forbidden. Therefore, the people of Chicago – indeed the people of America – dared to consume the forbidden fruit. The saloons, bars and cafés which were intended to close, stayed open and continued purveying alcoholic beverages. In addition, those who had previously brewed their own liquor, continued to do so. In the Italian and Sicilian communities especially, disregard for the prohibition law was widespread, as the families who had made their own wine back in the Old Country and who had carried on the tradition in the New World, saw no good reason as to why they should cease. Angelo Gibaldi was certainly no exception; from the time when he was a mere boy, he could remember his father fermenting his own unique brand of homemade wine and as Angelo developed into manhood, he too learned the family recipe. Indeed, when he had first begun work in the café, he had seen wine being sold to customers for 25c a glass and therefore could not understand why people should be denied that which they desired and more importantly, were willing to pay good money for. There were many more people who shared the same belief as Angelo, although these people were not already employed in the refreshment business. These were people who saw the new law as a way to make more money for themselves, who felt that the rewards on offer far outweighed the risks. In their desire to conduct their *'noble experiment'* the United States government had unwittingly created a fertile breeding ground for both crime and corruption, paving the way for the dawn of a new era. It was the age of decadence; it was the age of the boot-legger.

To the dismay of the federal authorities, it would be the bootleggers who would set the trend, promptly demonstrating the unenforceability of prohibition, whilst enthusiastically proving themselves to be one step ahead of the law. At 12.02am on January 17, 1920, – just two minutes after the National Prohibition Act became law – a small time hoodlum by the name of Herschel Miller, together with five of his cronies, drove a truck into the West Lake Street railroad yard on Chicago's West Side. Armed with pistols, they bound and gagged three security guards, raided the rail wagons and promptly made off with over $100,000 worth of whiskey; elsewhere in the city, four separate warehouses were simultaneously being relieved of their alcohol stocks.

* * *

Love – such a tiny word and yet it is used to describe an emotion of immense magnitude, indeed, it is one of the most powerful emotions known to man. When one falls in love, it is a very personal, individual experience. For some, it lurks around the corner, concealing itself and ready to pounce when you least expect it. For others, the feeling is a bolt from the blue, a revelation which knocks you off your feet with the force of a runaway train. In Sicilian, the latter is known as *'the thunderbolt'* and it was precisely this which hit Vincenzo Gibaldi when, on November 11, 1921, a new girl moved into the neighbourhood. Her name was Helena DeMore and she had moved with her parents to Chicago, from New York. Her parents had emigrated from Sicily whilst her mother was still pregnant and so, having been born and raised in America, Helena was deemed to be an American; even so, she would always vehemently state that she was Sicilian and proud to be so.

Vincenzo and Helena met one evening whilst he was on his way home from boxing training. It was love at first sight and the two of them were inseparable from that day forward. Up until that moment, boxing was the only love in Vincenzo's life, but in Helena, he saw a new meaning to being alive. He felt wanted and needed, as though his life had a renewed purpose. Vincenzo felt in his heart that he wanted to marry Helena and was over-joyed when she intimated that his feelings would not go unrequited. Their respective parents' happiness at their new found love was tinged with a certain sense of unease over the prospect of marriage: after all, the two of them had only known each other for a little under two weeks. Nevertheless, Vincenzo and Helena knew what their hearts desired and so they embarked on the first major act of rebellion either of them had ever committed. On November 24, 1921, the young couple eloped to DuPage County, Illinois, a county which could be considered to be the Gretna Green of America. As their looks belied their age, they managed – without too much difficulty – to obtain a hotel room and the following day, stepped into the offices of DuPage County Court to obtain a license to marry. This procedure involved the swearing of an affidavit to the effect that both parties were single, or if they had previously been married, they could prove that they were either divorced or widowed and, most importantly, that both parties were the required legal age of twenty-one. Whilst the swearing of an affi-davit was needed for a marriage license to be issued, the laws of DuPage County were somewhat lax, in the sense that no documentation was required to substantiate the applicants' declarations. Therefore, despite being only seventeen, Vincenzo gave his age as twenty-two and Helena's as twenty-three, when in reality she was one year his junior. Less than one hour later, having promised to love one another for better or for worse, for richer for poorer, in sickness and in health, Vincenzo and Helena emerged from the court building as husband and wife.

Needless to say, when they returned to Chicago to face the music, their respective parents' were less than satisfied with their deceit and somewhat unable to understand why they had failed to fully explain the depths of their feelings and to seek their permission. However, the fact remained that Vincenzo and Helena were indeed now legally married and as such, there was little that could be done, other than to wish them much health and happiness. Angelo and Josephine decided that they would try to give their son and new daughter-in-law the best start they could in their life together, after all, they themselves had married at a young age. So, as something of a belated wedding present and with the permission of Helena's parents, they gave the happy couple the first month's rent on a small house located at 1230 Oregon Avenue, on the outskirts of Little Italy.

Now that he had a wife to support, Vincenzo respectfully asked James Sawyer if he could have a small raise. Whilst such a request was relatively uncommon for someone in Vincenzo's position, James Sawyer was nevertheless impressed by the level of commitment that he had so far seen in this developing young man. He was still devoted to his boxing, never once missing a training session, or a day of work for that matter. Indeed, in Sawyer's opinion, Vincenzo was now proving himself to be a real man with his intention to take care of his wife, and it was primarily on these grounds, that a raise of $5 a week was granted.

Perhaps now that he was old enough to understand, Vincenzo was grateful to his father for the enormous risks he took, simply to ensure that in the future, his family would have a better quality of life. He had a well paid job - $15 a week was exceptional for a seventeen year old – he had a beautiful wife and a comfortable home and all this was considerably more than he would have had, should his father have chosen to remain in Sicily. Had he been asked about his feelings regarding his life, Vincenzo would have answered that in all honesty, he believed himself to be an extremely fortunate young man.

For Angelo however, life was not quite so good. Not that there was anything wrong with business, in fact, it could not be better. Fury Argolia, together with a somewhat sizeable fortune, had recently left America in order to return to his native homeland, a move which resulted in Angelo's acquisition of the café. Finally, after all the years of hardship and toil,

Angelo had fulfilled his dream of owning his own business. Prohibition had brought with it an increased volume of customers, and as the homemade wine which was now illicitly served at the café was undeniably good, there seemed to be an almost limitless demand. Nor was there anything amiss in his home life; once again, nothing could be further from the truth. Just as his son had done, Angelo had fallen in love with his wife the very moment he had laid eyes on her and, eighteen years later, he still had moments when he was almost overcome by the same wonderful feeling. One wonders therefore, where or what the problem could be?

The problem, it appears, came in the sinister form of *La Mano Nera* or The Black Hand. It was no coincidence that as the number of customers patronizing Angelo's café increased, the more interested in the business The Black Hand became. The Black Hand habitually preyed on either the naturally wealthy or successful Italian or Sicilian businessman. They dared not encroach on other members of society, such as wealthy Americans, for they knew that their activities would not be tolerated by these people. In doing so, they were exploiting the heavy prejudice which faced the Latinate community, for should an aggrieved businessman take his complaint to the police, it could almost be guaranteed that unless they were a famous star or entertainer – as in the case of Enrico Caruso – not a single finger would be lifted in assistance. However, should they attempt to threaten a wealthy *American* businessman, they could rest assured that the full force of the law would bear down on them so heavily, that they would be crushed into the ground like a bug. Yet, with approximately forty percent of Italians and Sicilians returning to their homeland with their fortunes made, the field of susceptible businessmen was slowly dwindling. Recently therefore, their avaricious eyes had begun to look around for more fair game, plump fruit which was ripe for the picking. Dismissing the infinite number of flourishing speakeasies, saloons and taverns as too high profile, the rapacious gaze of The Black Hand came to rest upon the café of Angelo Gibaldi.

CHAPTER FIVE

THE SCOURGE

It was the beginning of December, 1922, when Angelo Gibaldi took receipt of a characteristically formulaic letter which made his blood run cold. Signed with an inky black handprint – the sinister symbol of The Black Hand – the letter politely stated that they knew Angelo to be both a wealthy and reasonable man and as such, knew that he would not object to them wetting their beaks a little. The letter then went on to say that one of their collectors would pass by in a few days to pick up the 'agreed' payment. Angelo was a man not known for his naïvety; he knew that if he did not pay, his business and even his life were in severe jeopardy. Therefore, when as promised, the collector did arrive, Angelo was ready and waiting with the money. He would however, have preferred not to have discovered the collector's identity, for the man was notorious throughout the Latinate community. His name was Orazzio Tropea, although many people knew him simply as 'The Scourge.'

During the reign of The Black Hand, there were many fearsome collectors and enforcers, all of whom possessed the ability to fill hearts with dread. Men such as Salvatore 'Sam' Cardinella, who was known to the inhabitants of Little Italy and Little Sicily as 'Il Diavolo' meaning 'The Devil.' An obesely gargantuan extortionist with psychotically violent tendencies, Cardinella placed even the agents of law enforcement on tenterhooks in his presence. It was said that he had personally killed more than twenty unfortunates, who had been misguided enough to ignore his 'pay or die' demands. Then there was Nicholas 'The Choir Boy' Viana. Nicknamed 'The Choir Boy' because of his angelic appearance, his character could not possibly be further removed; Viana was in fact a highly accomplished killer by the tender age of eighteen, often hiring out his services to those members of La Mano Nera, who preferred not to get their hands dirty. More feared than Cardinella or Viana, was a man named Ignazio Saietta, better known to most as *'Lupo'* or *'Lupo the Wolf.'* A consummate kidnapper, Saietta was credited with the deaths or disappearances of more than sixty men, though the state's law enforcement only ever managed to convict him of one count of murder, thus sending him to prison for ten years. Compared to *'The Scourge'* however, these men were merely playground thugs.

Orazzio Tropea was himself a Sicilian man, one who had gained the reputation as probably *the* most sadistically lethal Black Hander who ever lived. It was a reputation which was not the least bit unwarranted, for when The Scourge was crossed, or even gained the remotest perception that he had been disobeyed or insulted, the result was catastrophic and usually came without warning. Many of Tropea's victims were taken to what became known as *'The Murder Stable,'* where they were tortured until they died, their blood curdling screams filling both the air and neighbourhood with terror. Needless to say, not a single soul ever dared to report the noise and so no investigation was ever instigated.

An example of Tropea's indulgence of his sadistic tendencies, was the day when one of his 'clients' found himself in financial straits and had therefore asked for a little extra time to pay. Within hours the man had disappeared; a few days later, his naked and mutilated body was discovered in a barrel and it was clear that he had died a truly horrendous death. His entire body was covered in cigarette burns and numerous ice pick wounds showed that he had been stabbed dozens of times, though each wound was purposefully not deep enough to kill. His skull was fractured, and most gruesome of all, his penis had been severed and placed in his mouth – though whether this act had been committed before or after death was never ascertained – whilst the actual cause of death was determined to be asphyxiation. Although it was widely accepted that the murderer was Tropea, the police conducted only a brief investigation and no arrests were ever made.

Following the macabre barrel discovery, fear descended onto Little Italy and Little Sicily. Indeed, just the very mention of Tropea's name, forced many citizens to cross themselves and say a Hail Mary or two. Almost everyone knew Tropea by sight, often seeing him strutting around the streets, revelling in the atmosphere of terror which he had created. Angelo

Gibaldi however, was closer to Tropea than most. Every morning, Tropea would patronize Angelo's café to partake in his customary breakfast of espresso laced with *grappa,* a powerful Sicilian liqueur. Angelo was fully aware of what Tropea was capable of indeed, Vincenzo had often heard his father say that the man had an evil aura around him and that to look in his eyes was to look into the eyes of the devil himself. It is therefore unlikely that Angelo informed his family either of the letter or of the collector's identity. Angelo was a proud man, and whilst there was certainly no disgrace in having been threatened by a man like Tropea, he may have felt somewhat ashamed to admit that he was unreservedly frightened. Besides which, as a father, he was fully aware that Vincenzo had increasingly pressing concerns of his own.

In March, 1922, Vincenzo's wife Helena had announced that she was pregnant with their first child. Whilst this was undoubtedly joyous news, the family's excitement was tinged with more than a slight sense of apprehension, due in no small part to the fact that in the early 1900's, the infant mortality rate was incredibly high. There were no drugs to control the seemingly epidemic proportions of Diphtheria, Polio, Cholera and Pneumonia and as a result, the amount of children who died within the first two weeks of life was a staggering one in five. There were many reasons why this figure should be so remarkably high, such as the connection between the high death toll and low income families. A study conducted in 1920, appeared to show that those families living at the foot of the income scale were stuck in a vicious circle, inasmuch as that when a child fell ill, the parents spent what little money they had on health care, with the extra expenditure further impoverishing the family. Therefore, when further treatment was required, it proved unaffordable and the child subsequently deteriorated. Another explanation was the high instances of mothers giving birth at home, a practice which was especially common throughout the immigrant communities. This was due primarily to an ingrained distrust of hospitals, in addition to unaffordable healthcare. Thus, should complications arise during labour, there was practically little or no medical assistance on hand. Consequently, the number of women who died during childbirth was also exceedingly high. Moreover was the ignorance of where, how and when diseases spread, and how children and adults alike could be best protected. All of this was compounded by the fact that complacency and neglect of the immigrant communities was almost as rife as the diseases themselves. Now, living as we do in an age of phenomenally advanced medical technology, it seems improbable that such diseases could ever have been allowed to claim so many infant lives and yet even today, the United States still has the highest infant mortality rate of most other industrialized countries.

In spite of the overwhelming impediments, on December 7, 1922, Helena successfully gave birth to a healthy baby girl. After surviving the critical two week period, the infant was eventually christened Helen Josephine, meaning *'ray of light'* and in honour of the two most important women in Vincenzo's life – his wife and mother.

At the end of December, 1922, Angelo Gibaldi announced to his family that he had filed his *'first papers'* to the Immigration and Naturalization Service, meaning that he had taken the initial steps to becoming an American citizen. This would give legitimacy in the United States not only to himself, but also to his family, as up until 1930, once the husband or father had been naturalized, wives and children were automatically included as American citizens. This was a huge step for Angelo to take, as it meant not only pledging allegiance to America, but also required of him to relinquish ties with his homeland. It was, in effect, changing both his and his family's nationality. All of this naturally took time, mainly due to the bureaucracy, but also to the sheer volume of people wishing to take part in the process. This massive step also indicated that Angelo – having paid off The Black Hand – may have disregarded the thought of any further threat. Had he known however, that Orazzio Tropea was both collector *and* sender of the initial letter, he would have undoubtedly taken the threat far more seriously. For the time being though, he was merely concentrating on the fact that it was just a matter of time until he and his family could refer to themselves as Americans. Unbeknown to Angelo or his family however, things were destined never to get that far.

Tuesday January 8, 1923, began as a day like any other. At 631 South Sangamon Street, Angelo Gibaldi rose as usual, ate his usual breakfast, before kissing Josephine and the children goodbye and heading off for another hectic day at the café. A few streets away, Vincenzo was also getting ready for work, telling Helena that he would be home a little later than usual, as he was going to stop off at his father's café on his way back from the factory.

As normal, Angelo's café was busy the whole day as women, taking a break from the pressures of shopping in the Loop, stopped for a refreshing cup of coffee, whilst their husbands came in later on their way home from work for slightly stronger refreshments. Almost as soon as the door was open, the café began to fill with customers; even if he ran out of tables, Angelo always tried to make space for his clients – paying guests were always welcome at his establishment. However, one face in the crowd was not quite so welcome, for it was that of the most vile, malevolent serpent of The Black Hand, Orazzio Tropea. He was there to collect further tribute, a fact unbeknown to Angelo due to Tropea's disregard for any further written correspondence. Exactly what happened next is unclear. Did Angelo politely inform Tropea that he was not expecting him and so did not have his payment to hand? Did he ask Tropea to come back later? Or did he make a stand against Tropea, and remind him of an age old Sicilian proverb that *'It is better to die standing, than live on your knees?'* Whatever words passed between the two men is something which is known only to them-selves, suffice to say that Tropea left without receiving what he had come for.

The rest of the day passed off without incident, as Angelo made sure that before they left, each of his customers was well sated. Then, in the late afternoon, the day became altogether more sinister. A black and aubergine Cadillac town car pulled up outside the café and out stepped Orazzio Tropea, accompanied by two other notoriously lethal Black Handers. The first accomplice was known purely by his nickname of *'Jimmy The Bug,'* which considering his chosen profession and the company he habitually kept, appears to be rather apt. Tropea's second companion was Willie Altierri, also known as *'Two Knife'* in reference to the two hunting knives which he never failed to carry.

Angelo was busy tending to a customer who had just handed him three Indian Head nickels in payment for his beverage, as the three men entered the café. Holding the nickels in his right hand, Angelo crossed the floor of the café, heading towards the cash register in order to get the customer his change. It is not known whether or not Angelo witnessed the three men enter his establishment, nor is it known whether he or anyone else, saw Tropea pull out a shotgun which had been concealed underneath his heavy winter coat. Undoubtedly, only Tropea himself knew that the shotgun was loaded with dum dum or hollow point bullets, ammunition designed to explode on impact, in order to cause maximum damage. So devastatingly lethal was this ammunition, that later on in history, they became the ammunition of choice for terrorist organizations such as the IRA.

Levelling the shotgun at Angelo, Tropea squeezed the trigger and fired. Angelo probably had very little time, if any, to react before the first bullet tore open his chest, the force sending him flying upwards and backwards through the air. As the shotgun blast resounded around the café walls, tables and chairs were tossed in every direction, as terrified and screaming patrons fell face down onto the floor for protection. Before Angelo's already lifeless body could hit the ground, Tropea fired again, this second shot hitting him square in the head and completely obliterating his face. Men and women alike cried out in horror, as pieces of skull and gouts of blood splattered out over their clothes and the white tablecloths. Angelo hit the ground with a sickening thud, blood pouring from the gaping wounds and forming a hideous pool of carmine around his body. With the subtlest of signals from Tropea, the three men exited the café and returned to the Cadillac; a few moments later, the murderous triumvirate had disappeared into the sprawling city. As the Cadillac drove out of sight, the shocked and horrified patrons slowly began to pull themselves up from the floor. Holding onto each other for support, not one of them wished to believe that lying in their midst, were the bloody, amorphous remains of Angelo Gibaldi.

Just at that moment, Vincenzo rounded the corner of West Harrison Street, heading – as promised – for his father's café on his way home from work. Seeing the thronging crowd of stunned onlookers, he naturally became a little concerned for his father's well-being, and after elbowing people aside, managed to push his way through the café door. It is difficult to imagine the shock and emotion which consumed Vincenzo's body when he reached the now somewhat nebulous form of his father. Legend has it that he soaked his hands in his father's blood and cried out for vengeance on his killers. In reality however, he was propelled into an acute state of prostration, an overwhelming weakness which brought him physically to his knees. As he knelt in his father's pooling blood, he did not shout, nor scream, nor curse; his was a muted grief, unwittingly stoic and yet each silent tear that fell was filled with the pain of a thousand heartbreaks. Death had come so instantaneously for Angelo that his reflexes had gone into spasm and his right hand still clutched the three Indian Head nickels. Seeing that his father's hand was clenched, Vincenzo pried open his fingers, anxious to discover what he held so tight. Upon discovering the three nickels he removed them, and feeling the poignant warmth which still emanated from them, held them, together with his father's hand, tightly in his own. Here he stayed for what seemed like an eternity, weeping silently and wondering how he could possibly tell his mother that her beloved husband, her one true love, was dead. He wondered too about his brothers and sisters, especially little Josephine who, at just three years old, would probably not understand why her father would never be coming home.

A short while later the police arrived and found Vincenzo still weeping by his father's side. After verifying his identity, an officer attempted to question him over what had happened. There was of course nothing that he could tell them, for he had neither seen nor heard a thing. Realizing his deep and emotional distress, a police officer was assigned to escort Vincenzo back to South Sangamon Street, where the heartbreaking news would be broken to the rest of the family.

It is at this point when it seems appropriate to mention a rather confusing aspect regarding the life and death of Angelo Gibaldi and his son Vincenzo. Many criminology writers believe that whilst Angelo was the paternal father, Vincenzo also had a step-father by the name of Angelo DeMore. They then go a step further by suggesting that it was Angelo DeMore who was killed that day, rather than Angelo Gibaldi. However, whilst both these claims are totally erroneous, the confused discrepancy of the names is easily explained. DeMore was the maiden name of Vincenzo's wife, Helena, who in a later statement to the FBI, stated that Vincenzo took her name at the time of their marriage. She went on to say that from then on, he would often refer to himself as Vincenzo DeMore.

Before being transferred to the Rago Brothers Funeral home, it is likely that the body of Angelo Gibaldi was taken to the Colombus Hospital.

Located on Cabrini Street, just two blocks west of West Harrison Street, the hospital was created by a young nun by the name of Frances Xavier Cabrini. Cabrini was a young Italian woman who was determined to become a nun, but whose ill health prevented her from entering the Holy Order. By way of compensation, she set about helping the poor and the sick of neighbouring Italian villages and eventually created her own order called the *Institute of the Missionary Sisters of the Sacred Heart of Jesus.* In 1897, she made a papal request to be sent to China to work as a missionary, but the pope refused, and instead sent her to Chicago to care for the Italian and Sicilian immigrants. In 1903, she set up the Colombus Hospital, a medical facility which soon became renowned for its treatment of poor Italian and Sicilian families.

Angelo's death had a profound effect upon the whole Gibaldi family, but most especially upon the young Vincenzo. For the days leading up to the funeral, he was in a world of his own. When faced with the death of a loved one, it is human nature to blame oneself, even though such blame is often misdirected. Vincenzo was certainly no exception and he continually played and replayed the moment of his father's death in his mind. Each time, the image was accompanied by a multitude of questions. What if he had left work slightly earlier? What if he had taken a shorter route to the café? What if he hadn't taken his time? For the grief stricken Vincenzo, there seemed to be a million and one *'what if's?'*

Yet amongst the tumultuous cavalcade of thoughts that assaulted his mind, one thought continued to return again and again – the thought of vengeance and how it could be achieved. He knew that the police would not obtain justice for him, for although they undoubtedly knew who the perpetrator or perpetrators were, they had no evidence whatsoever. So fearful were the community of Tropea, that no one would dare to speak out, let alone identify him. Vincenzo knew that if justice was going to be realized, he had to get it for himself, however for the moment, he would concentrate on leading and consoling his family in their grief.

Traditional Sicilian beliefs dictate that when a loved one passes away, their body should lie in an open casket in the family home for two days and two nights. It is of the utmost importance that the casket should remain open during this time, in order to allow the soul ample time to ascend to heaven. Should the casket be closed, it is deemed to be a grave insult to both the deceased and the grieving family. Yet in firing the second shot, Orazzio Tropea had ensured that the damage to Angelo's body was so extensive that an open casket would be all but impossible. Therefore, for two days and two nights, the body of Angelo Gibaldi lay in its closed casket in the front parlor of the family home at 631 South Sangamon Street. During this time, many friends passed by in order to pay their last respects and inevitably found Vincenzo kneeling beside his father's bier – as was his duty in Sicilian tradition – in an obvious state of great distress. Each of them bar one, brought him words of comfort and extolled the virtues of the immense healing powers of time. The one man who offered no words of comfort, was a man who had been one of his father's closest friends, someone who had been in the café at the time of Angelo's murder. Bowing his head in solemn deference before the casket, he slipped a small piece of paper into Vincenzo's hand. Upon it was written three names: Tropea, Jimmy The Bug and Willie Altierri.

Angelo Gibaldi was laid to rest on January 11, 1923, aged thirty-eight. After leaving the family home for which he had risked so much, his body was interred in the consecrated ground of The Holy Guardian Angel Church on Forquer Street, Cicero. Today, both the church and the cemetery have gone, whilst the street has been renamed Arthington Street, a telling testament to the perpetuity of time. Yet providence decreed that Angelo should never be forgotten, prompting some unknown person or persons to place a memorial gravestone in the grounds of Mount Carmel Cemetery, near to the final resting place of his beloved wife and son.

Funerals are often the worst part in the death of a loved one and the finality of his father's funeral hit Vincenzo hard. The cemetery looked somewhat surreal; the white blanket of fallen snow seemed to lend a certain dream-like feel to the occasion, whilst the Yew trees, legendary protectors of the dead, waited patiently to take charge of their latest ward. Standing at the graveside, it took all of Vincenzo's strength to conceal the multitude of emotions that were eating away at his very being and consuming his soul. His brothers and sisters were distraught to the extent that they cried themselves to sleep, whilst his mother was so grief-stricken by the loss of her husband, that each time he looked at her, Vincenzo's heart broke all over again. In his hand, he still held the three Indian Head nickels and at that moment, the idea of making his father's killers suffer for their heinous actions was the only thought which brought him solace. Having been raised in the Catholic faith, Vincenzo knew the bible's teachings well; he knew that god endowed us with the grace to forgive our enemies, yet he also knew that the book of Deuteronomy dictates that *'life shall go for life.'* The murder of his father had propelled his family's dream life into a waking nightmare and he knew that he would not, could not rest, until his death had been avenged.

In 49BC, Julius Caesar led his armies across the Rubicon, a small river situated in North-Central Italy. In doing so, he occasioned a civil war. The death of Vincenzo's father had set him on a collision course with the murderous Black Hand, a course from which he would not, indeed could not stray; a course which he had to pursue until its final, bloody conclusion. He would hunt for his father's killers like the animals they were and when he found them, would revel in their suffering before securing their violent passage through the gates of hell. Like Caesar so many centuries ago, Vincenzo had crossed the Rubicon.

CHAPTER SIX

LA VITA ANDRA PER VITA

It could well be argued that the art of vengeance – for true vengeance is indeed an art – was born in the heart of Sicily, a place where violence has long spewed forth from the mouth of Mount Etna to form the backbone of the island and where retribution has been intrinsically woven into the fabric of society. When a Sicilian cries out for vengeance, he demands not punishment, but justice, and in this smoldering cauldron of reckoning, justice takes on its most biblical form. Here, the teaching of Deuteronomy 19:21 *'and thine eye shall not pity; but life shall go for life, eye for eye, tooth for tooth'* is not dismissed as a flippant remark, but regarded rather as a code of conduct. If a Sicilian is hurt – for example, if a boy is beaten in the school playground – he will not take his complaint to the teachers, or his parents for that matter; he will take the beating and feel the bruises however, it can be guaranteed that in a matter of days or weeks, his assailant will suffer a similar attack on his way to or from school. Yet having taken his revenge, the boy will know that he himself may then be the target of a similar reprisal. It is a cycle of retribution that is as fundamental as the cycle of life itself.

Aside from love, the very word *'vengeance'* or *'revenge'* is so evocative as to have found a place in numerous literary works indeed, tales of righteous retribution have long flowed from the pens of some of history's most influential authors. In Shakespeare's *The Merchant of Venice*, Shylock proclaims that *'if I can catch him once upon the hip, I will feed fat the ancient grudge I bear him. If it will feed nothing else, it will feed my revenge,'* whilst in *Hamlet*, the Prince of Denmark decrees *'where the offence is, let the great axe fall.'* The Italian dramatist, historian and philosopher, Niccolo Machiavelli wrote that *'if an injury must be done to a man, it should be so severe that his vengeance need not be feared.'* The works of the great Oscar Wilde overflow with references to revenge; in *Vera, or The Nihilists*, the president of the Nihilists declares that *'as long as earth holds poison or steel, as long as men can strike or women betray, you shall not escape vengeance.'* More poignantly, in his classic play *The Duchess of Padua*, the young hero Guido cries out to god *'Listen, thou terrible God! Thou god that punishest all broken oaths and bid some angel write this oath in fire, that from this hour, till my dear father's murder in blood I have revenged, I do foreswear the noble ties of honourable friendship, the noble joys of dear companionship, affection's bonds and loyal gratitude.'* It was an oath which could easily have been sworn some thirty years later by Angelo Gibaldi's eldest son.

On the day of his father's funeral, as Vincenzo Gibaldi stared through the tears at the small piece of paper that had been handed to him, he made the silent asseveration *'La vita andra per vita'* meaning *'life shall go for life.'* He knew that his quest for justice would be an overwhelming obsession that time alone could not quell indeed, only when the ground was bathed in the blood of the enemy, would his soul be purged of its vengeful wrath.

For years, Orazzio Tropea had remained unchallenged, safe in the knowledge that his reputation preceded his name. His power rested on a pedestal of fear and he relished the look of dread on the faces of all those who saw him. In spite of the fact that he had committed grievous acts against numerous citizens, robbed countless families of their husbands or fathers, there was no one who would ever imagine to exact vengeance upon him. This was the reason why his power had endured, for whilst there were many people who would have dearly loved to have seen Tropea killed, not a single soul had the nerve to attempt it themselves. Even if anyone had plotted to kill him, there was always the nagging question as to what they would do should they miss. They could rest assured that if, by any chance, they left him alive, they could consider themselves as walking dead; after all, everyone could recall the poor soul who was discovered in the barrel.

The advent of prohibition only served to strengthen his tyrannous hold, for it gave him a new angle from which to work. The Italian and Sicilian families who made wine in their own homes, need only be threatened with the promise of the Prohibition Department bearing down on them and deporting them back to their homeland as lawbreakers, to make them come up with the money for their own protection. This would of course never have happened, but the average immigrant family was ignorant of the laws of this New World and as such, believed whatever they were told. Thus, Tropea basked in the despotic glory of his rule, never once considering the idea of anyone seeking to terminate his power, let alone his life. Yet on the day that he chose to gun down Angelo Gibaldi, he invoked a potent enemy, one who was carefully ruminating over the words of an emotive Sicilian proverb *'He who demands vengeance, must administer vengeance.'*

For Vincenzo, the vow which he had made over his father's casket was not an idle one made in the heat of the moment, a time when anyone would have acknowledged that he may have been blinded by grief. He had solemnly promised his father that his death would not go unavenged, and he knew that he would carry out his mission no matter what the consequences may be. He was however, very careful not to place his family in any unnecessary danger; he did not inform his mother or his wife of his plans, for he knew that they would worry and that in doing so, may attempt to enlist the help of a friend in order to try and dissuade him. Once someone else knew of his plans, neither he nor his family would be safe. It would be a secret that only he would know and a quest that he would carry out alone. Since the death of his father, Vincenzo's mind had undergone some dramatic changes. No longer was he the happy young man, content in working to support his new family; now he was a man possessed, possessed with a burning grief, anger and moreover, a desire for justice. His father could not obtain justice, so Vincenzo considered it his duty to do so for him. All his anger and grief would be channelled into his mission, for he knew that if he could not only control them, but also use them against Tropea and his impious cohorts, they may well prove to be his most potent weapon.

The day after his father's funeral, January 12, 1923, Vincenzo set the wheels of vengeance in motion. He had already decided that his weapon of choice would be a gun, the reasons for which were threefold. The first reason was that it would enable him, should the need arise, to pick off his target at a relative distance. This in turn led on to the second reason, that Tropea would never allow anyone to get close enough to him in order to kill him in any other way and indeed, he himself would almost certainly be armed, which made killing him in any other fashion even more hazardous. The final and most poignant reason was that his father's life had been taken by a gun, therefore Sicilian justice decreed that Tropea should die in the same way.

Vincenzo's first course of action was to obtain the weapon. He had never owned a firearm before in his life, let alone used one, after all up until now he had had no reason to; nevertheless, he was ready and willing to learn. That afternoon, Vincenzo did something he had never done before: he took a few hours off work and went on a shopping trip in the Loop. His destination was Robertson's Sporting Goods Store, an establishment located in the heart of the Loop and which sold all manner of sporting equipment and paraphernalia, including guns. In the America of today, generally a customer is required to present identification to a gun store owner, the details of which will be submitted to the Department of Justice for verification that the applicant is not prohibited from owning a firearm, i.e. due to a past criminal record etc. However, in 1923, no such laws applied and one could easily purchase all manner of weaponry without having to give so much as a name. The advent of prohibition had also caused an alteration in the attitude of the average citizen, a factor which resulted in many people simply ceasing to ask questions. Therefore, when Vincenzo informed the proprietor of Robertson's Sporting Goods Store that he wished to purchase a gun, one which could be handled with relative ease and which was ideal for target practice, he was shown a variety of weapons with no questions asked. Eventually, the proprietor directed Vincenzo towards a Daisy Repeating Air Rifle, also known as the American BB Gun. Originally styled on a military rifle that had been used in trench battles during The Great War, the Daisy was now widely recognized as the least demanding weapon for beginners. The proprietor explained that he believed this would suit Vincenzo perfectly, for it had a good wide wooden butt, adjustable rear sight and was ideal for target practice. Vincenzo handed over the sum of $12, comprising $10 for the gun itself and a further $2 for a box of BB pellets. Vincenzo only intended to keep the rifle temporarily, for once he had reached his optimum level of proficiency, he knew that a more suitably lethal weapon would be required. For now though at least, Vincenzo was in business.

The next stage of his plan was to target practice, or more to the point, find a suitable place and target with which to practice. In this respect,

Vincenzo was relatively fortunate for during that era of prohibition, there was one particular item which was in plentiful supply: empty beer kegs. Once the kegs were empty, the speakeasies would place them in the alleyways behind their buildings so that they could be collected by the beer delivery trucks. Since no one really knew, or indeed cared, how many kegs were supposed to be collected, it was easy for Vincenzo to simply help himself to any that he needed. The time of year also provided him with many opportunities for his practice sessions, for throughout the months of January and February, Little Italy and Little Sicily was home to all manner of feasts and pageants; Vincenzo reasoned that in the midst of such revelry, no one would think to wonder why he was not around.

One such feast took place on January 15, just three days after his gun purchase. Known as *'The Feast of San Mauro,'* it was the feast day of the patron saint of Palermo. The celebrations began with members of the local church carrying a statue of San Mauro through the streets of Little Sicily and were watched by almost everyone in the community. Later on in the day, because San Mauro was also affectionately known as *'the young man'* many young men and boys would set off celebratory firecrackers in the street. This provided Vincenzo with the perfect chance to attempt his primary practice session, for whilst everyone, including his own family, flocked out into the streets to witness the festivities, Vincenzo stole away into the labyrinth of alleyways behind the tenement blocks and began to tutor himself in the art of marksmanship.

Due to the fact that he had never held a weapon before in his life, let alone fired one, this first part of the session was a complete disaster; if he hit the beer keg with one shot, he was sure it was purely a fluke. Nevertheless, he told himself that perseverance was the key, and so reloaded and tried again…with much the same results. Out of sheer frustration, and before the second load of pellets had been exhausted, Vincenzo threw the rifle forcibly to the ground and lashed out at the walls of the alleyway in disgust. Had this been merely an attempt to find a new pastime, Vincenzo would have walked away there and then, however the thought that his father's killers would otherwise never be brought to justice, was enough to spur him on. Picking the air rifle up off the floor, he went into his next self tutored lesson with gusto.

His next session took place five days later on January 20, during the *Feast of San Sebastiano*, when the whole day was taken up with festivities, culminating at dusk with the lighting of a metal framework laden with fireworks, known as the *'vaporetto.'* In this session he fared a little better and the keg ended up with a few more holes than it had started with. With each subsequent lesson, Vincenzo became increasingly proficient and confident in handling his rifle, until eventually he felt ready to move on to live targets. Whilst he dearly yearned for his next target to be Tropea, he knew that even as confident as he felt, he was not yet ready to take on the man himself. Instead he decided that the easiest targets would be the birds that daily clumped together on the myriad of telegraph wires that crossed back and forth over the streets and alleyways.

Vincenzo had to wait almost two weeks before his whole family would leave the house and he could attempt his next lesson. Between February 2, and 5, the neighbourhood streets once again came alive with colourful festivals and pageants, such as *'The Stuzze,'* *'The Feast of San Biagio'* and *The Feast of Sant'Agata.'* These festivals were traditionally Sicilian and pagan in their origin and each revolved around the offering of foods and handicrafts, together with the lighting of several bonfires and the somewhat dangerous practice of throwing firecrackers. Once again, whilst his family and neighbours were busy enjoying the festivities, Vincenzo took himself off into the maze of back streets and alleyways and began his next stage of target practice. Popping the birds off the telegraph wires was more difficult than he had imagined, indeed, he found it to be almost impossible. This he put down to the fact that there was so much noise and so many firecrackers going off, that the birds hardly had a chance to settle on the wires before they were frightened off again. It was almost like the first time he practiced on the beer kegs, for it seemed that he could hit nothing but thin air. With practice however, his aim and accuracy improved, and he also discovered something quite remarkable. He found that the more he concentrated on the intense anger that burned like an inextinguishable flame in the pit of his stomach, the bigger the birds appeared and the easier they were to hit. Within a relatively short space of time, he found that he was able to hit two or three birds in flight in rapid succession. By the end of March, 1923, with his confidence soaring at heights he could never have imagined, Vincenzo felt ready to take on an even bigger target...Orazzio Tropea himself. Yet as any professional huntsman will testify, before one can kill their prey, one must first find it.

Vincenzo knew that in order to go after Tropea, he would require a certain amount of time, so he decided that it would be wise to have a talk with John Sawyer and found him to be much more accommodating than he had expected. Mr. Sawyer listened to Vincenzo's explanation of how the murder of his father was really only just sinking in and that he found himself desperately struggling to come to terms with his loss. Vincenzo also went on to explain that as his father had died suddenly, he had left no last will or testament and as such, it remained unclear as to what would happen to his father's business. At the time, US law dictated that if a person dies without leaving a will, their estate is passed into the hands of the Probate Department. This department calculates the total value of the estate, the total value of any expenses such as funeral costs, outstanding debts etc, and how many surviving relatives are entitled to receive a share of any remaining funds. However, as Vincenzo's mother was unable to read or write English, it was Vincenzo's responsibility to take care of all the Probate paperwork. Vincenzo also went on to say that his mother was devastated by her loss and that he was not comfortable with the fact that she was left alone each day to cope with the children who, he admitted, were equally distraught. He therefore wished to ask if it would be possible to have two weeks off work in order to get his emotions together and to comfort his family. Sawyer listened intently to what Vincenzo had to say and eventually replied that whilst he empathized with what he was going through, he could not spare him for a full two weeks. He could however, allow him ten days leave and that he hoped Vincenzo realized that it was the best he could do. Vincenzo felt that ten days would be adequate time to fulfill his mission and so, taking what was on offer, thanked Mr. Sawyer and promised to return in ten days time, fully refreshed and ready for work.

* * *

For all his brutality and cunning, Orazzio Tropea was a man of habit. Before he had gunned down Angelo Gibaldi, Tropea went to his café every morning for breakfast and now, as if to prove that he really did have no feel-ings whatsoever, he continued to go there. It appeared that everything had come full circle, for in a move which by-passed the US Probate Department, the café was now once again owned by a Greek man. Ten o'clock each morning, Tropea would sit at his favorite table by the window, drinking his customary espresso laced with *grappa*. The new owner of course knew all about Tropea and the abominable act that he had committed in this very establishment, yet to refuse to accommodate him would almost certainly be suicide. He had already been spared the extortion of Tropea by the simple fact that he was of Hellenic and not Latin extrac-tion, and on that point alone, he could consider himself extremely fortunate indeed.

The morning of April 10, 1923, found Tropea in the café as usual, however, there was something different about this particular morning. Parked just across the street was a claret and white Lincoln Town Car which had been borrowed from a family friend and inside, watching Tropea's every move, was Vincenzo Gibaldi. The sight of the murderous Black Hander, sat calmly drinking his espresso in the very establishment were he had murdered his father in cold blood, made Vincenzo feel as if the burning anger could erupt and consume him completely. He fought to restrain himself, battling the desire to kill the callous degenerate there and then. Somehow he managed to keep calm, telling himself that it was better to bide his time and to wait for the perfect opportunity to reap his timely justice.

After watching Tropea drain his coffee cup and, without even bothering to pay, leave the café, Vincenzo realized that he had a crucial advantage in this deadly game of cat and mouse. Whilst it was possible that Tropea had seen Vincenzo before, possibly when Vincenzo had dropped by to visit his father, he certainly had no reason to know who he was; for all he knew, Vincenzo had merely been another customer. It was therefore unlikely that Tropea would recognize Vincenzo even if he met him. Vincenzo watched intently as Tropea left the café and headed for his black and aubergine Cadillac Town Car. He waited until he had started the engine and begun to drive away, before starting his own car and pulling away from the curb. Vincenzo wanted to feel as though he knew Tropea better than he knew himself, to be able to instinctively feel what his next movement would be, and trailing his prey through the Chicago metropolis, he felt a strange, delicious chill of excitement coursing through his veins. He could not understand why he felt this way, but there was no time to consider the reasons; instead he simply allowed the feeling to wash over him. Vincenzo trailed Tropea from the café on West Harrison Street, travelling east until they reached South Jefferson Street. Here they turned right and then left on to West Cabrini Street, continuing along until they reached Tropea's headquarters: a dark, bleak looking bar on the intersection of West Cabrini and South Canal. Vincenzo stopped his car a few hundred yards from Tropea's and watched as he entered the building and disappeared out of sight. Then he waited.

He waited almost two hours before he finally spotted the object of his attention leaving his 'office' together with two other thugs, namely, Willie Altierri and Jimmy The Bug. At this point in time, Vincenzo did not know for sure that these were the two men who watched as his father was murdered. He thought they were, yet he did not have conclusive proof and unless he approached them and asked them to their faces, probably never would have. Relying on his gut feeling, he told himself that these were indeed the men he was looking for, though he realized that the luxury of killing them would have to wait until another time, for at this moment, his obsession was with the degenerate bastard who had pulled the trigger. Vincenzo watched as the three men entered Tropea's car before driving off, following the exact same route that had been taken to get to the bar. He tailed them back to the Loop before giving up the chase, reasoning that the last thing he needed to do was to become conspicuous and arouse suspicion. Pulling his car over to the curb, Vincenzo watched as Tropea and his cohorts disappeared from sight, knowing that he would be seeing them all again soon enough.

The following day, Vincenzo once again parked the claret and white Lincoln outside the café on West Harrison Street. Looking across the street, Vincenzo could see Tropea sitting at his usual table, sipping his usual espresso and as usual, affecting the air of a man who was the king of all he surveyed. Through the glass the features were unclear, but Vincenzo suddenly saw a disturbing malevolence in his eyes, one which could make the blood run cold and turn a heart to ice. He remembered something his mother had once told him, that the eyes are like windows, allowing light to pass to and from the soul, and that if you cannot see the light, it is because the soul is too dark. Tropea's eyes were like the eyes of a Great White Shark, black as night and with no hint of life or emotion. Vincenzo sat like this for over an hour, simply staring into the soulless void of his enemy's eyes, until finally Tropea rose from his seat and left the café, before stepping into his aubergine and black Cadillac just as he had done the previous day. Once again, Vincenzo waited until the Cadillac had pulled away from the curb, before falling in behind at a discreet distance.

The Cadillac took the same route that it had done the day before, once again coming to a halt outside the headquarters on the corner of West Cabrini Street and South Canal. Vincenzo watched as Tropea entered the building, disappearing out of sight behind the dank façade. As Vincenzo had previously observed, Tropea was a creature of habit and so he was not too surprised when, around two hours later, his quarry emerged from his lair with Altierri and The Bug and proceeded to head back downtown. Indeed, as Vincenzo would discover over the next eight days of surveillance, Tropea and his motley, murderous crew never once deviated from this course of daily action. It was almost as though a habitual pattern of behaviour was something of a prerequisite to being a Black Hander. On what was to be the final day of his observation, Vincenzo hardly even needed to follow the Cadillac, for by now he knew damn well which route it would take. As they returned from the bar, Vincenzo hung back and watched Tropea disappear into the sprawling metropolis, before guiding his own car toward the Chicago Harbour.

In the days and months following his father's internment, the young Vincenzo had grown up immensely. Whilst he could never have been considered to be well educated, he was nevertheless making up for his academical failings by educating himself in the ways of the street. He watched the street gangs and noted where they hung out, discovered the bootleggers' warehouses, and found where black market purchases could be made. During the course of his new education, he discovered that the prime area for contraband was the Chicago Harbour. Here, goods which had been unloaded from the thirteen thousand or so ships that drifted in and out of the harbour each year, were stacked in the immense dockyard ready for distribution to their final destination. In 1923, business was not conducted as rigorously as it is today, with the majority of goods that were shipped from major manufacturers being logged inaccurately, if at all. It was therefore inevitable that a portion of these untraceable goods found their way onto the black market.

A few days into his surveillance, Vincenzo had visited the harbour to make enquiries as to where he might be able to obtain both a gun and ammunition with no questions asked. Eventually, he was given information regarding a shipment of firearms that was due in from Greece on April 19. Now on the designated date, after parking his car close to the dockside, Vincenzo set out to find the Greek ship and its potentially lethal cargo. Before long he found the huge vessel, heavily laden with weaponry from some of the world's leading firearms companies, and it was with a little trepidation that he approached a member of the ship's crew and stated his business. The man he had chosen to approach spoke very little English and it took some time for him to properly understand exactly what it was that this young boy wanted. Eventually he understood, and promptly produced what Vincenzo instantly knew was the perfect weapon: a Remington .38 caliber revolver. The only stumbling block was the price, for the Hellenic seaman wanted the immense sum of $50; even in spite of the profitable sale of his father's business, Vincenzo could only afford $30 at the very most. On seeing the cash however, the seaman was soon persuaded to sell at a reduced price. All Vincenzo needed now was the correct ammunition, and for an extra $5, he was told that he could purchase a full box of dum dum bullets. Sicilians not only have an empathy with vengeance, but they are also extremely particular as to the way in which their vengeance is reaped. It is favourable that the act of vengeance should precisely match the original crime down to the smallest detail. Therefore, when he was offered the poignant box of ammunition, Vincenzo did not need to be asked twice, for he had long since decided that by having his body ripped apart by dum dum bullets, Orazzio Tropea would die in exactly the same fashion as his humble father had done. Vincenzo was now fully equipped and ready to make good the promise which he had made on that cold dark day, three months ago.

It was 9am, on the morning of April 20, 1923, when Vincenzo Gibaldi once again parked the claret and white Lincoln, outside the café on West Harrison Street. Tropea had not yet arrived, but Vincenzo needed to make sure that today, more than any other day in his life, everything went according to plan. In his left hand pocket was the loaded .38 revolver together with the remaining bullets, whilst on the opposite side, his fingers closed around the three Indian Head nickels. As he held them, he reaffirmed his promise and felt sure that he would indeed succeed in his mission. He told himself that even if he failed and was himself killed, he would at least fall where his father had fallen and would die clutching the last objects that his father had held. Vincenzo was fully aware of the enormity of his actions: he knew that before the morning was over, either he or Tropea would lie dead.

Vincenzo was shaken from his thoughts by the sight of the familiar aubergine and black Cadillac drawing to a halt outside the café. Vincenzo watched and waited until Tropea had entered the premises and had seated himself at his table, before opening the door of his own car and stepping out onto the street. Across from him, he could see Tropea being served with his customary espresso and as he crossed the street, he made sure that his eyes remained fixed on the devil-like vision before him. As he reached the door of the café he paused for a moment, steadying himself, before he entered the building and walked over to Tropea's table. The detail over whether any words passed between the two men has been lost in the labyrinth of folklore that has grown up around the story, but what is known is that a remark was made by Vincenzo's revolver, speaking in its own lethal tongue. The first dum dum bullet – expertly aimed – ripped open Tropea's chest, the force sending both him and his chair flying backwards through the air. To Vincenzo, everything appeared to happen in slow motion, as he watched the bleeding body of Tropea land with a heavy thud on the café floor. Calmly, Vincenzo walked over to where Tropea lay and as he stood over him, all the grief and anger which had been welling up inside of him, suddenly exploded into a furious and wanton torrent of vengeance, for now he wanted not only to kill Tropea, he wanted to make him suffer. Taking a deep breath, Vincenzo emptied the five remaining bullets into Tropea's arms, legs and groin. With each shot, the sadistic killer groaned in agony as his flesh and bone was blasted into a bloody, nebulous mass. The reverberations of gunfire around the café walls were punctuated by the sound of cups, saucers and cutlery crashing to the ground, as terrified patrons tossed their tables and chairs aside and fell to the floor in an effort to escape the deadly fusillade. Cowering behind the upturned furniture, everyone kept their heads bowed low, not wishing to be seen for fear that they may become the killer's next victim. None of them were to know that the only life which was destined to end that day, was that of Orazzio Tropea. Purposefully and methodically, Vincenzo removed a further six bullets from his left hand pocket, reloaded the revolver and began to fire once more into the body that was still writhing in agony on the blood splattered floor. Once again, Vincenzo emptied his gun into the soft tissue of Tropea's ample frame; he wanted to prolong the suffering, to make sure that Tropea could see the masked face of death waiting in the wings and know that the reaper was at Vincenzo's beck and call. Reloading for a third time, Vincenzo looked with satisfaction at the hideous, mutilated form and relished the sight of Tropea's life literally ebbing away with each heartbeat. He fired a further five times before offering his final insult, firing into the face of Tropea so that a closed coffin would be required, just as had been for his father. For the final finishing flourish, Vincenzo removed one of the three Indian Head nickels that he held in his pocket and calmly pressed it into Tropea's lifeless right hand. Quickly now, Vincenzo pocketed the revolver, stepped back over the body and exited the café, leaving the most dangerous Black Hander who had ever been destined to curse the earth with his presence, ripped apart in a sickening mass of torn flesh and gouted blood. Part one of his Sicilian vengeance had been served.

CHAPTER SEVEN

JUSTICE PART TWO

Despite the fact that it did not take a genius to piece together this jigsaw of vengeance and intrigue, it appeared that the Chicago Police Department was either unable or unwilling to solve the brutal murder of Orazzio Tropea. Indeed, whilst there were undoubtedly a few officers who were rather disgruntled at the sudden deprivation of their supplementary paycheck, it seemed that for the most part, both the police and citizens alike were rather relieved to have him out of the way. Even the witnesses who had been in the café at the time proved to be somewhat unenthusiastic when it came to identifying Tropea's killer; the most that anyone would say was that they had *'seen the shadow of a man, but that it had all happened so fast.'* Given the fact that they were all terrified for their own lives and had, throughout the duration of the onslaught, been hiding behind upturned tables and chairs, their testimonies were hardly inaccurate. Nevertheless, Vincenzo was worried and for the next couple of days, he spent his time hovering around the newsstands, in an effort to determine whether the police had any leads. However, the most that the police and media could offer was speculation as to the motive – the fact that Tropea was carrying a large sum of money which had been left untouched, meant that robbery had long since been ruled out – and also as to the meaning of the nickel that had been placed in his hand; the media especially had a field day with this aspect of the murder, claiming that it was the killer's way of expressing contempt for his victim, insinuating that it was the total value he placed on his life. Had they known that Angelo Gibaldi had held three nickels at the very moment he was killed, the riddle would have easily been solved, but as the days went by, it appeared that Vincenzo had executed his plan to perfection.

Across the city however, in Suite 202 of the Hawthorne Hotel, a young man was reading with interest the story of the brutal slaying of Orazzio

Tropea. He knew all about Tropea, in fact it was due to the activities of The Black Hand that he himself had come to Chicago and as such, was intrigued as to the existence of a soul whose audacity could lead him to take out Tropea in such an expeditious manner. The young man absorbed all the details of the killer's modus operandi, from the murder location to the use of dum dum bullets, from the fact that Tropea's bankroll was untouched to the Indian Head nickel; these final factors especially piqued his curiosity, for it suggested that the murder was not only the result of a personal grudge, but also that there was possibly more to follow. Of this fact he could not be sure, indeed only time would tell whether his prophecy would become a reality.

After his ten days leave had expired, Vincenzo returned to his work at the biscuit factory, however it was not long before things began to turn sour between James Sawyer and himself. So exhilarated was Vincenzo by his successful elimination of Tropea, that his mind was taken over by thoughts of going after Two Knife and The Bug. He began skipping work in order to undertake surveillance of his new quarry, graduating from occasional lateness to the point where he was missing whole days and all without any explanation. Finally James Sawyer decided that enough was enough. On one of the days he had decided to put in an appearance, Sawyer called Vincenzo into his office. Several times he asked for an explanation for his erratic behavior, reminding him that they had known each other for a while now and that if he needed any help in any way, he would try to do whatever he could. Despite all of James Sawyer's encouragement and sympathetic tones, silence was the only reply which was forthcoming. It was not that Vincenzo wanted to ignore or to cause offence to his boss, nor did he feel that had been done any disservice. He knew that he owed Sawyer an immense debt of gratitude for giving him a well paid job at such a young age, thus enabling him to take care of his family in a manner that many men twice his age could not aspire to. He had also given the young Vincenzo a certain amount of stability by displaying faith in his ability, a faith which Vincenzo had repaid by proving that he was someone who could be trusted, and treating his boss more as a friend than an employer. Yet the events which were, at this moment consuming his life, were such that he could not tell a single living soul; he had forsworn the ties of honourable friendship, affection's bonds and loyal gratitude. Therefore, when faced with Sawyer's barrage of questions Vincenzo's instinct inevitably took over, manifesting itself in stolid, unwavering silence. At the end of the meeting Sawyer felt that he had but one option left open to him and subsequently informed Vincenzo that his employment was terminated with immediate effect.

Vincenzo had mixed emotions over his sacking. On the one hand, he knew that it gave him the freedom to pursue his next intended targets without fear that someone would be checking up on his whereabouts, but on the other hand, there was now the worry over what he and his family would do for money. There were of course the proceeds of the sale of his father's café, but in Vincenzo's mind that was for his mother and his brothers and sisters; it would certainly not last long if they had to keep dipping into it just to survive. There was also the thought of how Helena would take the news that they would have to tighten their belts, for the moment at least. He knew that she would be disappointed, but what could he do? Nevertheless, it seemed that no matter how many factors there were to consider, the images of Two Knife and The Bug were at the forefront of his mind and he knew that the only way in which he could erase them, was to erase the men themselves.

In this quest, the first item on his agenda was to find his would- be prey. Whilst he knew that Tropea had most certainly been a creature of habit, whether Two Knife and The Bug would be given over to the same tendencies, he was yet to discover. Therefore, after once again borrowing the claret and white Lincoln, Vincenzo toured the streets of Little Italy and Little Sicily, searching for the Hadean-like visions that had been haunting both his days and nights. When this proved unsuccessful, he decided to try his luck at the bar on West Cabrini Street and South Canal, and it was here that he found exactly who he was looking for. In fact, it seemed that he had just brought his car to a halt outside the bar, when the two men came stumbling out of the door, completely inebriated. The funeral of Tropea had just taken place, and after witnessing his internment in Mount Olivet Cemetery, Two Knife and The Bug had gone to the bar to toast their associate. The sight of the duo drunkenly stumbling their way along the street, gave Vincenzo the idea that these two men were not quite so dangerous as Tropea had been; he believed that should someone be a self confessed menace, that someone would undoubtedly have enemies and as such, should never allow themselves to become too intoxicated to mount a defence to any potential attack. He realized that his surveillance would have to be put on hold, for today at least, for it was impossible to follow them at the moment, especially by car. Not that Vincenzo minded too much, for having waited this long, his patience could certainly stretch to another day.

The following day, Vincenzo intended to once again try his luck at the bar however, no sooner had he rounded the corner of West Cabrini Street, than he saw his quarry stepping into an aubergine coloured Lincoln and driving off down South Canal Street. Vincenzo waited until they had disappeared round the corner, before he began to follow them through the labyrinth of Chicago's streets. After a few miles, he saw the Lincoln pull into the curb just outside a tenement block on Tenth Street. Bringing his own car to a halt at a few meters back, Vincenzo watched as The Bug exited the Lincoln and entered the tenement block, not forgetting to notice that he entered the front door of the building with a key. His common sense told him that this was The Bug's residence and so he watched intently, wishing he could see which apartment he was heading for.

Approximately ten minutes later, The Bug reappeared, stepped back into the car and within a few seconds, the pair had set off again. Vincenzo fell in behind at a discreet distance however, he soon realized that they were merely heading back in the direction of the bar. He wondered why the two men had bothered to go all the way to The Bug's apartment, only to head straight back to the bar. Maybe they had gone there to collect something, but he had not seen The Bug carrying anything and in any case, why would they both have to go? Perhaps someone else at the bar had ordered them to deliver something, a message for example. Or, maybe they had their suspicions that they were being watched, after all, their boss had recently been murdered and perhaps they rightly believed that they were next. With all of these possibilities running riot through his mind, Vincenzo decided not to push his luck too far and pulled his car into the curb, allowing the murderous pair to continue on their journey undisturbed.

The next morning found Vincenzo parked a little way past the tenement block on Tenth Street; he did not wish to keep hanging around outside the bar, for fear of arousing suspicion. It seemed that he was waiting a few hours before he spotted the aubergine Lincoln pulling into the curb outside the building. He watched as once again The Bug stepped out of the car and entered the building, only to reappear a few minutes later before driving off again. This time however, Vincenzo was not going to follow on behind. Instead he left his car and hung around outside the building, watching and waiting for anyone entering or leaving. Finally, a young woman came to the front door on her way out of the building and without even thinking, Vincenzo approached her. He told her that he had a message to deliver to a man named Jimmy, whom he believed lived in her building, and he wondered if she knew of anyone by that name and if so, where he might find him. The woman replied that her husband was named Jimmy and that if he wanted to, he could tell her the message and she could relay it to her husband when he got home. Vincenzo insisted that he had to deliver the message personally and that it would be a great help if she could tell him where he might be found; in any case, they may not be speaking about the same man. The young woman said that her husband would be home around eight o'clock and that he could stop by then if he wished. Vincenzo professed his thanks and promised to return that evening, before returning to his car and heading home.

That night, the night of April 27, 1923, Vincenzo returned to the tenement building on Tenth Street. After parking his car around the corner, so as not to arouse The Bug's suspicion as to why there was a strange car parked outside his home, he crossed the street and headed for the front door of the building. He had no intention of entering, instead choosing to wait amongst the dim shadows that crept along the wall by the side of the entrance. Vincenzo glanced out onto the quiet street and felt the cool night air closing in around him. Tucking his hands deep into his coat pockets, he felt the reassuring form of the .38 revolver loaded with dum dums, together with the two remaining nickels. Confident that no one had seen him approaching the building, he crouched down in the camouflage of the half light and waited; the seconds ticked slowly by, each second seeming like a minute, each minute like an hour. It was almost eight o'clock; any minute now, he told himself.

It felt as if he had been in the shadows for an eternity, when he suddenly heard the distant growl of an engine and saw the familiar shape of the aubergine Lincoln looming large on the horizon. Vincenzo watched carefully as the car pulled into the curb outside the tenement block; he steadied himself, sure that it was The Bug, yet needing to be one hundred percent positive. As the man stepped from the Lincoln, his face was briefly illuminated in the glow of a street lamp, clearly identifying him as the wanted man. Leaving his car, Jimmy The Bug started along the pathway to his building, blissfully unaware that these would be the last steps he would ever take. Vincenzo's gaze followed him up the path and he felt his grip almost autonomously tightening around the revolver. Slowly pulling the gun from his pocket, he took a deep breath, steeling himself for the moment of vengeance. At the very moment that The Bug approached the front door, Vincenzo cocked the safety catch. The click instantly grabbed The Bug's attention and he stopped to turn towards the noise, rapidly trying to adjust his eyes to the darkness of the shadows. In the instant that he looked towards him, the retort of Vincenzo's revolver rang out, the bullet catching its target square in the forehead. As though propelled by some fierce, unseen hand, The Bug was lifted clean off his feet and thrown backwards through the air. He landed just to the side of the pathway, the shock induced spasms causing his body to jerk violently like some demented marionette. Calmly, Vincenzo stepped from the shadows, his own face briefly illuminated by the street lamp as he crossed the path to where his victim lay. A pool of blood was already forming around The Bug's head, glistening slickly like some ghastly halo. Whilst his hatred for Jimmy The Bug was not as overpowering as the hatred he held for Tropea, he nevertheless wished to replicate the contemptuous insult that had been bestowed on his father. Thus, as he stood astride the body, Vincenzo levelled the revolver towards the middle of The Bug's face and fired, reducing the once proud features to an amorphous, gruesome mass. The noise of the gunfire reverberated around the neighbouring buildings, drawing inquisitive citizens to their windows to see the cause of the commotion. Satisfied that his two shots would suffice, Vincenzo coolly pulled one of the two remaining nickels from his coat pocket and pressed it firmly into The Bug's right palm, before hurriedly stepping back over the body and returning to his car, pocketing the revolver as he did so. As he started the engine, Vincenzo wondered whether anyone had seen him and if so, whether they had seen enough to identify him. It was this thought which prompted him to avoid driving back past the tenement block, anxious to avoid the possibility of anyone being able to identify his car. Events had gone so well up until now, that it was pointless to spoil it all at this late stage by tempting fate.

In the days subsequent to the killing, Vincenzo once again nervously scanned the papers at the newsstands, searching for information as to whether the police had any leads concerning the two murders which he had committed. He was sure that they must at least have had an idea as to why these crimes had taken place, so it was with a great sense of relief that he read that the police were dumbfounded by the perpetration of a second brutal killing in the space of a week. The reports stated that whilst the police knew that the two victims were members of The Black Hand, their murders did not bear the hallmarks of gangland slayings. The police also admitted that they were baffled by the fact that both men had been carrying in excess of $500 which had, in both cases, been left untouched. The reports went on to say that with no motive, no murder weapon and, more importantly, no suspects, the police were appealing to the public for information. Once again, it seemed that the young Vincenzo had planned the second install-ment of his vengeful crusade to perfection.

Back in Suite 202 of the Hawthorne Hotel, the young man sat back in his luxurious leather armchair, reading the story of the killing of Jimmy The Bug. He could see the pattern that was emerging, but he was not about to let the police in on the secret. Instead, he set about doing a little investiga-tive work of his own, starting with uncovering the secrets of the café on West Harrison Street.

The success which Vincenzo was experiencing in tracking down his father's killers was bringing about certain changes in his personality. When he had first set out on his mission of vengeance, he felt in his heart that once his mission had been completed, he could then return to a normal life; go back to being the reticent Vincenzo Gibaldi, factory worker, doting father and loving husband. With the wisdom of hindsight, it is unfortunately all too clear that he was blinding himself to the reality of the situation, for it is impossible for anyone who sets out to willingly take the lives of three people – albeit with justifiable reasons – to expect that their own lives will ever be normal again. The events of the past few months had irrevocably changed his life; once the Rubicon is crossed, it is impossible to cross back, yet this was a fact of which Vincenzo was painfully unaware. Buoyed by his remarkable success, he felt that he could do anything, take on anyone, even take on the world. Before he could take on anything else however, he had to take on Two Knife.

CHAPTER EIGHT

TWO KNIFE

In terms of danger, Willie 'Two Knife' Altierri was almost on a par with Orazzio Tropea. He was certainly not as sadistic, yet he was nonetheless just as pernicious, treating murder more as a pastime than a heinous act. In today's society, Two Knife would undoubtedly have been locked away in a mental institution, for not only was he clearly a psychopath, he also had what can only be described as affection for his weapons. He cleaned them regularly, almost caressing them as he did so and had often been heard to refer to his knives as 'friends.' When it came to killing, Two Knife would do it anywhere, anytime and with the least provocation. One of his most famous *'rubouts'* or hits, was that of a small time Irish hoodlum named Eddie MacFarland, also known as *'Charleston Eddie'* because of his love of the popular dance. Charleston Eddie had made the mistake of stepping into Two Knife's collecting territory, an offence for which, in the case of a minor hood such as Eddie was, a strong warning would be given which would normally serve as a sufficient deterrent. Two Knife however, was a man not known for his conversational skills, or his diplomacy for that matter, and a few days later, Charleston Eddie's body was found in a local cinema, where he had been enjoying a matinee film. His throat had been cut so viciously that his head had almost been severed, yet the killing had been performed so adroitly that it was over in seconds and not a single person in the cinema had seen or heard a thing. Despite all his psychopathic malevolence however, to Vincenzo, Two Knife was simply the last of the cold blooded bastards who had stood and watched as his father was executed. Vincenzo had one nickel remaining; a personified malediction was about to descend on Two Knife, a fact of which the Black Hander was blissfully oblivious.

There is a saying that it is possible to have too much of a good thing, and for Vincenzo, the luck which he had so far experienced in his quest for vengeance was about to work against him. For Two Knife, being more than a little alarmed at the sudden demise of his two associates, unexpectedly dropped out of circulation. Whether he had an inkling as to the identity of the perpetrator or what the motive for the killings may be is unclear, though one suspects that if he had known who the killer was, then Vincenzo would undoubtedly have found himself as the hunted rather than the hunter. Nevertheless, Two Knife was smart enough to figure out that someone had certainly borne some kind of a grudge against Tropea and The Bug and so maybe, also against himself.

Throughout the past few months of his surveillance, Vincenzo had learned a great deal about the behaviour of the Black Hand, or at least the three members with whom he was concerned. He considered himself to be something of an expert on their psychology, often going over in his mind what he thought their next move would be. He had observed the deals which they had effected and had learned that, despite all their supposed secrecy, this ruthless gang of freelancers were hardly as sophisticated as they would have people believe, with many deals being done out on the street. Vincenzo had also been able to work out quite accurately, in which areas of the city the three men operated. Tropea had held the whole of Little Italy and Little Sicily as his dominion, but had allowed The Bug and Two Knife to ply their trade in the South and East sections, the two sectors which were predominantly inhabited by southern Italians and Sicilians. Of all that he had learned, it was this knowledge in particular which now gave him the edge that he needed in order to track down Two Knife.

Vincenzo had all the time in the world; not once during the past few months had he ever felt hurried to take out the murderous triumvirate. He had often told himself that it was better to take his time, to meticulously plan his each and every move, for revenge is never done well if it is done in a hurry. Two Knife on the other hand, was living on borrowed time and in more ways than one, for in spite of his reluctance to show his face around his stomping ground, financial necessity would inevitably force him to continue with his old rounds: no one can survive without money. Therefore, just three days after the murder of The Bug, Two Knife once again began hustling the heads of a few of the Sicilian households in the East section of Little Sicily.

When shaking someone down, Two Knife used the tried and tested technique of calling on the head of the household in the evening. This was because husbands and fathers were generally at home in the evenings with their families, a factor which generally made them easier to intimidate. For example, should the demand for payment be met with resistance, the man's wife and children would also become the target of his threats. During the evening of April 30, and May 1, 1923, Vincenzo observed these goings on from his car, watching as the Black Hander called on various innocent and unsuspecting families. As he watched, he thought about his father, for he now knew that it was likely that he had also been threatened in this way. This was a fact over which he had reproached himself time and time again, for in his mind, he should have known what was going on, or at least seen the warning signs. He wished he could have been there when the demand was made, for he felt sure that he would have killed the filthy pig right there and then with his bare hands. Not once had Vincenzo felt any form of guilt or remorse for taking the lives of two men indeed, at this very moment in time, the thought of them lying in their own blood, their eyes staring life-lessly skyward, was the only thought which brought him comfort.

As he caught sight of Two Knife leaving one of the houses, he suddenly realized that this particular killing would have to be his most daring yet. He had never attempted to follow Two Knife back to his residence, for he reasoned that he would surely be on his guard in that respect. He had also noticed that the Black Hander had ceased to patronize the bar on West Cabrini Street, which made it impossible to take him out there. Vincenzo now knew that if he was to take out Two Knife, he had to take him on the street.

May 8, 1923, found Two Knife once again demanding money with menaces, this time from a house located on Twelfth Street – now renamed Roosevelt Road – the natural border between Little Sicily and Greek Town. The house was the home of the Abbandando family, a relatively wealthy family originating from Palermo. That night also found Vincenzo sat in his parked car opposite the house, watching intently as Two Knife knocked on the door before entering into a brief conversation with the man of the house and making his way inside. Vincenzo's experience told him that the dealings should not take more than a few minutes, so he had little time to lose. As the front door of the house closed, Vincenzo left his car, crossed the street and walked up to the house, stopping at the end of the pathway that lead up to the door. Pushing his hand deep inside his coat pocket, he allowed his fingers to close around the cold metal of his revolver and took a deep breath; this was the moment for which he must steel himself, call on every fibre of his resolve, for should he panic, there was a chance that he would merely hit the masonry rather than his intended target. A few moments later, the front door opened and out stepped a smiling Two Knife, followed by the ashen faced husband and father of the family. For a moment, this sight threw Vincenzo a little off guard, for he had not counted on any member of the family being in such close proximity to his prey. However, if that was the way it had to be, he told himself, then that was the way it had to be. Calmly and steadily, Vincenzo raised his gun, took aim and fired, catching Two Knife who was in the process of turning back to speak to the man behind him, in his left shoulder. The man of the house ducked back behind his front door to escape the fusillade, whilst the shock of the impact spun Two Knife around to face his assailant; there was a look of astonishment in his eyes, as though he could not quite believe what had happened, followed by a look of pure, unadulterated rage. Instinctively, Two Knife fumbled for his weapons, but the dum dum bullet had shattered his shoulder, causing his left arm to hang inertly from its splintered socket. Before he could react further, Vincenzo fired again, this time hitting Two Knife in the upper part of his chest. A spray of blood suddenly erupted from his gaping wounds, illuminated by the light of the open doorway like some hideous carmine fountain. By this time, the heavy sound of gunfire had brought the lady of the Abbandando house to the door. When she caught sight of the bleeding figure that now lay on the ground, fighting for each breath, she screamed and promptly fainted. Aware that time was fast running out, Vincenzo reached into his pocket, pulled out the final Indian Head nickel and tossed it onto the dying body of Two Knife, before running as hard as he could back to his car.

That night and the following day were the most worrying that Vincenzo had experienced since he first embarked on his mission, for not only had at least two members of the Abbandando family witnessed the shooting, he was also convinced that he had left Two Knife alive. If this was true, then he knew that his life, as well as the lives of his wife and child was in serious danger. Unable to sleep, Vincenzo rose before the sun and went to the only source of information he could rely on: the newsstands. Sure enough, splashed across the front page of the newspaper was a report of the shooting.

'THIRD MYSTERY MURDER' ran the headline, the word murder causing Vincenzo's heart to skip a beat with relief. The report went on '*Willie 'Two Knife' Altierri, a notorious hoodlum and reportedly a member of the infamous so called Black Hand, was last night gravely wounded in a shooting. He was taken to the Cook County Hospital, where he died three hours later.*' Also contained in the report was the fact that despite witnessing the killing, the Abbandando family had been unable to assist the police in identifying the gunman. Mrs. Abbandando truthfully claimed that she had seen only the body of the victim before she had passed out, whilst her husband had spent the entire episode hiding behind his front door. As yet, the police had made little headway in their investigation of the killings of Orazzio Tropea and Jimmy The Bug, and now this latest killing only served to confound them further. The presence of the nickel, the lack of a motive and witnesses was just too perplexing and to many officers in the force, the murders were unsolvable.

Angelo Gibaldi had been shot down in cold blood on January 8, 1923 and now, exactly four months later, the circle of vengeance had been closed. After reading the report on the death of Two Knife, Vincenzo visited his father's grave at the Holy Guardian Angel Church, to tell him that justice had been done and that the last of the three gunmen had paid the ultimate price for his crime. Vengeance had been both demanded and obtained in a way which truly reflected Vincenzo's Sicilian heritage and moral disposition. His father was dead and he knew that no words or actions could ever reverse that horrible fact, yet he believed that his father's soul could now finally rest in peace. His own soul could also rest, having at last been purged of the vengeful animal which roared within.

The killings had all been seemingly high profile, catching both the attention and imagination not only of the community, but also of the media, who took delight in hypothesizing as to the identity of the perpetrator and what his motive may be. In the ensuing days, the Italian and Sicilian neighbourhoods came alive with gossip over the possibility of a vigilante, single handedly waging war on the extortionists and who, at the moment at least, appeared to be winning. The newspapers fanned the conjectural conflagration, speculating on when the next murder would occur and who the victim may be. As it was, there was only the young Vincenzo Gibaldi and the young man residing at the Hawthorne Hotel who knew why these men had been killed.

Having laid his ghosts to rest, Vincenzo had set himself free and could now concentrate on getting his life back to normal. He planned to obtain new employment, to work hard as he always had done in order to make a success of his life. He was looking forward to making up for lost time with his wife and daughter and had promised himself that one day, he would tell little Helen the truth as to what had happened to her grandfather. Despite all the goodwill in the world however, Vincenzo could never go back to being who he was. Just as the merry-go-round appears somewhat boring in comparison to the thrill and excitement of the rollercoaster, would Vincenzo, after experiencing the thrill that he admittedly felt in taking the lives of three men, consider his old life to be equally jejune?

In the mid and latter parts of 1923, it seemed that he indeed could go back, as the lives of both himself and that of his family, slowly began to return to an even keel. Almost as a carbon copy of his father's early years in the New World, Vincenzo managed to obtain a part time job as a cleaner in a local café, allowing him to bring home a small but nevertheless steady income. Baby Helen was approaching her first birthday and was developing in leaps and bounds, whilst the terrible emotional wounds suffered by Josephine at the loss of her beloved husband, were being slowly eased by the soothing poultice of time. Vincenzo and Helena began to make up for lost time in their marriage, and whilst Vincenzo was sure that his wife was aware that he now owned a gun, he was relieved that she never once questioned him about it. Eventually, Vincenzo began to look back on the events that had occurred in the preceding few months as just an extraordinary chapter in his young life. Although it was true that, at the age of eighteen he had encountered more events than most people come across in a lifetime, it had merely been a period of craziness that he could now put behind him. Yet if he thought that his life had so far been a little strange, it was all about to get completely bizarre.

CHAPTER NINE

THE YOUNG MAN

The Hawthorne Hotel – a four storey, brown brick building located on Cicero's West Side, itself a suburb of Chicago – was in its day a four star establishment, though by today's standards it would be regarded as little more than an elaborate motel. Situated at 4823 Twenty Second Street, one block west of the main arterial highway that runs north to south through Chicago, it was one of the most prominent buildings in the city. The rooms on the third and fourth floors of the hotel were entirely suites, the grandest of all being Suite 202. In order to obtain access to this room, a visitor would have to walk the length of a passageway, twenty-five feet long and decked out on either side by chairs and small tables. At each table sat an armed guard, huge gorilla like men whose fingers hovered constantly over their loaded pistols and who would have already been alerted to the visitor's presence by a lookout, stationed in the hotel lobby. It was here in this passageway, in the latter part of 1923, that a nervous Vincenzo Gibaldi found himself standing.

The reason for Vincenzo's visit was that his presence had been requested by the guest currently residing in Suite 202. Despite his youth – for he was just twenty-four years of age himself – the guest was nevertheless beginning to make a name for himself, not only on Chicago's streets, but also in the pages of the city's tabloids. The guest was signed in as Al Brown, though he was more commonly known by his real name: Al Capone.

Capone was a man who took great pride in knowing everything, a man who made himself aware of every small detail about anything that was happening in his city. This thirst for knowledge had led to his attention being grasped by the murder of Orazzio Tropea and his motley crew. So intrigued was he as to who would have balls big enough to take on Two Knife Altierri and The Bug – let alone Tropea himself – that he had used his contacts on the street to look into their recent activities. Before long, his contacts had relayed details of the circumstances surrounding the murder of Angelo Gibaldi, including the fact that Tropea had been the lead gunman. Therefore, whilst the Chicago police were hunting for any possible leads concerning the three mysterious and apparently motiveless murders, Capone was preparing to receive Vincenzo Gibaldi, the young man whom he considered to be the prime suspect. Hence, Vincenzo now found himself about to enter the main suite of the Hawthorne Hotel, ready to meet the man who would, in time, be regarded as the most famous, or rather infamous gangster who ever lived.

Vincenzo of course had no knowledge as to why he was there, for he had simply received a message that it was in his best interests to come. Once he had entered the room and the two men had exchanged pleasantries, his nerves were assaulted by overwhelming shock and horror, when Capone announced that he knew it was he who had murdered Orazzio Tropea, The Bug and Two Knife Altierri. At that point in time, Vincenzo believed that no one had knowledge as to the killer's identity and for a moment, was somewhat perplexed as to how to react. His mind ran riot with thoughts as to what this accusation, albeit an accurate one, could possibly mean. Was Capone angry because he had committed these murders without permission? Had Tropea been an ally of Capone, thus making him desire vengeance on the man who had killed his friend? How had Capone discovered his identity? Was his family in any danger? Vincenzo's heart beat frantically and so heightened were his senses, that it felt as though he could actually hear the rhythmic rushing of his blood as it was pumped to his desperately frayed nerves.

Finally, after what seemed like an eternity, Vincenzo decided to rely on his instinct, strenuously denying that he had had any involvement in the murders. Capone countered by telling him that he was obviously not aware who he was speaking to, and reiterated that he *knew* that Vincenzo was the killer. Realizing that outright denial was doing him no good whatsoever, Vincenzo nervously asked how Capone knew that he had perpetrated these crimes. Capone's reply was concise: it was his job to know. Having basically admitted his guilt, Vincenzo's next question was whether he was going to be arrested. A low ripple of laughter flowed between Capone and his bodyguards; no, he was not going to be arrested. Capone explained that he was certainly no friend of The Black Hand, for he himself had travelled to Chicago in order to help rid his friend's uncle of the parasitic menace. Capone continued that he had simply wished to meet Vincenzo, to congratulate him on a job well done and also to extend a proposition to the young assassin. Vincenzo felt a wave of relief sweep over him and for a moment, his entire body seemed leeched of energy. Slumping back into a luxurious armchair, he struggled to regain his composure as sheer desperation was replaced by a wonderful sense of calm, followed by a curious sense of unease. This, Vincenzo put down to the fact that he now expected Capone to require him to carry out a favour, as a sort of 'thank you' for not informing the police as to his recent activities.

After a few moments, Capone outlined his proposition, telling Vincenzo that he wanted him to come to work for the Outfit – as Capone's organization was known – as a hit man, on a starting salary of $200 per week. If ever there was a dilemma, then it was in that very suite and was staring Vincenzo straight in the face. At this point in time, his cleaning job allowed him to bring home the minimal sum of just $8 per week; $200 per week was more money than he could possibly imagine. His mind was suddenly awash with thoughts about what he could do with that kind of money; Helena and little Helen would want for nothing; he could take care of his mother, thus leaving the proceeds of the sale of his father's café to be used for his brothers and sisters education, or to help them later on in their lives. Being somewhat distracted by the vision of dollar signs dancing before him, Vincenzo momentarily forgot his nerves and confidently asked for a drink while he considered the proposal. Almost instantaneously, a cold glass of bourbon on-the-rocks was proffered by a burly bodyguard, his outstretched arm causing his immaculate jacket to fall open, revealing a holstered revolver. It was this sight which brought Vincenzo crashing back to reality, for he suddenly saw the flip side of this most valuable coin. True, he had killed three men without so much as a raising of his heart rate, but he had killed with justifiable reasons. Should he accept this position, he would be required to kill people whom he may never have met, or who had never wronged him in any way. There was also the thought that whoever he killed would be someone's husband, father or son, and whose death may have the same devastating effect as his father's death had had on his own family. As Vincenzo was mulling over this barbed predicament, Capone announced that as a gesture of goodwill, he was willing to pay him a week's salary in advance, before proceeding to peel off $200 from a roll of bills big enough to choke an ox. Strangely, in sitting in this opulent suite, Vincenzo was in essence continuing with his street education, for he was fast discovering that cash is a remarkably potent weapon in the placation of the conscience, as well as providing an unchallengeable lubricant for the wheels of business. Without delaying his decision any further, Vincenzo accepted the seemingly unbelievable offer.

During the course of his lifetime, each man makes his own decisions, never knowing or realizing that the decisions that he makes today, may leave an indelible impression on the rest of his life. There is a train of thought which suggests that our destiny is mapped out for us from the very moment we are born into this world and this, in all probability, could be true. Yet it is also true that we as individuals have the power to alter the course that our lives may take by the choices that we make. Albert Einstein once said that *'fate is what life gives you, but destiny is what you do with it.'* If this assertion is correct, then the life of Vincenzo Gibaldi had been charted for him from the very moment that he emerged from his mother's womb, yet when he resolved to seek vengeance from Tropea and his cohorts, and now as he chose to accept Capone's offer, he exercised his right to irrevocably transform his life. Whether or not these choices would have a positive or detrimental effect on his life, was something which would be only be revealed in the fullness of time.

For Vincenzo, aside from the dilemma that he had initially faced when the option of taking up a position in Capone's Outfit was set forth, he now found that he had another, quite familiar quandary to deal with: specifically, the question of his name. He did not take delight in the thought of his wife or mother discovering who his new employer actually was, and this would surely be all too easy should he use his real name. To solve this problem, he reverted back to the name that he had used during his old boxing days, although the nickname would of course be dropped. With his *nom de guerrre* firmly in place, the legend of Jack McGurn was reborn.

Later that evening, as Vincenzo sat down to dinner with Helena, he thought more about the meeting he had had with Capone and how he could break the news to his wife. Rightly or wrongly, he felt a strange sense of excitement about his new position, as though he were embarking on something of an adventure, that he was on the verge of a thrilling new chapter in his life. He knew that he would have to tell Helena that he was no longer a part time cleaner and wanted, more than anything, to be able to share his excitement with her, to tell her that she need never worry about money ever again and that they had a wonderful, bright future ahead of them. Yet the fear of being disappointed by her reaction prevented him from revealing the whole story. Vincenzo told Helena that earlier in the day he had had a meeting with a businessman who owned a large and popular business, and who had offered to take him on as a full time employee. He went on to say that this new job would provide a significant increase in income, but that he may have to work longer and less sociable hours; he also said that he wanted to know if Helena agreed before he accepted the job. To Vincenzo's surprise, Helena's response was to ask if the new job was either dangerous or illegal, a question which he had certainly not expected and for which the only reasonable answer was an outright lie. No, he told her, it was neither dangerous nor illegal. Helena rejoined that in that case, if it was something that Vincenzo wanted to do and if it would make their lives more financially viable, then it was fine by her. Having received his wife's blessing, Vincenzo felt able to look forward to his new position as an employee of Al Capone.

★　★　★

Whilst he had initially been hired as a hit man, Jack McGurn would spend his first few weeks at the Chicago and Northwestern Rail Terminal, located at the intersection of Madison and Canal Street, working in Capone's fruit market racket: a relatively simple, yet remarkably profitable operation involving the seemingly innocent trade of grapes. A somewhat prosaic product by normal gangster standards, this racket was nevertheless an immensely lucrative iron in Capone's fire. Each day, railcar loads of grapes would enter Chicago via the aforementioned Rail Terminal. The fact that grapes are used in the manufacture of wine meant that during prohibition, the fruit was big business. Capone placed McGurn in charge of exacting tribute from the grape merchants, such tribute being in the form of three to five cents per carload of grapes. Of course, the merchants were perfectly within their rights to refuse to pay such tribute, as they would then be forced to pass on this extra expenditure to their customers and in this competitive market, as in any market, the lower the price, the higher the sales. However, should McGurn stumble across a recalcitrant merchant, he would employ the forces not of truculence, but of the Railway Inspector's Union. Thus, a refractory and uncooperative salesman would suddenly discover that his entire cargo had been impounded and that the only way to secure its release was to pay the demanded tribute. As grapes are a delicate and perishable cargo, the salesman soon realized that it was far better business to pay the extra money, than risk losing his entire stock and income.

Given his recent history, the fact that McGurn was in charge of exacting tribute from merchants who were merely trying to make a living, appears to be something of a perversity and one wonders whether his mind ever drew a parallel between his new line of work and the activities of Tropea. True, the merchants were never threatened with the loss of their lives, yet McGurn was nevertheless aiding the extortion of innocent traders. However, it seems that he had drawn a veil over his past and looked upon his new profession merely as an easy way of making money; besides which, *all* the traders were subject to the additional levy, not just those from a particular extraction. At this moment in time, he had no doubts whatsoever that his decision to join Capone was one of the best he had taken in his entire life.

The profits from the fruit market racket were certainly incredible to say the least. A carload of grapes being sold at the Chicago and Northwestern Rail Terminal, would generally sell for around $50. An FBI investigation ascertained that the number of carloads sold at the terminal, generally averaged between five thousand and twenty-five thousand per week. This meant that the tribute of three to five cents per carload, would equate to an income of somewhere between $150 and $1,250 per week. Such an amount, although paltry by the Outfit's usual standards, was nevertheless a significant profit from the sale of mere grapes.

The FBI investigation into the activities at the Chicago and

Northwestern Rail Terminal, stemmed from an initial approach by Mr. Charles Irrgang, leader of the Fruit Labourer's Union. He informed the agents of the racket which was being employed within the terminal and suggested that he would personally fund the positioning of two undercover agents at the terminal itself. His idea was that he would purchase a carload of grapes for the agents, who would then attempt to sell them at the terminal. Irrgang assured them that before the day was out, they would be approached by a man named Vincent DeMore, who would request the payment of a tribute. (DeMore was in fact Jack McGurn, who had, as previously mentioned, taken to using his wife's maiden name after their marriage)

Upon receiving the authority to go ahead with the investigation, the agents stationed themselves at the rail terminal in order to sell their previously acquired carload of grapes. What the agents did not know – nor did Charles Irrgang for that matter – was that Irrgang's office was home to an Outfit employed rat, one which squealed to McGurn. McGurn pondered for a while as to the best solution to this problem, for there were many, equally expedient options open to him, the most obvious of which was to arrange for the agents to be denied access to the terminal. However, he quickly dispensed with this idea, for he realized that such an evasive course of action would merely add fuel to the fire of suspicion. Eventually, and after much consideration, McGurn decided to allow the investigation to proceed as planned, though not before he had ascertained – through various Outfit contacts – the identities of the agents and arranged for them to be allotted a specific place within the terminal. McGurn then put the word out amongst his fellow collectors that the dealers in this particular area were strictly off limits and were not to be approached.

When the day of the investigation arrived, the two undercover agents (names withheld under Section C of the Freedom of Information and Privacy Act) together with their carload of grapes, entered the Chicago and Northwestern Terminal building and were quickly assigned a lot at the far end of the trading area. People came and went, some merely inspecting the goods with a keen, judgmental eye, whilst others bartered with the newcomers over the price. At the end of the day, the agents left the terminal, having sold their wares yet having failed to garner any evidence as to any scam or racket whatsoever.

A few days later, Charles Irrgang again contacted the FBI to say that he was sorry for wasting their time, but that he would no longer be cooperating with them. When asked for a reason – after all, he had made the initial approach – a noticeably shaken Irrgang, stated that he had made a dreadful mistake and as such, was now in fear of his life. This show of influence and power from Capone's Outfit was certainly not lost on McGurn who, in spite of the infancy of his new found career, was already beginning to realize that the tentacles of gangland are more pervasive than the so called long arm of the law. Even so, he was careful to both acknowledge and learn from the fact that it had been a close call.

CHAPTER TEN

BRINIGAN

In the 1990 movie, *'The Godfather III,'* Michael Corleone advises his nephew Vincent, to *'keep your friends close, but keep your enemies closer.'* It was a piece of advice which could so easily have been given by one of the most outwardly amiable men ever to grace the streets of Chicago, a man who referred even to his mortal enemies as *'swell fellows.'* His name was Dean Charles O'Banion, though from his early childhood he was known as Dion rather than Dean.

Born to Irish immigrants Charles and Emma O'Banion, Dion was the second eldest of three children (Charles and Emma actually had four children together, however their daughter, born before Dion, died before she could reach the age of one year) The family resided in Aurora, Illinois, a small town situated approximately twenty-five miles west of Chicago. Despite being afflicted by a genetic disorder which caused his left leg to develop at a slower rate than his right, young Dion was a happy, healthy, well balanced child, slowly blossoming in the bosom of a warm and loving family. Tragically however, this innocent childhood bliss was about to change. In 1904, when Dion was only six years old, his mother Emma contracted Tuberculosis; she died five days later, aged just twenty-nine. It is something of an analogy that just as the death of his father had shaped the life of Jack McGurn, the death of Dion's mother would prove equally fateful.

In an effort to escape from bad memories, Charles O'Banion moved his family to Chicago. Wrapped up in his own grief, he was oblivious to the changes that were happening in the psyche of young Dion. The quiet child became a wild spirit, a real daredevil with no fear of danger. So daring was his nature that his boyhood pals nicknamed him *'Brinigan,'* after a mythical Irish sprite that was always looking for mischief. This love of danger carried through into his adult life and in 1919, secured his first and only spell in Chicago's Bridewell Jail. O'Banion, together with a childhood friend, Samuel 'Nails' Morton, had stolen a safe from a warehouse and were in the process of cracking it open when they were caught red handed. The pair was charged with robbery and each sentenced to one year.

After this event, Dion tried to go straight, securing employment under Moses L. Annenberg, who at the time was co-owner of the Chicago Tribune and whose son, Walter, later went on to be the British Ambassador to Ronald Reagan. O'Banion was employed as the Chicago Tribune's political writer, his job being to write propaganda columns for the Republicans and Democrats. Then, with the advent of prohibition, O'Banion seized his opportunity to get rich quick. Leaving the newspaper business behind, he embarked on a new career as a bootlegger, a move which saw the mischievous Brinigan evolve into Mephistopheles.

Dion O'Banion was a paradoxical man. From the moment that he entered into the bootlegging business, to his acquisition of Chicago's North Side, he was at best, pathologically reckless; at worst, he bordered on the suicidal. Yet there was another side to his nature, a more genteel – perhaps even feminine – side, for behind the idiosyncratic inanity lay a keen florist, a lover of all things floral. So intense was this passion that when the opportunity arose to purchase a flower shop located at 738 North State Street, O'Banion grasped it with both hands. The shop was named Schofield's, after its original owner Bill Schofield, and despite the takeover, O'Banion kept the name. The rear of Schofield's flower shop served as O'Banion's headquarters, with liquor transactions being sealed amongst the chrysanthemums and carnations. Notwithstanding this moderate side to his nature, O'Banion's wildness and incredibly foolhardy behaviour would inevitably take over, so much so that within the first ten months of 1924, O'Banion would not only commit a murder in which he would implicate Capone, but would also attempt to start a gang war, and all this in addition to swindling Capone out of $500,000!

February 1, 1924, was the day that Jack McGurn had his first encounter with Dion O'Banion. It was Election Day in Chicago and McGurn, along with many other Capone henchmen, had been ordered to the polling stations to ensure that everyone voted the right way: the right way, being for Joseph Z. Klenha, the Capone backed Democrat candidate for Mayor. At that point in time, O'Banion was an ally of Capone and as such, had sent some of his own gunmen to join the cause. McGurn encountered O'Banion at a polling station on the corner of Twenty Second Street and Cicero Avenue and according to all reports, disliked him straight away. Later that evening, at a meeting in Capone's suite at the Hawthorne Hotel, McGurn allegedly warned Capone about O'Banion, virtually guaranteeing that Capone would have problems with him. The warning however, did not register with Capone, for although he knew that O'Banion had little or no mental equilibrium, he believed he could handle him.

It took just nineteen days for McGurn's prophecy to become reality, with the murder of a man named John Duffy. Duffy had a girlfriend named Maybelle Exley, a hooker who Duffy had met when he visited the brothel where she worked. On the evening of February 20, 1924, Duffy and Maybelle were engaged in a drinking session in a North Side saloon when the couple got into an argument, one which ended with Duffy shooting Maybelle in the chest, killing her instantly. Suddenly sober and desperate for help, Duffy wound up at Schofield's flower shop and begged O'Banion for assistance. O'Banion told Duffy not to panic, but to go and collect the body and then meet him in The Four Deuces; a Capone owned club located at 2222 South Wabash Avenue. When Duffy arrived at the club, he found O'Banion waiting for him, together with Philip Goldberg, Carl Hein, Julian 'Potatoes' Kaufman and William Engelke, four of O'Banion's North Side cronies. The next day, Duffy was found shot to death in a snowdrift in between Cicero and Joliet, firm Capone territory. The Chicago Police subsequently announced that Capone was their prime suspect, not only because of the location of the body, but also because the last place Duffy had been seen alive was in Capone's club. However, in spite of an intense investigation, no charges were ever brought in connection with the killing, primarily due to the fact that any potential witnesses suddenly developed a peculiar loss of memory, something which O'Banion would later call 'Chicago Amnesia.'

Following on from this incident, Capone began to listen to McGurn, began to take an increasing amount of notice of him. After all, he had been right in his assertion that O'Banion would be trouble and he had only met the guy once. Yet even McGurn had grossly underestimated just how much trouble O'Banion would be.

Capone's other major allies were the Genna's, a violent Sicilian clan of six brothers who, during the era of prohibition and with the passing of Tropea, dominated Little Italy and Little Sicily. Salvatore was the eldest of the six, followed by Vincenzo, Pietro, Angelo, Michael and Antonio; together they ran their business empire from 1022 Taylor Street, in the heart of Little Sicily. In the first few weeks of 1924, a corrupt lawyer named Henry Spignola – whose sister Lucille would later marry Angelo Genna – conceived the idea of helping the brothers to obtain a license to produce medicinal alcohol. This they did and within weeks, the brothers were producing legal raw alcohol from the three storey warehouse on Taylor Street, an address which soon became their headquarters.

The brothers then hit upon the idea of placing stills in the homes of families living in Little Italy and Little Sicily. Their plan was simple. A family would be supplied with both the still and the ingredients to make beer. Then, once a week, a collector would come by, remove the full still, replace it with an empty one and pay the family the handsome fee of $15 for their trouble. Whilst it sounded like relatively easy work on the part of the families, the job did not come without its hazards, due to the potential volatility of beer fermentation. The ideal fermentation temperature for beer is seventy-five degrees Fahrenheit; this temperature ensures that the beer ferments at a good, steady rate. The lower the temperature, the slower the fermentation process; the higher the temperature, the faster the brew would be ready to drink. The Italian and Sicilian families were under a great deal of pressure to make sure that the beer was ready for the weekly collection, prompting them to raise the temperature of the still as high as they dared during brewing. Consequently, incidences of stills actually exploding were not uncommon. It appears that during prohibition, there was little, if anything, which was not without its risks.

Before long, the Genna brothers discovered that they were producing more alcohol than they could sell within their own territory and thus began to encroach onto the North Side of Chicago...O'Banion's fiefdom. Incensed by their blatant disregard for his patch of turf, O'Banion vowed to strike back, to teach *'them lousy Sicilians'* as he called them, a lesson. As the

Genna's were renowned for their capriciously violent nature, this was O'Banion's stupidity running at full speed. Capone knew that should O'Banion be allowed to pursue his intended course of action, a bloody gang war would engulf the streets of Chicago. He therefore dispatched his newest recruit, McGurn, to talk to O'Banion, to rationalize with him and make him see sense. It took some time, but eventually McGurn succeeded in mollifying the Mephistophelean O'Banion. There remained however, the question of how to pacify the Genna clan, who demanded that O'Banion should pay the highest price for what they saw as a deliberate insult. For this task, Capone turned to a man who was the then head of the Unione Siciliana.

An organization dedicated to the improvement of the Italian and Sicilian community in Chicago, the Unione Siciliana had begun its life as a non-profit concern, although over the years it had mutated into a shadow of its former self and was now unquestionably a criminal association. Like the Mafia, the Camorra or indeed, the Brigado Rosso, the Unione Siciliana had undergone something of a metamorphosis, from a society designed to fight for the rights of its people, into an evil enterprise. The man at the helm was Michael Merlo, a man who was respected by both the community and gangland alike, so much so, that now only he could appease the brothers' Genna. Finally, after much placation and negotiation, Merlo prevailed in cooling their smouldering Sicilian tempers and for now at least, another O'Banion created crisis was averted.

Jack McGurn had developed almost overnight, from a quiet, reserved teenager, into a sharp individual, disarmingly astute and fully aware of his environment. His new found wealth meant that he could dress with the style and flair that had previously eluded him. He had always been perceptive of the latest fashions, yet he had never had the income to warrant the seemingly extravagant purchases of custom made suits, shirts, ties and shoes. Now, not only could he afford to provide himself with such luxuries, he could also take care of Helen, Helena and his mother with equal extravagance. The shabby slacks, shirts, worn shoes and *borsalino* cap that he had habitually worn, were replaced by grey spats, ivory white shirts accentuated by crimson braces and silver grey ties, whilst ebony black waistcoats and gray jackets completed the ensembles. His shoes were no longer tatty and dilapidated, but custom made of the finest leather. His naturally wavy black hair was now pomaded straight and slicked back, enhancing his appearance with the very essence of cool. Capone even arranged for him to take possession of his own car: a brand new maroon and black 1924, Cadillac. Aside from his appearance, there was a further and quite curious transformation taking place, for it seemed that whatever McGurn turned his hand to, it was if he had done it all his life. An example of this was when McGurn accompanied Capone and his entourage to the Hawthorne Race Track and Kennel Club, an Outfit owned concern. During the visit, McGurn was asked – along with a few others – whether he would like to try his hand at horse riding. Not wishing to appear afraid, he accepted the offer and to everyone's amazement, including his own, he rode almost like an experienced jockey. Needless to say, the rest of the party was greatly impressed and for the remainder of the day, McGurn revelled in his being the center of attention. This flood of adulation merely served to enhance his perception that his decision to join the Outfit was the best he had ever made.

McGurn's emerging astuteness once again came into effect when he heard talk that Capone was planning to enter into a business partnership with Dion O'Banion. The partnership was to be between O'Banion, Capone's mentor John Torrio and Capone himself, and involved the ownership of the Sieben Brewery. A huge concern located at 1464-75 North Larrabee Street, the Sieben Brewery had – until the advent of prohibition – been one of the most productive breweries in Illinois. The funds to purchase the brewery were being supplied solely by the three men, yet McGurn still refused to trust O'Banion; why should he after all the recent shenanigans? Regardless of O'Banion's past performances however, Capone and Torrio were not to be dissuaded and pressed ahead with the deal. Nevertheless, it seemed that on this occasion, McGurn was wrong about O'Banion. Within a few months, the brewery was making each of its three partners more money than they could ever have envisaged, eventually churning out more beer than they could sell. They decided to branch out and began to sell their beer to all the other gangs in Chicago, in addition to stocking their own speakeasies, clubs and saloons.

One of the conditions of this working partnership was that O'Banion would take care not only of the local police, but also of the recently formed federal government agency, known as the Prohibition Department. It was

O'Banion's duty to ensure that each week, a package was delivered to the police captain of each precinct in the Loop, the North Side and Cicero; these packages would contain anywhere between $5,000 and $20,000 depending on the size and strategic importance of the precinct. The precinct captain would then distribute the funds amongst his men who would, in return, turn a blind eye to the activities of Capone, Torrio and O'Banion. This finely balanced relationship worked exceptionally well until May, 1924, when O'Banion's sense of mischief awoke the Faustian devil which slumbered within him.

Ever since the peace between O'Banion and the Genna's had been brokered, the rumblings of discontent had nevertheless continued. Occasionally these rumblings would threaten to erupt, especially when O'Banion hijacked a truckload of Genna beer, yet somehow the fragile accord remained intact. It was no secret however, that everyone both inside and outside the Outfit – including McGurn – wondered just how long this agonizing stand off could continue. Suddenly, O'Banion proffered a solution which appealed to everyone...he was going to retire. O'Banion told Capone and Torrio that he had grown tired of the whole booze business and that he had decided that the rewards on offer were no longer worth risking his life for. O'Banion added that it was clear to him that he and the Genna's would never be able to resolve their differences, something which only served to bring constant aggravation that everyone could do without. Therefore, he proposed to make the best out of a bad situation by suggesting that if Capone and Torrio bought his share of the brewery for $500,000, he would hand over the keys, close his flower shop and leave Chicago for good. Capone and Torrio felt that they could not pass up on the opportunity to rid themselves of their troublesome partner. So, whilst McGurn smelled a rat, O'Banion was arranging to meet Capone and Torrio on the morning of May 19, at which time he would seal the deal by handing over the keys.

On the morning that the transaction was due to take place, a particularly large shipment of beer was set to leave the brewery, heading for delivery to all the major gangs in Chicago. Torrio and Capone arrived at the brewery to meet O'Banion as arranged, however O'Banion was not there. In his place was the Prohibition Department, brandishing a warrant for the arrest of the brewery's owners, along with a governmental order to seize the brewery. Torrio and Capone were immediately arrested and taken down to the Cicero precinct, where it soon transpired that the trustworthy O'Banion had been neglecting to ensure the weekly delivery of their package. After a while, the precinct captain decided that he was no longer willing to ask his men to turn a blind eye and as such, had informed the Prohibition Department of the trio's activities. Because of the fact that this was Capone's first prohibition violation (that anyone could prove) his punishment would be a laughable fine. Torrio on the other hand, had a previous liquor conviction, meaning that for him, a jail sentence was inevitable.

In the days immediately following the Sieben Brewery debacle, McGurn would certainly have been forgiven for saying *'I told you so,'* yet he knew that it was not a wise move to put his boss's nose even further out of joint. Instead, he waited for Capone to give the obvious order to take O'Banion out of the picture…permanently. So easily said, yet it would not be so easily done, at least while Michael Merlo was alive. Merlo called a meeting with Capone, to find out what his next move would be and was not surprised to find him baying for O'Banion's blood. Whilst Merlo empathized with Capone, he was renowned for his desire to find peaceful solutions to gangland's problems, and so attempted to talk Capone out of this drastic course of action. Although Capone had no reason to answer to Merlo, he nevertheless held the utmost respect for the man, a factor which prompted him to give Merlo his assurance that he would not be the one to go after O'Banion.

'The luck of the Irish:' if anyone in the world had it, then that person was Dion O'Banion, for not only had he successfully conned Al Capone and John Torrio out of $500,000, he had also gotten away with it. Secure in the knowledge that Merlo had talked Capone and the Outfit out of seeking revenge, he was now – quite literally – laughing behind their backs. He felt himself so invulnerable that he did not see the leaving of Chicago as a necessary move, indeed he continued with his bootlegging business with impunity. However, O'Banion would have been wise to understand that even the luck of Irish cannot last forever.

In addition to the battle that Merlo was fighting in order to keep O'Banion alive, he was also waging his own personal war against cancer.

Very few people knew of his illness, and even fewer knew that it was a war he was losing. Finally, his frail body could take no more and in the early hours of the morning of November 8, 1924, Michael Merlo died peacefully in his sleep. His death was significant for many reasons, not least of which being that he would be the last head of the Unione Siciliana ever to die of natural causes. Also, as Merlo died, the accord which he had brokered in order to save the life of O'Banion died with him.

Since Dion O'Banion had taken over Schofield's, it had blossomed to become the central flower store in Chicago. Whether it be for birthdays, anniversaries, marriages, births or funerals, Chicagoans recognized Schofield's as *the* place for all their floral needs. Therefore, O'Banion was not too surprised to find that the death of Michael Merlo was extremely good for business, as everyone who had ever known him ordered large floral arrangements to help them pay their last respects. So O'Banion saw nothing unusual when, on November 9, a telephone order came through for a $2,000 arrangement, with the customer proposing to come by to collect the order the following day around noon.

Once the news of Merlo's death reached the Genna's, they immediately contacted Capone, to see if he had any objections to a hit on O'Banion. Of course he did not indeed, as a gesture of goodwill, he offered to send his newest recruit, Jack McGurn along to assist. McGurn had mixed emotions over this, his first major assignment since joining the Outfit thirteen months ago. Due to the fact that he had so far been assigned to more mundane tasks, McGurn had, for the most part at least, almost forgotten the true nature of his employment. It was not that he had second thoughts; on the contrary, he saw nothing wrong in killing O'Banion, for he knew that the good-for-nothing firebrand was little more than dead wood blocking the course of a great ship. It was more like first night nerves, when the overwhelming desire to do well and to impress can be either a positive or negative influence, depending on its use. The fact that this was his chance to prove himself both to Capone and the Outfit, was one which was not lost on McGurn and whilst he was determined to succeed, he was a little anxious over the alacrity with which the hit was planned. Nevertheless, in spite of his history, he knew that he was relatively new to the role of hit man and as such, told himself to try to sit back and simply let the impending events unfold.

McGurn began to relax a little when he was told that three other experienced gunmen would be joining him on the hit. Frankie Yale, a close friend of Capone from New York, would lead the group, indeed it was he who had placed the floral order from Schofield's. The two other gunmen would be John Scalise and Albert Anselmi, the Genna's most heartless and pitiless executioners. The four men would be driven to and from Schofield's by Angelo Genna.

November 10, 1924. Midday. A dark, silver trimmed Jewett pulled into the curb in front of Schofield's flower shop on North State Street and out stepped McGurn and Yale, followed by Scalise and Anselmi. Leaving Angelo Genna waiting in the car, the four hired assassins made their way into the shop and upon entering, discovered that O'Banion was not alone; another man by the name of William Crutchfield, was on hand to help with the last minute floral arrangements. The following story is taken from Crutchfield's testimony. O'Banion was working on an arrangement with Crutchfield when the hit man quartet entered the premises. As the men came inside, O'Banion asked Crutchfield to go and fetch a broom from the back of the shop and sweep up the abundance of petals that were strewn over the shop floor. Crutchfield left to get the broom and as he did so, glanced over his shoulder to see O'Banion shaking hands with one of the men. He was in the back room when he heard O'Banion say *"Hello boys, you from Mike Merlo's?"* before another voice, laced with a heavy New York accent, replied *"Yes."* The next thing Crutchfield heard was a shot and, according to his testimony, he ran to the partitioning door which separated the back room from the main store. So frightened was he by what he saw that despite being impelled to flee, he stood rooted to the spot. The man who had initially shaken hands with O'Banion, was now holding O'Banion's hands in both of his own, thus preventing him from reaching for either of his two pistols which he habitually carried. Two other dark haired men (Yale and McGurn) were standing at either side of O'Banion, each firing shots into his incapacitated body, though Crutchfield was too frightened to remember exactly how many shots were fired. Afraid that his own life may be in danger, he ran back into the rear of the shop and exited through the back door.

O'Banion was in fact shot six times. Two of the shots hit him in the chest, whilst the next two, fired almost simultaneously from the left and right, ripped open his throat. The fifth shot hit him in the side of his face, almost completely shattering his jaw. The sixth and final shot served as the *coup de grace* and was fired from such close range into the center of his forehead, that powder burns were clearly evident on the skin.

After fleeing out of the back door, William Crutchfield carried on through the alleyway which ran the entire length of the left side of the building, stopping just before he reached the street. Peering cautiously around the corner, he was just in time to see the four men pile out of the shop and into the dark, silver trimmed Jewett. Whilst the murder of O'Banion had been relatively straightforward, it did have one curious detail, one which only became evident as Crutchfield described the getaway. Crutchfield stated that the Jewett had its motor running, nothing unusual there, but then as the car pulled away from the curb and sped away down North State Street, six other identical cars pulled away and blocked the intersection of North State Street and Superior Street, so as to impede any pursuit of the lead vehicle. As soon as the initial car carrying the four gunmen had disappeared onto Dearborn Street, one of the remaining six cars gave a short blast of its horn and, as quickly as they had blocked the street, all six cars returned to their original positions and then vanished. In its detailed report of the murder, *The New York Times* claimed that '*in the ploys brilliant simplicity, the existence of a mastermind was revealed.*' That '*mastermind*' was later determined to be none other than Jack McGurn.

The police officer assigned to investigate the murder of Dion O'Banion, was Captain William Shoemaker, known simply by his fellow officers as '*Shoes*.' Upon taking charge, he immediately instigated the rounding up of all the usual gangland suspects, including Capone and Torrio. Both men insisted that they and O'Banion had been friends indeed, they had placed a joint order of flowers totaling $10,000 with him just the day before. Needless to say, the remaining suspects proved to be equally helpful. During this roundup, it was only McGurn who was not arrested and questioned, simply because at that moment, he was a total unknown to the police. Eventually, Captain Shoemaker gave up and declared that, unless they got lucky, they would not find the killers and even if luck were on their side, it was doubtful that they could make the case stick. Even their star witness, William Crutchfield, claimed that he would not recognize the killers if he saw them again. In the end, the police had no option but to declare the case unsolved, which it officially remains to this day.

November 13, and 14, 1924, proved to be something of a vaudeville experience for the people of Chicago. November 13, saw the funeral of Michael Merlo and upon closer inspection, the somber occasion was the very essence of a lesson in corruption; the Mayor of Chicago, William E. Dever, (despite Capone's backing Klenha had been defeated in the polls) Robert E. Crowe, Illinois State Attorney, Morgan A. Collins, the Chicago Chief of Police and Cook County President, Anton J. Cermak, all conveniently forgot their legal and moral obligations in order to serve as honorary pallbearers. The funeral cortege consisted of two hundred and sixty six-cars, eighty-eight of them carrying members of the Unione Siciliana, whilst the remaining cars contained nothing but flowers. Following the service, a crowd of ten thousand mourners watched as the body of Michael Merlo was buried in the grounds of Mount Carmel Cemetery.

November 14, was the day of Dion O'Banion's funeral, an occasion which rivalled even Merlo's obsequies chic. So vast were the crowds that resident Chicagoans were raking in the profits by charging extortionate fees for premium vantage points. Whilst Capone and Torrio could barely hide their delight at finally being rid of the troublesome O'Banion, they nevertheless kept up the public charade of mourning for a dear, departed friend. It is at this point however, that it appears apt to mention something of an anomaly regarding the detail of Capone and Torrio's involvement in the funeral of O'Banion. It is generally accepted that Capone and Torrio expressed their delight in his passing, by arranging for O'Banion to be buried in a $10,000 silver and bronze casket, which they had delivered by special freight from Philadelphia. However, the Probate Record for Dean C. O'Banion contains the written order from Sbarbaro & Company, Funeral Directors, upon which it clearly states that the casket was made from copper and cost $7,500. This discrepancy is nonetheless easily explained, for over the years, many legends have grown up around these fascinating gangland characters, adding somewhat inaccurate romance to their already intriguing lives.

It took more than twenty-four cars simply to transport the flowers from the funeral home at 708 North Wells Street to Mount Carmel Cemetery, where a solemn Capone, Torrio and McGurn stood amongst the mourners waiting by the graveside. The only dampener which was put on the occasion was that Cardinal Mundelein ironically refused to allow a funeral mass in the Holy Name Cathedral, where the young O'Banion had enjoyed a brief spell as an altar boy. He also refused to allow O'Banion's body to be interred in the consecrated ground of Mount Carmel, citing that *"a person who refuses the ministrations of the Church in life, need not expect to have the ministrations of the Church in death."* Perhaps if O'Banion had died a little more slowly and had been able to recant on his deathbed, the Cardinal may have shown a little more compassion. Nevertheless, the copper casket, inscribed with the words *'Suffer the little children to come unto me'* was lowered into the unconsecrated ground of the cemetery.

Five months later, O'Banion's wife Viola, had her husband's body secretly exhumed and reburied in consecrated ground. It is strange how in life, we can choose as to whose company we keep and whom to stay away from, yet this is a luxury which is denied to us in death. As such, Dion O'Banion, murderer, thief, extortionist and rejecter of the ministrations of the Church, now lies just eighty feet from a Bishop.

For McGurn, the funeral brought back poignant memories of his own father's burial. The solemn face that he wore at the graveside could hardly be called an act, yet the irony that he himself had committed an act that had itself been perpetrated against his own father, was lost on him. The young boy who once wanted only to become a successful boxer, now wanted to be no less than a successful gangster. Somewhere along the road of his life he had lost something, but it seemed that the exact point of its disappearance was now little more than a blurred memory. Having received, to a certain extent, both a conventional and street education, McGurn was now receiving a third education. He was learning that people are fascinated with gangsters, for the simple reason that they *are* gangsters. Anyone who lives by their own rules, who is willing to take death as part and parcel of their business, who is willing – though they would much rather not – to die in public and who thumbs their nose at the establishment, will always be fascinating. Jack McGurn was slowly beginning to realize that if he played this game to win, he would be a star and that is a proposition which is hard for anyone to resist.

McGurn's life was now on the up and up. He had won the respect of Capone with his brainstorming idea of the decoy cars and as a reward, had been presented with a xenium in the form of a belt buckle with his initials encrusted in diamonds. So charming was his manner that most of the Outfit virtually fell in love with him. He got on famously with the Genna's, holding them in great esteem, especially when he discovered that they originated from the same area of Sicily as himself. Regardless of all this adulation however, McGurn and indeed the whole Outfit, had overlooked one point, a detail which would, in a relatively short space of time, prove to be a costly misjudgment. Buoyed by their success in the killing of O'Banion, the Outfit regarded the North Side as now being ripe for a takeover, not realizing that the perpetual backslapper had numerous followers who were not quite as amicable and nowhere near as manageable. With his passing, it was O'Banion's best friend who stepped into the fray, baying for revenge on those who had murdered his friend. In the post murder euphoria, the Outfit had failed to recognize the threat now posed by a personified time bomb named Hymie Weiss.

CHAPTER ELEVEN

NO GOOD NORTH SIDERS

In 1916, Brigadier General John Taliaferro Thompson, invented what he called a *'submachine gun,'* a weapon to be named after himself and which was capable of firing more than eight-hundred rounds a minute. In doing so, he unwittingly changed the way in which future gangland wars would be fought. The good Brigadier General had, of course, not intended for his baby to be used within the realms of gang warfare, despite the fact that war had been the instigating factor behind the design. The outbreak of The Great War engendered something of a revolution in terms of weaponry and the Thompson submachine gun or *'Tommy Gun'* as it became known, was part of that revolution. Initially described by its inventor as a *'broom'* which could be used to *'sweep the trenches and kill as many men as the technology of our day allows,'* the Tommy Gun – in addition to its immense firing capabilities – held many advantages over other short range weapons of the day. Before The Great War, all long barrelled weapons emitted a brief flash of flame when fired, meaning that if fired in darkness, the enemy would still be able to identify where the gunfire was emanating from at any one time. The Tommy Guns however, where laden with Roburite, a smokeless, flameless derivative of nitro-benzyl which prevented the weapon from emitting flame, thus affording the allies an immense advantage over the enemy. Nevertheless, a lengthy development program meant that the Tommy Gun would not be ready for use before the conclusion of the war.

During the halcyon days of peacetime, the Tommy Gun rapidly fell into disuse and in 1922, the Auto Ordinance Corporation began to look for ways in which to offload its stockpile of fifteen-thousand weapons. As has been previously stated, before 1923, American gun laws were, amazingly, even more lax than today, a factor that resulted in advertisements for these destructive weapons being placed in almost every daily newspaper. Thus, via such advertisements, or a sporting goods store, a gun enthusiast could purchase a Tommy Gun for around $175, or $225 if the one-hundred round drum-like magazine was also required. Despite all their best efforts however, the Corporation found that demand for the guns was in extremely short supply, due in most part to the fact that in 1922, few people could afford such a huge sum. Another contributing factor to the weapons' redundancy was that it had never actually been used in combat. Had they been employed for the purpose for which they had been developed, they could have undoubtedly been advertised as *'the gun that won the war.'* As it stood, it had not been used in a single battle, though it would be used extensively during America's participation of WWII, with the US Army ordering ninety-thousand pieces a month.

Inevitably, a number of Tommy Guns found their way onto the Black Market, where of course, the price skyrocketed. In this illegal marketplace, a new gun complete with a one-hundred round drum and with the serial number filed away (few people knew that all Tommy Guns also contained a 'secret' identification number, which could only be read upon dismantlement of the gun) sold for around $2,000 and in 1922, only one sector of the community could afford to part with that kind of money. Gangsters considered a couple of grand as small change, so it was not too long before these disseminates of death landed in the wrong hands.

A dangerous pair of these wrong hands belonged to Earl J. Wajciechowski, a Polish immigrant who, at some indeterminate point in time, decided to change his surname to *'Weiss'* and to adopt the nickname of *'Hymie.'* Quite why a devout Catholic would wish to take on the incredibly Jewish sounding name of Hymie Weiss is a mystery, though one theory suggests that the reason could lie within the xenophobia of society. Just as anyone with a surname ending in vowel was immediately segregated into a lower social class, anyone with a surname ending in *'sky'* or *'ski'*, was unfailingly classed as Jewish and as a Jew, one could expect to encounter a great prejudice, more so even than the Italians and Sicilians. Therefore, society's racial intolerance and stereotypical ideals came together to ensure that *'Hymie Weiss'* sounded somewhat less Jewish than *'Earl Wajciechowski.'*

Hymie Weiss was the best friend of the now dearly departed Dion O'Banion, and with his passing, now reigned as the self appointed leader of

the North Side. As captain, Weiss subsequently named his principal lieu-
tenants as Vincent 'Schemer' Drucci and George 'Bugs' Moran. Together
the three of them certainly made a motley crew; Weiss with his unkempt
appearance and wildly staring eyes, Moran with a smooth shaven, dimple-
chinned face which belied a hair trigger temper and Drucci looking at best
vacant and gormless, it was difficult to take them seriously. Whilst Drucci
and Moran possessed little felonious acumen, Weiss was an unmanageable,
kaleidoscopic individual, mercurial to the point of insanity. Separately, the
three were truly impotent, yet together they were an extremely volatile
combination, far too dangerous not to be taken seriously. Weiss believed
himself to be on a mission whose goals were threefold. The first was to
avenge the death of his best friend, whilst the second was to overhaul and
completely dominate the North Side territory. The third, and most
outlandish goal, was to annihilate Capone, take over the Outfit and emerge
as supreme ruler of Chicago.

January 12, 1925, and Jack McGurn sat in Capone's cream coloured
Cadillac outside the Hawthorne Restaurant, in the heart of Cicero. Situated
next door to the Hawthorne Hotel, The Hawthorne Restaurant was a large,
airy and luxuriously appointed establishment, with round, white cloth
covered tables encompassing the dark wood floor. The façade of the
building was taken up with two huge plate glass windows bordering a
central doorway, whilst a sign which simply read *'Restaurant,'* protruded
from above the entrance. McGurn was accompanied in the car by another
bodyguard, Philip D'Andrea, and Sylvester Barton, Capone's chauffeur; a
few moments earlier, Capone had also been in the car, but had just asked
Barton to stop at the restaurant so that he could place a lunch order.
McGurn and D'Andrea watched Capone step through the door of the
restaurant, before McGurn turned away to look back onto the street. As he
did so, he noticed a dark coloured sedan heading towards them on the
opposite side of road. McGurn watched curiously for a moment, for whilst
there was nothing outwardly unusual about the car itself, it was nevertheless
barely crawling along. His instinct warning him of trouble, McGurn nudged
D'Andrea and nodded towards the slow moving automobile. As it drew
almost level with their car, the sudden realization hit the two men almost
simultaneously and in unison, they yelled at Barton to get down as they

themselves dropped to the floor. The dark automobile, driven by George Moran, pulled alongside the Cadillac, as Weiss and Drucci – who had so far been secreted in the back – opened fire with their newly acquired Tommy Guns, peppering the automobile with a lethal spray of lead. Surrounded by the weapon's deafening roar, the windows imploded, showering the cowed occupants with shards of glass, whilst round upon round of ammunition reduced the Cadillac's flawless bodywork to little more than an elaborate colander. The action stopped as quickly as it had begun, the deafening noise replaced by an equally deafening silence, as the North Side triumvirate sped away believing – or perhaps rather hoping – that they had succeeded in their attempt to kill Capone.

Cautiously confident that the onslaught was over, McGurn and D'Andrea pulled themselves up from the floor of the Cadillac. Having reacted almost simultaneously, both men had escaped the fusillade unscathed however, it immediately became apparent that Sylvester Barton had not been quite so lucky. Gangland inexperience meant that he had failed to react as swiftly, resulting in his being hit five times in the arms and chest. Bizarrely, he made no noise, something which alerted McGurn and D'Andrea to the fact that he had been seriously wounded and, after clambering into the front of the vehicle, they found the barely conscious Barton bleeding profusely from one or all of his wounds; it later became clear that one of the bullets had severed a major artery. Despite his terrible injuries, Barton miraculously survived, probably due in the most part to the fact that a nearby store called for an ambulance as soon as the gunfire had ceased. However, following his recovery, he wisely decided that his spell as Al Capone's chauffeur was over.

The attempted hit was an exquisite display of the North Side's new firepower, yet it was also a perfect example of their uncontrolled and imprecise aggression. Whereas precision, skill, timing and ingenuity would have been the four components of an Outfit orchestrated hit, Weiss's team appeared to have just two: point and shoot. Had they taken a little more time over their attempt, maybe passed the car a few times to ensure that Capone was actually inside, then history may not have been quite as intriguing.

Standing inside the restaurant, Capone had heard the gunfire and upon exiting the establishment, was shocked to see the extensive damage that had been inflicted not only to his car, but also to his trusted chauffeur. A few moments later, the ambulance arrived and promptly transferred the badly injured Barton to the nearest hospital. Despite the destructiveness of the attack, Capone nevertheless realized that had it not been for the suspicious nature of McGurn, the consequences could have been dire. As a reward, Capone took the decision to promote his new recruit to the level of chief bodyguard and principal hit man, a move which made McGurn one of the key members of the Outfit. McGurn was sure that this career elevation was not purely a reward, for he firmly believed that every fibre of Capone's body would be crying out for a retaliatory attack and that his promotion effectively meant that it would be he who carried out the hit. As it was however, McGurn was to be disappointed, for the expected order never came. This caused a miscellany of thoughts, not least of which was why the order had not been given. Was it that Capone had inside knowledge of the North Side gang and as such, knew that the time was not yet ripe to strike back? Could it be that Capone had to answer to his own boss and mentor, John Torrio and as such, was being prevented from launching a revenge attack? After all, everyone knew that Torrio was a peace loving man, something of a contradiction in terms for someone who chose such a violent profession. McGurn asked himself whether he should go to Capone, tell him that he was willing to accept the job and that in his view, it was best to strike while the iron was hot. He quickly dispelled this thought however, for common sense told him that it was not his place to tell Al Capone what to do. Whilst he could not quite work out why the order never came, he resigned himself to the fact that Capone knew what he was doing and that when the time was right, he would get his call.

The North Side attack shows a dramatic change in the character of McGurn, for it appears that rather than being shaken by the fact that he could, in all probability, have been injured or even killed, he was somehow buoyed by the gangland thrill. The high that came from the pure, unadulterated adrenaline rush was like nothing he had ever known or felt before, a feeling which, instead of prompting him to reconsider his profession, led him to almost crave the moment when the sensation could be replicated.

Having tasted the bitter sweet fruit of the underworld, McGurn was hooked.

★　★　★

The advance in Jack McGurn's career was a staggering achievement for one so young and prompted a massive augmentation to his lifestyle. With his promotion came a salary increase, from $200 to $300 per week; in the modern economy, this equates to over $3,000 a week. Justifiably, he felt that his family's residence should reflect his higher income and status and as such, decided to move from their old house in order to purchase a higher class of property for Helena, Helen and himself. McGurn had to be relatively particular in his choice of abode, for his new position meant that he had to be as close as possible to Capone at all times. Jack and Helena viewed dozens of properties, before eventually deciding on 1522 Edgemont Avenue, a beautiful house situated a mile or so from Oak Park, the crème de la crème of the city.

The new house was an attractive two storey, red brick property, complete with its own driveway and rear garden. Their neighbourhood was comprised of high class businessmen, bankers, financiers and insurance brokers, who all came to regard their new neighbours as any other ordinary, successful couple. Everyone remarked upon the appearance of Jack and Helena; he was charming and gregarious, she was elegant and sophisticated, whilst their daughter Helen was simply adorable. Not one of them ever suspected McGurn's true occupation, though one suspects that they would not have said anything even if they had. The only snag as far as Helena was concerned, was that their existing furniture would not match the décor in their new house. For a couple of years now, money had not been an object and so Jack was able to solve that problem in one go. Giving Helena a thick roll of bills, he told her to go shopping and pick out any furniture that she liked and have it delivered to the house. If she didn't like the décor in the new house, then she should call a decorating company and have them come and refurbish it to her liking. Jack absolutely adored being able to treat his wife this way; with $300 a week rolling in, he could be as generous as he had always wanted to be. At this point in time he felt wonderful, as though he could go anywhere and do anything, that the world was his oyster with which he could do as he pleased. At no time did he actually stop to consider at what price all this happiness came, yet it would undoubtedly have made little difference if he had.

Love is a wonderful blindfold for life and from Helena's point of view, it certainly held the ability to shield her eyes from what, to anyone else, may have been blatantly obvious. The change that had come about in her husband was too visible to ignore, yet Helena chose not to question it, chose not to ask where all the money came from or who his employer actually was. Whilst most wives would want to know where, who, how, why and when, Helena simply accepted what Jack chose to tell her. Quite why she chose to think in this way is unclear however, love is the primary reason which springs to mind. When you love someone with everything you have, including your soul, you are prepared to forgive them for anything, even if it means purposely blinding yourself to reality. It is entirely possible that Helena deliberately blinkered herself to the fact that her doting husband was now not the man she had married. The other reason of course, is money, for having been raised as the child of a struggling immigrant family, held back by prejudice and denied the rights of any other American citizen, why should Helena question how they could afford this lavish new lifestyle. What did it matter what her husband was doing for a living, as long as he was making sure that he and his family wanted for nothing? As Shakespeare wrote in *'The Merry Wives of Windsor'* *'O, what world of vile, ill favoured faults, looks handsome in three hundred pounds a year.'*

★   ★   ★

Just twelve short days after the attempted hit on Capone, McGurn was dining in Suite 202 at the Hawthorne Hotel, when the word came through that the North Siders had shot Capone's mentor, John Torrio outside his home on Clyde Avenue. Having been used to seeing his boss calm and composed, McGurn was stunned to see what can only be described as a rampageous side; such was the audacity of the hit, that Capone could scarcely believe that it had actually been carried out. McGurn knew that the Outfit would now have to be placed on a war footing, for aside from hitting

Capone himself, this was *the* worst act that the North Siders could possibly have committed. As chief bodyguard and in the absence of a regular chauffeur, McGurn was commissioned to drive Capone to the Jackson Park Memorial Hospital where, they had been told, Torrio had been taken.

Once there, they were informed that Torrio was in surgery and that the doctors were doing all they could to save him, but that they should be in no doubt that he was gravely wounded. It seemed that all they could do now was to simply wait in the corridors and pray for some good news. Eventually, Capone was told that the surgeons had managed to remove five bullets from Torrio's body however, in spite of the fact that he had survived the surgery, they held out little hope that he would live through the night. Upon hearing this news, Capone became demoniacal with overwhelming grief and rage and began ranting over and over *"The gang did it, the gang did it,"* at which point McGurn thought it best to remove him from the hospital. Even with such an ambiguous statement, he realized that his boss may have already said too much; even hospital walls have ears.

Mercifully, Torrio did live out the night, thanks not only to the skills of the surgeons, but also to incredible inaccuracy on the part of the North Siders. Weiss's intention had been for Torrio to die in exactly the same way as O'Banion: five bullets to the body, before the final *coup de grace* to the forehead. The North Siders had caught Torrio just as he was coming back from a shopping trip with his wife, pulling alongside his car as he unloaded packages from the back seat. Upon spotting Torrio, Weiss and Co had immediately opened fire however, Weiss had missed with his first four shots, in addition to Moran missing with three. As Drucci was acting as driver, this meant that they had only five bullets left between them. Therefore, when it came time to deliver the final fatal shot, both Weiss and Moran were out of ammunition. Panicked by the fact that Torrio may now live, the North Side trio fled the scene; had either Weiss or Moran been a little more accurate, then Torrio would never have even made it to hospital, let alone through the night. Nevertheless, there was no escaping the fact that they had once again failed in their mission and had left Torrio alive.

After a few days, the medical staff declared that Torrio was now stable enough to be questioned by the police. Time and time again, Torrio was asked whether he had seen his assailants, or if he knew who might wish to see him killed. Each question was met with the same stoic answer: he had not seen a thing and had no idea as to who would wish him any harm. Whilst he would not divulge the names of the attempted killers to the officers of law enforcement, he would gladly do so to Capone, leaving Hymie Weiss and his potluck party to consider the full gravity of their actions.

After three long weeks, John Torrio was released from hospital and upon leaving, made a shock announcement to Capone and the Outfit. He told them that a peace loving man such as himself was in grave danger in these modern day rackets, and had therefore decided to preserve his life and retire. As was his right, he had already chosen his successor, subsequently announcing that overall control of the Outfit and all Outfit businesses were now in the hands of Capone. Despite the surprise, this was indeed great news, not just for Capone who, at just twenty-six years old held almost the entire city of Chicago as his fiefdom, but also for McGurn. Just two years after he chose to join the Outfit, McGurn now found himself in the position of chief bodyguard and principal hit man to the underworld king of Chicago. He felt that the gamble he had taken with his life was now paying dividends and, more than ever before, he knew that he would never go back to his old life. Not that he could have done even if he had wanted to, for as Capone would say over and over again *"Once you are in the rackets, you ain't never coming out."*

In view of recent events and now with Capone at the helm, McGurn was even more confident that a retaliatory hit on the North Side would be ordered. Having once attempted to assassinate Capone and very nearly succeeding in killing Torrio, McGurn knew that there was little more, if anything, that the North Siders could have done to provoke a reprisal. Bizarrely however, the order still failed to be given, and now McGurn began to become just a little concerned as to the reason. Since joining the Outfit, a friendship had developed between himself and Capone, one which allowed him to speak more openly than most other members, yet despite this, he refrained from questioning Capone as to his motives for holding back. Once again, McGurn told himself to simply sit tight and trust that Capone knew what he was doing.

As head of the Outfit, Capone set about making certain changes, the first of which was the physical fitness of his men. The condition and stamina that McGurn still retained from his boxing days, was not lost on Capone, for he realized the advantage it gave over any potential enemy. He therefore declared a new policy: from now on all combatants, that is body-guards and hit men, were to use the gymnasium at the Hawthorne Hotel at regular intervals. This new rule of course did not sit well with all of the combatant members of the Outfit, most of whom were more than happy to while away their free time smoking cigarettes and drinking espresso. Notwithstanding this fact, a rule was a rule and in gangland, rules are broken only under the most mitigating of circumstances.

As the months went by, Jack McGurn was uneasy; he felt that there was something afoot, yet he was unsure as to exactly what it would be. He had been correct in his assertion that the Outfit would consider themselves to be at war with the North Siders, yet the enemy had been too quiet for too long. The last that had been heard from them was the day that they had shot John Torrio and that was four months ago. They had not even been sighted in or around the city; it was as though they had simply evaporated from the face of the earth. There were, of course, innocuous reasons for this apparent lull in the action and McGurn wondered whether they had finally realized the grave error they had made in leaving Torrio alive and well enough to iden-tify them to Capone. Maybe their fruitless endeavours had brought them to the conclusion that their impending *coup d'etat* was a virtual impossibility. However, McGurn preferred to air on the side of caution, believing that this lull could, in all probability, be the calm before the storm and may very well be the last chance that anyone would have to be at ease. Whilst he did not know it, he was about to be proved right; something was about to happen, yet as with most enemy action, it was the one thing that no one had even dared to consider.

May 25, 1925, a perfect spring day with ideal conditions for taking a drive. Angelo Genna – now a fearsome force to be reckoned with within the realms of Little Italy and Little Sicily – was making his way down Ogden Avenue, the heart of his territory, in his brand new roadster. He had just taken possession of the vehicle, paying the dealer $6,000 from the roll of over $17,000 he held in his pocket. Suddenly, a dark sedan drew level with his roadster, before the retort of a shotgun blast shattered the tranquility of the day. The bullet pierced the bodywork of the pristine automobile and witnesses stated that Angelo then accelerated at great speed, before another shot blew out the front tyre, forcing the car to spin wildly out of control. Angelo hit the brakes as hard as he could, forcing his car into a screeching slide, before a lamppost violently halted its travel. The sedan, which had been pursuing the erratically driven roadster, now pulled up alongside. Two men – namely Hymie Weiss and Vincent Drucci – then leapt from the vehicle and fired several more shots into the now seemingly concussed Angelo, before jumping back into their sedan and speeding away into the metropolis. Undoubtedly, this mission was relatively more successful than their two previous incursions into enemy territory, as Angelo Genna was killed, albeit not instantly as the North Siders had hoped.

A few moments later, an ambulance took the barely conscious Angelo to the Evangelical Deaconesses Hospital, a private medical facility, where Dr. A.J. Schoenberg and Dr. John Pearl, operated to remove three bullets from his body, one of which had shattered his spine. Angelo managed to hold on for a further three hours, ample time for his brother Salvatore to arrive and to whom he identified those who had shot him. The fact that Angelo was taken to a private hospital and not the Cook County Hospital as has previously been believed, suggests that the Genna family may have been informed as to the events which had occurred *before* an ambulance was called, thus allowing them to make arrangements for their brother to be afforded the best medical care.

Angelo Genna was laid to rest in Mount Carmel Cemetery, though unlike Dion O'Banion, Cardinal Mundelein permitted his body to be interred in consecrated ground. A possible reason for this change in attitude is that Angelo Genna, extortionist, racketeer, bootlegger and murderer, had recently paid a large sum of money for urgent repairs to be carried out on a local church steeple. Perhaps therefore, there is hope for a great majority of today's society, for it seems that by the correct displacement of sufficient funds, anyone can attain eternal life.

The reasons why the North Siders had chosen to strike at the Genna's were twofold. Firstly, the brothers were important and valuable allies of Capone, thus prompting them to believe that by weakening the Outfit's strongest partnership, the Outfit itself would be subsequently enervated. Secondly, Angelo's killing was a revenge attack for his participation in the murder of Dion O'Banion. Despite the fact that Weiss had desired revenge on the Genna's, the belief that to weaken their clan was to weaken the Outfit, was little more than a fantastical illusion. In their haste to prove that they were the toughest and most competent gang in Chicago, they had unfortunately failed to see the whole picture.

When news of Angelo's death reached the Outfit, Jack McGurn felt he could hold back no longer and began to subtly tout the idea of a retaliatory attack to Capone. McGurn justifiably ascertained that the North Siders, no matter how lubberly they may be, were nevertheless dangerously out of control and he for one saw that the rot must now be stopped as quickly as possible; after all, they would have to be inordinately stupid or exceptionally violent to have intentionally taken on the Genna's, a gang whose own violence was so whimsical, that Angelo had long since acquired the sobriquet *'Bloody Angelo.'* Capone however, believed that the killing of Angelo would be the last fling that the North Siders would undertake. McGurn on the other hand, realized that if anything, they would now be buoyed by their success and would, in all probability, be planning the next installment of this deadly series. McGurn had an advantage over Capone, for he knew all too well where Weiss was coming from. He knew all about personal, vengeful attacks and, having experienced the self same emotions that Weiss was now undoubtedly feeling, he knew that his spirit would be soaring after such a notable hit. His own experiences during his young and already turbulent life meant that he had a full insight into the mental workings of Hymie Weiss and it was precisely this which now disturbed him. Capone appeared to be waiting for the North Siders to simply self destruct, but McGurn felt that to do so was to enter into a deadly battle of wills. However, without Capone's permission to make a move, there was little that McGurn could do, save of course, to endeavour to foresee and thus prepare for the enemy's next move.

In an attempt to understand just how this battle may pan out, McGurn decided that he should make covert enquiries – both within the Outfit and via their allies – as to just what Hymie Weiss was all about. What he discovered shook him to his core, for he ascertained that his boss and mentor Al Capone, a man who would in years to come become a legendary figure, was afraid of no man...except Hymie Weiss. By his own admission, Capone was a man who liked to be able to predict events as accurately as possible, to know instinctively what a person was thinking or what their next move may be. Yet Weiss was anything but predictable, his kaleidoscopic personality making him even more complicated and unmanageable than Dion O'Banion. In Capone's mind, this translated as a mere fear of the unknown, yet it was a fear nonetheless and McGurn knew that if Weiss or any of the North Siders knew of it, there was no telling what they would attempt next. McGurn saw that if anything in this life was certain, it was that the North Siders did not fear Capone or the Outfit, a factor which put the Outfit itself at an increased disadvantage. After mulling over the problem, McGurn hit upon an idea that he believed may redress the balance.

Albert Anselmi and John Scalise, the two men who had participated in the hit on O'Banion, were now in McGurn's sights. The duo had landed in America in the early 1920's, when an impending murder prosecution forced them to take flight from their Sicilian homeland. Soon after their arrival in New York, the pair gravitated towards Frankie Yale and in short order, were put to work as bodyguards. A few months later he dispensed with their services and sent them to Chicago, where they were soon employed by the Genna brothers. Upon the brothers' realization of the potentially enormous bootlegging profits, Scalise and Anselmi were given the task of enforcing – through whatever means they saw fit – the sale of Genna beer. Since that time, they had earned their reputation as the most heartless and pitiless gunmen in Chicago, a reputation which was perpetuated by their frequently used technique known as the *'Handshake Hit.'* Its method was simple and had been used to great effect in the killing of O'Banion. Anselmi, being physically stronger than his counterpart, would extend his hand in greeting to the victim. Once his hand had been accepted, he would then hold the victim's hands and wrists in a vice-like grip, while Scalise shot the poor soul in the face. McGurn knew that any gang which held the services of these men during a time of war would immediately have a natural advantage. According to Frank Nitti, Al Capone's debt collector and enforcer, the men had *'an evil aura around them, one which made it impossible to relax in their presence.'* McGurn had the idea that if Capone could manage to woo the duo away from the Genna clan, it would undoubtedly give the North Siders something to fear. Thus, a few days after the funeral of Angelo Genna, Scalise and Anselmi received a secret offer from Capone to join the Outfit, together with a goodwill gesture of $10,000 each and two diamond rings. Their reply was that they would consider it.

McGurn had another idea which might also serve to swing the balance of war into the Outfit's favour. As chief bodyguard and principal hit man, he was entitled to supply his crew with any equipment he deemed necessary. With Capone's approval, he set about furnishing the bodyguard and hit man entourage with the newest and deadliest weapon on the market: the Thompson submachine gun. McGurn organized practice sessions for the men, observing that the weapon's power to weight ratio was such that during sustained fire from shoulder height, it had a tendency to pull upwards, making it difficult for some men to handle. In addition to the power aspect, should the gun be fitted with a one-hundred round drum, the gunman inevitably received one-hundred simultaneous kickbacks. This took an enormous toll on the body and often left the gunman in question with either heavy bruising or, in extreme cases, a dislocated shoulder. However, after having personally fired a 1928 Thompson submachine gun, I can testify that when fired from waist height, it is a remarkably easy, if not accurate weapon to handle. Indeed, within the Outfit, there were only three men who would succeed in deploying the weapon with precision. These men were, Philip D'Andrea, Frankie Rio and Jack McGurn.

John Scalise and Albert Anselmi began to consider Capone's offer much more carefully when, on June 13, 1925, a little over two weeks after the murder of Angelo Genna, his elder brother Michael discovered too late that he was the North Siders next target. Hymie Weiss and Co found him, as usual, driving around Little Italy and chose to attack at the intersection of Sangamon Street and Congress, Jack McGurn's old stomping ground. Unable to get a clean shot, the gang fired wildly at Michael's car, before fleeing the area at high speed, convinced that they must have hit their prey. For once, they were correct in their belief, as one of the many bullets fired had pierced the bodywork of his car before ploughing its way into his leg and severing an artery. After driving himself to hospital, Michael lost consciousness and eventually slipped into a coma. He died a few hours later with his remaining brothers by his bedside. Unlike Sylvester Barton, Capone's chauffeur who also suffered a severed artery, Michael's decision to drive himself to the hospital merely prolonged the duration of his blood loss, a factor which undoubtedly contributed to his death. The Genna clan was now severely weakened and, like rats deserting a sinking ship, Scalise and Anselmi jumped overboard to join the good ship Capone.

In the aftermath of their excursion into enemy territory, the North Side once again fell eerily silent; indeed, nothing was heard from their part of the city for over two weeks. McGurn began to wonder whether it was all over, that maybe after hearing about the Outfit's acquisition of new men and fire-power, Weiss had decided that the game had become far too deadly. As the days continued to flit silently by, McGurn stopped wondering and began believing that this must indeed be the case. However, for the first time in his career, he was to be proved wrong.

Twenty-five days after the murder of Michael Genna, the lethal North Side triumvirate struck again, this time at Antonio, the youngest of the brothers. On July 8, 1925, Antonio was exiting a grocery store on Grand Avenue, owned by father and son Charles and Vito Cutaia, when two slugs were pumped into his back from close range. Despite the fact that no one could positively identify the killers, it was and indeed still is, generally assumed that the ambush was the work of the North Siders. One reason for this train of thought is that a witness told the police that there were two men involved and proceeded to give a description of one of them: it was a description which fitted Weiss perfectly. The witness went on to explain that she remembered him in particular because he was not wearing a hat. Throughout the decade of the 1920's, and indeed on into the 1930's, a hatless man was an extremely unusual sight. The second piece of evidence that points towards the hit being the work of the North Siders was that, despite having fired from point blank range, they had failed to kill Antonio instantly, due to the fact that they had chosen to fire into his back rather than his head. Nevertheless, in spite of the maladroit way in which it had been executed, their scheme was extremely impressive. Weiss had first elim-inated Angelo and Michael, the fighting force of the clan, thus reducing the possibility of any immediate revenge attack. They had then struck at Antonio, the brains of the clan, eliminating the risk of a tactical strike.

The remaining Genna brothers, Salvatore, Vincenzo and Pietro, having seen their numbers halved in just forty-two days, wisely decided that it was in the best interests of their health, to dispense with bootlegging and return to Sicily. The three brothers would return to America in the 1940's, this time choosing to make their living from the legal trade of importing Italian cheese and olive oil. They also took the decision to have the bodies of their brothers exhumed and placed in a mausoleum which they commissioned from the Italian Monument Company. Today, all six brothers can be found in the very same mausoleum, reunited in peace in the grounds of Mount Carmel Cemetery.

The killing of Antonio Genna only served to reaffirm McGurn's opinion that it was suicide to take the North Side gang too lightly. He was convinced that the final episode of their master plan had not yet taken place. After discussing his thoughts with the rest of his crew, he discovered that they too were of the same opinion; something was indeed about to happen though it was unclear as to just what that something would be. McGurn went back to Capone and pleaded with him on behalf of the entire strike force, to allow him to organize a strike against the North Siders. He argued that as far as he knew, Chicago had not seen a war like this for some time and that many of his crew had been around long enough to recognize the danger signs. The North Side had already been allowed to go too far and it was now time to gatecrash their party, before it had a chance to get out of control. Despite all his pleading and reasoning however, he could not convince Capone, who seemed more certain than ever that now that the North Siders had eliminated the Genna's, peace would descend onto the cities streets. McGurn could not help wondering whether this was indeed his real opinion. Could it be that Capone was too fearful of Weiss to authorize a strike? Without Capone's approval however, McGurn's hands were tied and so the waiting game continued. As it happened, the Outfit was destined to wait a long time, for it was to be a full year before McGurn and his crew discovered just what the elusive 'something' would be.

CHAPTER TWELVE

THE DEMISE OF WEISS

During the year 1925, to 1926, the Outfit saw a tenfold increase in its annual revenue, with every speakeasy and saloon in Cicero, the South Side and the Loop, taking delivery of Capone's liquor. There were five-hundred speakeasies in Cicero alone and each *'speak'* took delivery of approximately forty-eight barrels of beer a week, at the wholesale price of $50 a barrel, meaning that the Outfit was pulling in around $1,200,000 a week from just one section of the city. Added to this were the regular shipments of bourbon from the Bahamas and rye whiskey from Canada. A crate of good Bahaman bourbon sold for around $4,000 and it is from these shipments that the expression *'The Real McCoy'* was born.

In that era, the crème de la crème of bourbon was distilled by a man named John McCoy. Operating from the juristic sanctuary of the Bahamas, McCoy would evade the US Coastguard by packing his bourbon into crates which would then be tied to a Hessian sack filled with salt. A red float would then be attached to the top of the crate and the whole package would be taken by boat into American waters, where it would be thrown overboard. The weight of the salt would drag the crate and the float beneath the waves, however once the salt had dissolved, the float would bring the crate back to the surface where it would be collected by rum runners. McCoy's bourbon was of such high quality, that many people – as is always the case with premium goods – attempted to copy it. Unfortunately however, the counterfeit product fell far below the original's high standard, leading to a great many dissatisfied customer. In an effort to solve this problem, John McCoy began placing a stamp on all his crates and bottles: any crate or bottle without this stamp could not be sold as McCoy's. Therefore, all bottles and crates bearing the stamp came to be known as *'The Real McCoy.'*

The Hawthorne Restaurant was, by Capone's own admission, his favourite place to eat, serving what he described as *'the best food in Chicago.'* When eating at the Hawthorne, Capone and his party always took the same table, one which stood against the rear wall but facing the entrance; being seated at this table meant that they could be sure that no one could approach them from behind, whilst still being able to observe everyone within the large, airy establishment, as well as all who entered or left. It was at this usual table that Capone and McGurn were seated around lunchtime on September 20, 1926. The two were chatting idly between themselves when, almost simultaneously, they heard a distinctive and disturbing sound coming from outside: the rattle of machine gun fire. Almost inaudible at first, it gradually grew louder and louder as it neared the restaurant. Finally, a black sedan with a Tommy Gun toting man leaning out of the rear window rolled past the restaurant, causing all the patrons – including Capone and McGurn – to hit the floor for cover. As the car rolled out of sight, the rattle of machine gun fire ceased as quickly as it had begun, leaving only silence in its wake.

Puzzled, Capone pulled himself from the floor, dusted himself off and proceeded to walk to the plate glass windows at the front of the restaurant in order to see what or who had interrupted his lunch. McGurn was puzzled too, but for an altogether different reason: it was too quiet. There was no sound whatsoever, no breaking glass, no screams, no police sirens...nothing but absolute silence. Suddenly it hit him – the machine gun they had just seen and heard had been firing blanks, a ploy designed to arouse curiosity and draw the inquisitive to the windows. In an instant, McGurn leapt to his feet and raced after Capone, before rugby tackling him to the floor. Capone struggled to get free but McGurn kept tight hold of him, telling him *"Stay down boss, it's a stall...the real stuff ain't started yet."* Reluctantly, Capone relented and allowed himself to remain pinned to the floor and sure enough, the real action suddenly began. Ten black sedans, each identical to the first and all with Tommy Guns protruding from the rear windows, rolled past the restaurant. As each one drew level with the building, the guns blazed away, spraying the outside with *real* shells. The plate glass windows exploded, sending pieces of shattered glass flying onto the cowed patrons, whilst chunks of masonry were gouged from the immaculate façade. The noise was deafening, with the roar of the machine guns punctuated by the screams of terrified women and children. As the last car drew level, it rolled to halt, allowing a man carrying a machine gun and two drums of ammunition, to step out. Calmly kneeling in the splintered glass, he raised the gun to his shoulder and began to fire into the interior of restaurant, slowly moving the machine gun from side to side in a smooth, sweeping action. Whilst he was aiming low, from this position, the nature of the Tommy Gun was to pull upwards, meaning that anyone standing would have been cut down from the waist up. When the first drum of ammunition ran dry, the gunman quietly reloaded, before once again raking the interior with lead. As soon as the second drum was empty, he rose and returned to the waiting sedan. Then, at the mere toot of a car horn, the entire convoy disappeared into the city. This entire episode had been masterminded by the increasingly maniacal Hymie Weiss.

For all its pomp and circumstance, the second attempted hit on Capone had once again proved fruitless. Weiss and his North Siders had demolished the interior and exterior of the Hawthorne Restaurant with over one-thousand rounds of ammunition, yet had failed to hit a single person, let alone kill their intended target. Indeed, the only reported injury was to woman who had shards of glass embedded in her arm. When the noise had died away and the dust had settled, the fact remained that the North Siders had left Capone shaken, but otherwise uninjured and very much alive. In his attempt to pull off the most extravagant hit in gangland history, Hymie Weiss had effectively signed his own death warrant.

Of all the Outfit members, it was undoubtedly Jack McGurn who enjoyed the closest relationship with Capone, a relationship which allowed him to speak openly and frankly to the crime czar with little risk of retaliation. In the aftermath of the attempted hit, McGurn took full advantage of this special relationship, and for the third time of asking, demanded to be allowed to strike back. Capone was somewhat stunned at being spoken to in such a forthright manner, and sensing that he may have overstepped his boundary, McGurn quickly followed up his demand with an explanation. He told Capone that the North Siders were obviously growing increasingly desperate, so desperate in fact that they were willing to place the lives of non combatants in serious jeopardy. McGurn stressed that there had been women *and* children in the restaurant, and that with a group of uncontrolled desperados such as they, soon no citizen would be safe. They had taken out the Genna's, had almost taken out Torrio, and this latest attempt on the Outfit had been too close for comfort; by McGurn's reckoning, Weiss had not simply overstepped the mark, he had damn well vaulted over it. Capone knew that McGurn was right; he also knew that had it not been for him, the Outfit would now be searching for a new leader. Finally, but better late than never, Capone did what he had to do and gave McGurn his blessing to strike. He told him that it could be his operation, he could pick his own crew and have whatever materials he saw fit, but if anything went wrong, the consequences would be on his head. McGurn agreed.

Jack McGurn now found himself back in familiar territory. Not since the killings of Tropea, Two Knife and The Bug, had he been able to construct his own hit from start to finish. True, it was he who had contrived the idea of the identical automobile blockade on the O'Banion hit, but this was different, this was his thing, his call. He knew that to get at Weiss was to use a certain amount of psychology. Weiss, as he had come to realize, was a bumbling idiot most of the time, yet he was nonetheless as dangerous as a primed grenade. McGurn also knew that a cool, calculated and methodical killer, can often be far more effective than an aimless and unsystematic one. Eventually, a plan began to form in his mind, a plan which if executed to perfection, would culminate in the death of Hymie Weiss.

After having given his spoken consent to a retaliatory North Side strike, events took a rather unexpected twist. Capone received a telephone call from a low ranking member of the North Siders, who stated that he was merely a messenger who had been instructed to deliver the message that Weiss wanted peace, and to ask whether Capone would agree to a meeting. The entire Outfit was exceedingly skeptical, after all, O'Banion had used almost the exact same words before double crossing Capone and Torrio over the Sieben Brewery. If Capone had learned anything from his time under Torrio however, it was that peace was always more beneficial than killing one another. So putting cynicism aside, Capone agreed to the meeting on the condition that, for security reasons, he would not appear personally. Instead, he would send Antonio Lombardo, the new head of the Unione Siciliana to speak on his behalf. Weiss agreed, and the meeting was arranged for October 4, 1926, and was to be held at the Hotel Sherman in downtown Chicago.

As the day of the meeting dawned, Capone gave Lombardo two strict instructions. Firstly, he was to make it clear to Weiss that Capone was willing to agree to anything within reason in order to secure a peace agreement. Secondly, he was to ascertain exactly what it was that Weiss wanted in return for such an accord. The first part of the message only served to confirm the Outfit's fears that Capone was indeed afraid of Weiss. Why else would he state that he was willing to agree to anything, albeit within reason? McGurn for one knew that if he was not afraid, Weiss would have been dead a long time ago.

The meeting went ahead as planned, and on the same afternoon, Lombardo telephoned Capone with Weiss's demands. Lombardo informed Capone that Weiss had expressed his willingness to forgive him for the fact that he had given his consent to the murder of O'Banion. In spite of the fact that Dion had been his best friend, he was nevertheless ready to forego his vengeance to secure peace. However, Lombardo added that Weiss had stated categorically that he could not forgive the man who had pulled the trigger and as such, the Outfit member who had participated in the hit had to go. Capone asked for clarification as to what Weiss meant by that demand, to which Lombardo replied that Weiss wanted Capone to hand over Jack McGurn. Capone told Lombardo to go back and tell Weiss that that was something he was not prepared to do indeed, he *"wouldn't do that to a yellow dog."* Lombardo returned to the meeting and informed Weiss of Capone's reply, adding that he could ask for anything else and peace would be his. However, when Lombardo next telephoned Capone, it was to inform him that upon hearing his response, Weiss had stormed out of the meeting and had promised that Capone would live to regret his decision. Unbeknown to Weiss however, the meeting was not a reprieve for Capone, but for himself, and that by refusing to waver on his unreasonable demands, he had effectively destroyed any chance that his own life could be preserved.

Rightly or wrongly, Capone informed McGurn of Weiss's demands. The news had a strange effect on him, for aside from feeling relieved and indeed flattered by Capone's refusal, he also felt the same sense of excitement that he had felt during the North Side's onslaught on Capone's car. It was as if the threat to his own personal safety was a delicious risk and that rather than making him afraid, it thrilled him, aroused him even. Just as a wild animal is most dangerous when it is hurt or threatened, so it was with McGurn. Weiss's actions had ensured that McGurn would not only seek to kill him, but that he would actually enjoy doing so.

On October 5, 1926, the day after the meeting at the Hotel Sherman, a young man who gave his name as Oscar Lundin, visited a boarding house located at 740 North State Street, next door to Schofield's flower shop. Even after O'Banion's demise, the shop still served as the North Side head-quarters and as head of the North Side, McGurn figured that Weiss was sure to turn up there eventually. Lundin was told that the only space avail-able in the house at the present time was a bedroom in the center of one of the halls; Lundin took the room, but also reserved a second floor front bedroom to be allocated to him the moment it became vacant. The following day, the reserved second floor room suddenly and mysteriously came free, and the boarding house manager allowed Lundin to move in immediately. As with many boarding houses in the city, the rooms could hardly be described as elaborate, indeed it was something of a falsehood to even depict them as comfortable. However, this particular room had one redeeming feature, namely a panoramic view of North State Street, Superior Avenue and Holy Name Cathedral. Removing a large roll of bills from his pocket, Lundin paid one month's rent in advance and left, never to be seen again. The boarding house manager later stated that he saw another man move into the room, a man whom he described as tall, dark haired, charming and well dressed. The man was Jack McGurn.

For five days, McGurn, together with Frankie Rio – one of the only other Outfit men able to deftly handle a Tommy Gun – lived in the room overlooking the Cathedral, watching and waiting for the arrival of Weiss. The two men were in no particular hurry. Weiss was technically a walking dead man; it mattered not whether they got him in one day, one week or one month. It was set not to take that long however, for on October 11, McGurn and Rio saw their chance, as a large sedan – which they had previously identified as belonging to Weiss – slowed to a halt on Superior Avenue, directly outside Holy Name Cathedral. Accompanied by his lawyer William W. O'Brien, his chauffeur Sam Peller and another bootlegging crony named

Patrick Murray, Weiss was returning to his North Side HQ after attending the murder trial of one of his most influential allies, Joe Saltis. Stepping from the sedan, Weiss proceeded to walk over to Schofield's, before stopping to turn and talk to his lawyer. It was to prove a costly discussion.

Sitting at the second floor window in the building opposite, McGurn and Rio were taking aim, bringing their Thompson submachine guns level with Weiss and his counterparts. Worried that at any moment Weiss could disappear inside the flower shop, the two assassins grasped at the opportunity which now presented itself. Suddenly, the roar of machine gun fire echoed through the streets, resounding around the buildings that lined the Avenue. Weiss was the first to be hit, his body jumping like some demonic marionette, as the bullets tore through his flesh. William O'Brien tried to react, and in an effort to escape the merciless fusillade, ran back to the relative sanctuary of the sedan, a move which caused him to catch hot lead in his arm, ribs and stomach. McGurn and Rio were now in full flow, cutting down the North Side quartet with unforgiving and unparalleled accuracy. Having been standing next to Weiss, Patrick Murray was caught like a deer in the headlights, before seven slugs ripped into his torso, sending him crashing to the floor in a bloody heap. Sam Peller was still standing by the sedan, his position as chauffeur ensuring that during the onslaught, he remained partially covered by the bodywork of the auto. Despite this however, he was caught by a deflected bullet which embedded itself in his abdomen. In spite of being gravely wounded, both Peller and O'Brien would survive, though they would not be released from hospital for some time. Patrick Murray was not quite so fortunate; one of the seven slugs had pierced his heart, killing him instantly.

To Rio and McGurn, the three other casualties had simply been in the wrong place at the wrong time and were little more than collateral damage. What mattered most to them was that their primary target lay in a bloody mass, his body ripped apart by ten machine gun slugs to the torso and head. Not wishing to remain too long at the scene of the crime, McGurn and Rio fled before a fleet of ambulances arrived. The ambulance crews found that Weiss was barely alive, though his injuries were so severe that they could do little to save him; two bullets had ploughed their way into his forehead, shattering his skull and blowing two sizeable holes above his left eye. Hymie Weiss, the Outfit's would-be conquistador, died before he could even reach the hospital.

In addition to the damage inflicted upon Weiss, the shots fired from McGurn and Rio's Tommy Guns, also took their toll on the cornerstone of the Holy Name Cathedral. Inscribed on the stone was an excerpt taken from St. Paul's Epistle to the Philippians and before the shooting read *'At the name of Jesus, every knee shall bow – those that are in heaven and those on earth.'* Following the onslaught however, the inscription simply read *' every knee shall bow –   heaven and on earth.'*

Detective Chief William Shoemaker was once again assigned to investigate the murder of a gangster and, once again, he rounded up all the usual suspects, even though he knew full well that he was wasting his time. When he arrived at the Hawthorne Hotel to arrest Capone however, Shoemaker spotted the *'new boy'* McGurn. He decided to haul him in for questioning, reasoning that if he was new and inexperienced, he may prove easier to crack. Nevertheless, as he suspected, his best efforts were thwarted, as all those arrested expressed both shock and disbelief that Weiss was dead, in addition to swearing that they had verifiable alibis. McGurn – at whose hands Weiss had died – put on the best show, claiming that he was horrified that someone could kill his fellow man like that. McGurn's statement exposes the fact that he did indeed, feel no remorse whatsoever for the crime he had committed: he truly had relished the sight of Weiss dying before him. With no evidence forthcoming, Shoemaker had no option but to release all those arrested. His frustration was self evident, for when asked by a reporter for his views on the recent events, Shoemaker replied *"I don't want to encourage this business, but if somebody is going to be killed, it's a good thing that the gangsters are murdering themselves. It saves trouble for the police."*

Whilst McGurn took pleasure in the killing of Weiss, it is pure speculation as to whether he enjoyed killing in other circumstances, or whether he treated it purely as an aspect of his profession. It is entirely possible that he felt both these emotions; taking pleasure in the killing of those whom he believed should be killed, whilst in other cases, it was merely business. Either way, the killing of Weiss and his deft handling of the Tommy Gun, led the other Outfit members to christen him with the nickname *'Machine Gun.'* No longer would his name simply be Jack McGurn, but 'Machine Gun' Jack

McGurn, and for the rest of his life, indeed in perpetuity, that name would remain. McGurn would later tell a friend that he did not mind the nickname, but that he did think that it a little inaccurate, as his weapon of choice was actually a revolver. Quite whether history would have supported the legend of 'Revolver' Jack McGurn is something for which we can merely speculate.

Like those who had fallen before him, Hymie Weiss was buried in the grounds of Chicago's Mount Carmel Cemetery. The Church remained resolute in its declaration that gangsters are unfit to be buried in the hallowed ground of the cemetery, or to be allowed a funeral mass. Whether this is a correct assertion or not is undoubtedly a great argument, one which immediately brings one particular thought to mind. The Lords Prayer asks God to *forgive us our trespasses, as we forgive those who trespass against us.'* It therefore appears to be rather a simulation of virtue for the Church to go against the words of an established prayer and decree that some people are not worthy of such forgiveness.

The murder of Weiss appeared to have a marked effect on the remaining members of the North Side hierarchy. In mid October, 1926, Vincent 'Schemer' Drucci had a brainwave, realizing that should the war between the Outfit and themselves be allowed to continue, there would be no one left to rule anything. The result of this notion was that Capone once again received an offer for peace, and a meeting was subsequently scheduled for October 20, 1926, to be held once again at the Hotel Sherman. This meeting was set to be even more important than the last, for it would not only be a meeting of the North Siders and the Outfit, but of the entire gangland of Chicago. As with the previous meeting, the impartial Antonio Lombardo would preside as chairman, however unlike the previous meeting, Capone would attend personally, with McGurn serving as *consigliore*.

At the meeting, it was agreed that the war would end and that Drucci and Moran would relinquish their right to vengeance. In return, Capone would hold his own territory of the South Side, Near West Side, Cicero and Stickney. The North Side would remain under the control of Drucci and Moran; in addition, their territory was to be extended to encompass the North of Madison Avenue, East of the Chicago River. The entire East Side was to be the dominion of Spike, Miles and Klondike O'Donnell, brothers who had, up until now been impartial, although it was generally accepted that if it came to an all out war, they would line up against the Outfit. The West Side would remain under the control of the Saltis-McErlane Gang (Joe Saltis having been unanimously acquitted on the charge of murder) Each party shook hands and agreed the deal, with Capone giving his word that he would not be the one to break the agreement. As the parties exited the Hotel, a new peace looked set to descend on the city.

Just after Thanksgiving, Capone announced that he was greatly indebted to his young parvenu, Jack McGurn, for the way in which he had saved his life. He was also duly impressed by how adeptly he had handled the affair with Hymie Weiss. For these reasons, together with the fact that he was growing increasingly fond of his rising star, he was giving him a reward in the form of his own club. Many Outfit members held a share in a club or two, though none of them – except Capone's brother Ralph who owned the Cotton Club – owned any speakeasy outright. The club that Capone had in mind had originally been opened in 1907, at 4802 North Broadway Street under the name Pop Morris's Gardens. It was subsequently taken over three year's later and renamed The Green Mill Gardens. Now known simply as The Green Mill, it could be described as a lively speakeasy, with live entertainment in the form of singers and dancing girls, appearing every night. Capone declared that he was now transferring ownership of The Green Mill solely to Jack McGurn. The news came much to the chagrin of various other members of the Outfit, not least of whom was Frank Nitti, who regarded himself as more than worthy of such a reward. Not that anyone would dare speak their mind to Capone, from whom they already received an outstanding income; in any case, to do so would simply be regarded as jealousy. Nevertheless, jealous they were and in gangland, jealousy can be an extremely volatile emotion indeed; a trigger happy gunman whose eyes have turned green with envy, can be quickly become his comrade's mortal enemy. However, McGurn was known as Capone's boy, his protégé and as such, was one on which no one could make a move. Yet despite the fact that Capone could control the actions of his men, he could by no means control their thoughts.

In spite of all the best intentions, the newly brokered peace was not set to last, though as promised, it would not be the fault of the Outfit. Once again, the blame would lie squarely with the North Side, or more specifically, George Moran. Since the death of his one time friend and leader, Dion O'Banion, Moran had smouldered with vengeful thoughts and now with the death of Hymie Weiss, these smouldering ashes were set to erupt into a fireball. Of the entire North Side gang, Moran had to be the craziest, yet he also had a certain intellect when it came to revenge. Whilst he could never be described as a well read or learned individual, he was aware of Shakespeare and of one Shakespearean quote in particular: *'You never hurt the one you hate.'* Notwithstanding his deep seated hatred for Capone, it was not the crime czar who was now in Moran's sights.

The end of 1926, loomed on the horizon, and oblivious to the ruminations of Moran and what was left of the North Side cronies, the Outfit was reflecting on a rather torrid, yet highly successful year. Capone and McGurn were certain to enjoy their Christmas, having just received invitations to attend a Christmas party in New York. The party was to be thrown and hosted by long time Capone friend, Frankie Yale.

CHAPTER THIRTEEN

THE ADONIS CLUB

Towards the end of 1926, it appeared that life was heading steadily upwards for Jack McGurn and his Outfit cohorts. Certainly, the past twelve months had brought its share of problems, yet aside from these distractions, business was booming and it seemed that there was nothing that could stop the tide of money from flowing in. McGurn was currently in the process of overseeing renovations to The Green Mill. Under his guidance, and with a little help here and there, he was determined to make his club the best and hottest entertainment nightspot in the whole of Chicago. His excitement was heightened upon reflection of the fact that this new and indeed profitable acquisition, would serve to add a considerable boost to his already sizeable income. His turbulent past, together with its heterogeneous consequences, was already a distant memory and now looked set to pale into insignificance in a glorious haze of wealth. A few hundred miles away in New York however, Frankie Yale would have gladly wished that his own problems could so easily fade.

Born Francesco Ioele, Yale had spent his formative years in the southern Italian town of Calabria. Calabria is about as far south as you can go on the Italian mainland, a port situated right in the toe of the *'boot.'* In 1902, at age nine, the young Francesco had been brought to America, and like a great majority of his country cousins, he and his family attempted to settle into a new life in New York. Before long, Francesco noticed – just as Vincenzo Gibaldi had done – the incessant prejudice facing people of his ilk. Unlike Vincenzo however, Francesco was in the group of immigrants who chose to merely Americanize their names, rather than change them completely. Therefore, Francesco became Frankie and Ioele became Yale, and the new Frankie Yale was now ready to face the world.

It was not long before the now adolescent Frankie fell in with the various gangs which thrived on the streets of New York, the most notable of which was the Five Points Juniors. As soon as he was old enough, Frankie gravitated towards the Five Points Gang, the adult version of the Five Points Juniors and widely regarded as the most powerful street gang in New York. In this heady world of youthful violence, Frankie worked hard to make his way up through the ranks, until eventually he had accrued enough money, power and respect to make it on his own. He bought his own club on Coney Island, named the Harvard Inn, an acquisition which proved to hold the key to his future success. The massive income generated by the club led Frankie to realize that money breeds power and vice versa in a perpetual chain reaction. Before long, his followers had increased tenfold and his tentacles of influence reached into every corner of the city; he ran the ice, soft drinks, laundry and coal unions; he was on first name terms with the Mayor of New York, Jimmy Walker (who was later investigated on corruption charges) and regularly invited high ranking members of City Hall to dinner. In an effort to ingratiate himself with the local community, he even funded the repair of the local church. Eventually, the community came to regard Frankie Yale as *the* man to go to, for he was a man who could solve all of life's unsolvable problems. There was of course, a more sinister side to his nature, a side which was kept hidden from public view at all times and witnessed only by those who caused vexation. It was this flagitious side that occasioned his associates to adorn him with the sobriquet *'The Prince of Darkness.'*

One of the fallouts of the street gang culture is gang rivalry; indeed, as long as street gangs or clans of any form remain, it is a rivalry which will inevitably continue. Even before the streets of New York had heard the name of Frankie Yale, they had heard about the various gang related shootings, knife attacks and horrific mutilations which occurred in and around his city. Thus, Frankie Yale's rise to power had not been as swift and as effortless as it may seem. From the beginning of his tenure he was beset with problems, emanating primarily from the vicinity of a gang of Irish hoodlums calling themselves *'The White Hand,'* a name chosen for two specific reasons. Firstly, they mistakenly believed that Frankie Yale was the head of the notorious Black Hand which, as a gang of freelance extortionists, does not have a head at all. The second, and indeed most disrespectful reason, was that they often referred to the southern Italians and Sicilians as *'blacks'* or *'niggers'* in reference to their olive complexions. The White Handers were led by Richard 'Pegleg' Lonergan, a man who had taken over as leader from his brother-in-law William 'Wild Bill' Lovett, after Lovett had been murdered by a squad employed by Yale. Lonergan had gained his nickname after a childhood accident resulted in his left leg being amputated below the knee.

Over the years, the bad blood between Yale and Lonergan had grown increasingly rancid, with each side suffering heavy losses during the conflict. Undoubtedly however, it was The White Handers who had so far fared worse, so much so that by the year 1926, Lonergan had only five men that he could actually call followers. Yale was only too aware of the depletion of Lonergan's ranks, and it was this knowledge which had led him to believe that there would now be and end to the bloodshed. He was however, infinitely mistaken, for Lonergan was planning to even the balance. Calling his five disciples together, he formulated a plan that was so outrageously desperate as to be suicidal; the plan was to wipe out as many of Yale's men as possible in one fell swoop.

Pegleg knew that every year, Yale threw a Christmas party for his entire crew and their families. The party was habitually held at the Adonis Social and Athletic Club, and this year was to be no exception. Lonergan's plan was to gatecrash the party and once inside, he and his men would begin blazing away with revolvers which were hidden in their overcoats. They would fire wildly and indiscriminately, taking out as many *'blacks'* as possible, thus redressing the balance. However, the hopelessness of The White Handers cause had led Pegleg and his cohorts to blind themselves to the fact that their ingenious plan was destined for failure.

Unbeknown to Lonergan, Frankie Yale had an informer by the name of Eddie Lynch. Lynch and Lonergan had, at one time, been bosom buddies, but had recently had a falling out over a woman. In the ensuing argument, Lonergan had branded Lynch a *'yellow dog,'* an unforgivable and irrevocable insult even between best friends. In an effort to get even with Lonergan, Lynch pretended to shrug off the insult, whilst secretly approaching Yale with regards to employment as an informer. Initially, Yale was more than a little skeptical, yet once he had verified the story, took

Lynch on board wholeheartedly. Previously, the information which Lynch had supplied had been of little consequence, yet the tree of betrayal was about to bear the sweetest fruit. Informed of Lonergan's plan for the ambush, Yale could hardly bring himself to take it seriously; the thought of The White Handers – all six of them – attempting to wipe out Yale's entire crew, was ludicrous. After much persuasion however, Yale was eventually convinced that this was indeed a serious threat. Following much contemplation and negotiation, Frankie Yale decided to place a call to his old friend and country cousin in Chicago.

It was hardly surprising to find that Yale had specifically requested that Jack McGurn accompany Capone to New York, for having worked with McGurn personally on the O'Banion hit, he had first hand experience of both his working methods and skill. Of course, Capone was only too delighted to be able to assist Yale in the resolution of the predicament in which he now found himself; over the years, Yale had been an unwavering asset to the Outfit, providing outside firepower as well as intelligence. Yale now saw that just as he had been the cool headed, yet unknown gunman in the slaying of O'Banion, so too would McGurn be to Lonergan and his pestilent White Handers.

Upon arrival in New York, Capone and Yale came to the agreement to allow McGurn to chiefly decide on the best course of action. So far, McGurn had proved himself to be adequately adept in both the planning and execution of a hit, yet he had never been given cause to plan a hit of oversize proportions. In allowing him majority control, Yale and Capone could further observe what they both believed to be hidden potential; they could see that McGurn could very well be a gangland star in the making. Yale expressed his view that he wanted to meet the ambush party in the street, to shoot them down before they even had a chance to reach the club, however McGurn warned him against the use of such a tactic. He reasoned that they could not be sure that Lonergan really did only have five other gunmen at his disposal; he could have more waiting in cars, imported gunmen with nothing to lose and everything to prove. If they attacked them on the street without knowing for sure how many men they would be dealing with, there was a high probability that their counter-ambush could degenerate into a bloody street battle, something which much be avoided at all costs. The idea that McGurn was toying with involved the element of surprise, that way they would have the upper hand from the beginning. Finally, McGurn managed to persuade Yale that the best course of action was to do nothing, to make not a single move which could alert their would-be assailants' suspicions. McGurn's idea was to make everything appear as normal as possible and to allow Lonergan and his men to enter the club as if they were never expected. Once they were inside, The White Handers would be trapped, to be dealt with as Yale, McGurn and Capone saw fit. When McGurn had completed the outline of his plan and presented it to Yale, he was duly impressed; he knew that if everything went according to plan, the spoils of war would belong to them.

December 24, 1926, the day of the party. In previous years, the merriment had begun at around 9pm, with the partygoers not returning home until late Christmas morning. This year would be no exception. McGurn had instructed Yale to inform all those attending the party as to what was to happen that night, for in a situation such as this, the last thing any of them needed was an ignorant bystander who could potentially blow the whole shebang out of the water. The party would begin as normal and the security men would be at the door as usual: everything would be just as it should be.

McGurn and Capone arrived at the Adonis Club at 9pm prompt. McGurn carried two revolvers – his preferred weapon – concealed in the pockets of his heavy winter overcoat, as did Capone. At first, Yale had wanted to use Tommy Guns, but had eventually decided against it when McGurn pointed out that should the enemy be watching, then it would appear highly unusual that the partygoers were armed; if their weapons were small enough to be concealed, they would be none the wiser. In any case, the Tommy Guns were somewhat cumbersome and could not be unlimbered with any urgency. To add to the charade, the doormen, who were expected to stop and search anyone entering the club, had been issued with descriptions of Lonergan and his men and were under strict instructions that these revellers were to be allowed unimpeded access. McGurn wanted to ensure that The White Handers could enter the club with as little fuss as possible.

It was only after their arrival at the club that Yale, and indeed Capone, got a true idea of just how cool McGurn was. Knowing what was about to go down, it would have been perfectly understandable if McGurn had been slightly tense, quiet at the very least, yet it was fair to say that the opposite was true. He was perfectly relaxed, sharing a joke here and there with the other guests, indulging in the fabulous buffet and even taking to the dance floor with a few of the attending ladies. The only obvious anomaly was that he did not drink any alcohol whatsoever, though it is generally assumed that this was purely to keep a clear head and a straight shot. On any other night, bourbon would have been his beverage of choice. As the evening wore on and the merriment continued, Yale, McGurn and Capone expected that the Irish gatecrashers would show up at any moment however, by 2.30am, there was still no sign of Lonergan or his men and everyone began to wonder whether they would show up at all.

It was shortly before 3am and McGurn was leaning on the bar, enchanting Elvira Callahan with his Sicilian charm. Elvira – a cigarette girl who was working at the club that night – tall, slender and exceptionally attractive, truly was Jack McGurn's type. After purchasing a pack of ciga-rettes from her, McGurn asked her if she had a light. She did not, and so he turned to get a match from a book which was lying on the bar. As he did so, he caught sight of a stranger – one whom he guessed was Lonergan – enter the room. McGurn guessed that it was Lonergan from the mere fact that he had blonde hair and blue eyes, features which were strikingly unusual among Italians. Lonergan was followed into the room by his five compan-ions: Aaron Harms, Cornelius Ferry, Patrick Maloney, Joseph Howard and James Hart. As the six men walked into the club, they began abusing the guests with names such as *'wops'* and *'dagos.'* The guests had been instructed to allow the Irish intruders to say whatever they wished, for should an argument begin, then events may ignite a little earlier than planned. McGurn had arranged for a few chairs to be placed along the length of the bar, so that the only standing space available was at either end of the bar. As planned, Lonergan and his men stood at the end nearest the entrance, directly opposite from where McGurn was standing. Despite the fact that they appeared inebriated – perhaps due to a little too much Dutch courage – the six men were permitted to have a beer. At 3.10am, McGurn glanced over to Capone who was standing a few feet away to his left, talking to a group of guests whom he recognized from his days in New York. With

the most subtle of confirmations from Capone, McGurn took another cigarette from his packet, before turning to ask the barman whether he had a
light. This was the signal for the barman to turn out all the lights in the club,
except one: the one which was to remain lit was a small spotlight at the end
of the bar, just by the entrance.

In an instant, the room was plunged into darkness, leaving Lonergan,
Harms, Ferry, Maloney, Howard and Hart, illuminated by the solitary spotlight. Panicked by the vulnerable position in which they now found themselves, Lonergan and his men forgot their battle plan and fumbled for their
weapons, oblivious to the fact that a man by the name of Sylvester Agoglia,
had appeared behind Pegleg Lonergan. Through the darkness there
suddenly came the sickening thud of cracking bone and splitting flesh, as a
butcher's meat cleaver – wielded by Agoglia – tore open Lonergan's head,
sending him crashing to the floor in a bloody heap. That was McGurn's
cue. Removing his revolvers from inside his coat, he began firing at the illuminated group. Capone too, unlimbered his own weapons and joined the
onslaught. Under a hail of lead and in an effort to save their own skins,
Maloney and Howard fled towards the exit, remarkably making it out of the
club without a scratch. Despite having his left leg torn open by three separate bullets, James Hart also managed to make it out of the club; he was later
found by a patrolman, crawling along the street in audible agony. However,
Lonergan, Harms and Ferry were not quite so fortunate. The massive head
wound that had been inflicted by Agoglia, had killed Lonergan instantly,
whilst Ferry and Harms had each been shot three times in the head and
chest. McGurn and Capone had hit one man each, with the shots coming in
such quick succession, that the two men fell dead on top of each other, not
even having time to draw their own guns.

Within minutes the action was over, and upon a brief signal from
McGurn, the lights were flicked back on. In the now brightly lit room, the
guests laid their eyes on the sickening carnage before them. Lonergan – the
meat cleaver still buried firmly in his head – now lay in a pool of his own
blood, whilst the blood stained pile that was Cornelius Ferry and Aaron
Harms, blocked the entrance. Upon viewing the bodies, not to mention the
copious amounts of blood, Elvira Callahan screamed before promptly
fainting, as did many other women in the room. Nevertheless, everything

had gone according to plan and despite the fact that three White Handers had escaped, Yale was not overly concerned. He knew that the escapees did not have enough standing in gangland to command any further reprisal. McGurn too was satisfied, safe in the knowledge that not only had he completed a successful assignment, but he had also enabled an already powerful Outfit ally to become the undisputed king of New York. The potential of having such a potent friend was not lost on him, for he saw that one day, in true gangland style, he may also be in a position to call on Yale to return the favour.

McGurn was not the only person to realize that Yale would now be in a position to return a favour. Capone too understood this fact, though unlike McGurn, he had decided to call in that favour while he was still in New York. Capone was aware that Yale controlled the Longshoremen's Union, meaning that he effectively had control of the whole of New York's Dockland. This advantageous position meant that Yale could determine which goods – including booze – passed into and out of the dockyards and in what quantity. Capone however, was not interested in just any old booze, after all, there was enough rotgut beer and bathtub gin to sink the entire United States. What Capone wanted most of all, was high quality bourbon: The Real McCoy. If Capone could corner the market of supplying The Real McCoy to the speakeasies of Chicago, the Outfit would see its profits go through the roof. Capone also saw the potential of wholesaling the liquor to all the other Chicago gangs, at an even greater profit. Obtaining the liquor was the easy part, a task which any fool could do single handedly. However, safely transporting the liquor from New York to Chicago without incurring the risk of hijackings or prohibition raids, was a task with which anyone would need assistance. That was where Yale came in.

When McGurn heard about the impending deal, he conferred with his boss as to whether he too could be in on it. Having just taken charge of a new club, McGurn knew that in order to achieve greater success, to get more paying clients than any other establishment, he would have to offer something special, something which no other club provided. The obvious attractions, such as high class entertainment, beautiful dancing girls and big names from both stage and screen, were already in place, yet McGurn still felt that there was something missing. He now realized that, if in addition to all these major attractive features, he could offer the best liquor that money could buy, The Green Mill would be well on its way to becoming the best joint in town; McGurn could simply sit back and watch the money roll in. So before preparing to leave for Chicago, Capone and McGurn struck a deal with Yale. Once a month, Yale would receive payment for twelve truck-loads of The Real McCoy. In return for the favour carried out by his Chicagoan friends, Yale would oversee the safe transportation of the liquor between New York and Chicago. Ten of the truckloads would be delivered to a Capone owned warehouse, whilst the remaining two would head directly for The Green Mill. On December 30, 1926, the triumvirate of Capone, Yale and McGurn, indulged in a celebratory dinner, to toast Yale's newfound standing and also the deal that had been reached. It was at this dinner however, that McGurn discovered some information so provocative, that it would test his powers of restraint to the limit.

During the course of the evening, the conversation eventually turned to the subject of employees, in particular, the difficulty in finding people who were both honest and loyal. The three men gave their respective ideas as to whom they considered to be trustworthy and reliable in their respective crews. It was at this point that Yale mentioned the names of John Scalise and Albert Anselmi, informing his fellow diners as to how faithful and depend-able they had been under his employment. This certainly came as a surprise to McGurn, for up until now, he had no knowledge that these men had ever worked for Yale. Yale then proceeded to relay the story of how, having heard rumours that a notorious Chicago Black Hand extortionist was in need of a couple of enforcers, and more importantly, was willing to pay good money for them, he had contacted the man in question and offered to send Scalise and Anselmi. Once he had received word that his offer had been accepted, Yale dispatched them to Chicago forthwith. McGurn's interest was now suddenly piqued and out of sheer curiosity, he asked Yale as to the identity of the man in question. If ever there was a point when McGurn wished he had kept his mouth closed, it was now, for Yale nonchalantly replied that he had sent these two faithful soldiers to work for Orazzio Tropea. As devas-tating as this information was, there was worse to come, for Yale coolly added that he had sent them to Chicago just before New Year of 1923. The news rocked McGurn to his core, for that was the very year when his own father had had his life cruelly snatched away after ignoring that malevolent serpent's *'pay or die'* threats; to think that Scalise and Anselmi were allied with Tropea was, in effect, to relive the nightmare. Should he not know these men personally, then perhaps his old wounds would not have been so cruelly and painfully reopened, but the awful truth was that he did not merely know these men, they were under his command. As chief hit man and bodyguard, he was effectively the boss of the entire hit crew. Still reeling, Jack McGurn realized that he was now in the unenviable position of working alongside men who were allied to his father's murderer.

The possible implications of the situation played on his mind all the way back to Chicago. The circumstances in which he now found himself were so perplexing, that he did not feel fully equipped to deal with them. His mind ran riot with thoughts on how best to handle the predicament. Should he inform Capone that he was no longer able to continue in that particular employment? Should he confront Scalise and Anselmi directly, ask them point blank as to whether they had a hand in his father's death? Should he simply assume that they had and deal with them in the same way that he had dealt with Tropea himself? Then again, maybe it was all a test set up by Capone, after all, he knew that it was Tropea who had killed his father; maybe Capone was testing him, to see how he would handle the most emotionally demanding of situations. Eventually, McGurn decided that the best course of action was inaction, a reasoning which was based more on common sense than personal feeling. In gangland – as in any other community – there are laws which dictate how its members should behave, one of which is the absolute prohibition of murder on mere suspicion. The member in question must have firm evidence and even then, permission had to be sought from his superior, especially if the purported perpetrators were in that members own crew. McGurn also rejected the idea of asking Capone for advice, believing that it may prompt Capone to believe that he was allowing his heart to rule his cool and objective mind. Nevertheless, in spite of the fact that he would relay his true feelings to no one else, he would certainly be keeping a close eye on his two *'dependable'* colleagues.

★   ★   ★

Over the past few months, as Jack McGurn became more and more involved with Capone and his duties within the Outfit, the relationship between Helena and himself had begun to deteriorate to the point where it felt as if they hardly knew each other at all. McGurn's acquisition of The Green Mill had led to an increase in the hours that he was away from home; occasionally full days and nights would pass before Helena and Helen would see him. Naturally, this relative isolation resulted in Helena feeling increasingly neglected and as such, when Jack finally did come home an argument usually ensued. Jack's response was little more than stoic defiance followed by him leaving once more to spend the next few hours at The Green Mill, where he would drown his sorrows in flirtatious conversations with a few of his female guests. Though neither Jack nor Helena was willing to admit it openly, they nevertheless knew that the road on which they were now travelling could lead nowhere except to heartbreak.

The information gleaned from Frankie Yale in New York had done little to improve McGurn's mood, and so it was with a heavy heart that he arrived back in Chicago in the late afternoon of New Years Eve, 1926. Whilst Capone returned immediately to the Hawthorne Hotel, McGurn – somewhat reluctantly – went home to see Helena and Helen. Late that evening, a New Years party was to be held at the Hawthorne and the idea was that McGurn and Helena would join the party later on. Helena was glad that her husband had decided to come straight home, for she was about to give him some news that would turn the evening into something of a double celebration: she was pregnant again, with the baby being expected sometime in September, 1927. McGurn was ecstatic at the news. It gave him a brief respite from the trials and tribulations of his duties with the Outfit and, more importantly, it took his mind away from the thought of Scalise and Anselmi. McGurn hoped that this baby would be a boy, a son to carry on the Gibaldi name and perhaps, in some way, cathartically repair all the wrongs in his own life. With respect to their relationship, the news seemed to be just the tonic it needed, for it gave Jack and Helena a fresh incentive to make their marriage work. Helena hoped that Jack would now be home more often, for she had long since realized the temptation which was being thrust upon her husband day after day at the club. Not that Jack had ever considered being unfaithful to Helena – far from it – yet he was only human and Helena knew all too well that if the situation should continue, there may come a point when the question would not be *if* Jack would succumb, but *when*. In the words of Oscar Wilde *'The only way to get rid of temptation is to yield to it.'*

The year 1927, promised to be a year which was just as good, if not better, than the last. The peace accord that had been brokered between the various gangs at the Hotel Sherman appeared to be holding out, and whilst minor scuffles occasionally broke out, the full scale gang wars had all but ceased. Prohibition too was still going strong, ensuring that business would effectively continue on the up and up. Even politically, events looked set to turn in the Outfit's favour. The current Mayor of Chicago was William E. Dever. Nicknamed *'Decent Dever'* he was a reform politician, and had come to power with the election spiel that he would rid Chicago of the gangsters and turn the city from *'wet'* to *'dry'*. However, since his election in 1923, his tactics had failed to prevent a single criminal act in Chicago; the reform mayor had failed miserably on the very policy he stood for. Dever's election had ousted the then mayor, William Hale Thompson, a man who was as wet as the Atlantic Ocean and, more importantly, was a Capone backed politician. Now – to the delight of the Outfit – he was preparing to run for another term in office. Knowing that it pays to have allies in such a powerful position, Capone ensured that Thompson was given as much financial support as was needed, whilst ensuring that on polling day itself, all voters were *'encouraged'* to vote the right way. In the end, when all the votes had been collected and counted, Thompson had won a marginal victory…512,740 to Dever's tally of 429,668. The most incorrigibly corrupt politician since 'Hinky Dink' Kenna or 'Bathhouse' Coughlin, was in power and in Capone's pockets.

★ ★ ★

At the end of January, 1927, Jack and Helena were dealt a crushing blow. One night, Helena awoke with severe abdominal pains. A doctor was called, and after performing a brief examination, ordered that she be immediately taken to the nearest hospital. A few hours later, a nurse broke the news that Helena had suffered a miscarriage. The news was devastating, more so considering that the first pregnancy had gone so well, with virtually no problems whatsoever. The reality of the situation dealt a hammer blow to their already fragile marital state, shattering the hard work that they had both put in over the past month. Jack found himself unable to fully accept the news and left the hospital without even consoling Helena. Up until this point, the prospect of having a second child had begun to have the intended effect, bringing the couple closer together to the point where they could almost make up for lost time. Now however, the panacea had deteriorated into a grotesque, festering wound which threatened to poison the very essence of their relationship.

In order to make sense of the situation, McGurn felt that he needed to get his head together, to deal with the events in his own way. One of those ways was to throw himself completely into his work, both with Capone and at The Green Mill. The club especially, with all its hustle and bustle, the incessant music and the constant chatter, left him little time to contemplate the devastation that had just entered his life. Within The Green Mill he felt he could escape and so once again, he began to spend an increasing amount of time away from home; when he did go back, it seemed that Helena was either crying, or the civility which, for the sake of Helen was now somewhat forced, would inevitably degenerate into a full scale argument. So, night after night, McGurn would sit at his corner table at The Green Mill, sipping his Real McCoy bourbon and laying on the charm for all those who desired his company, whilst secretly hoping that he could avoid returning home that night.

It was this situation which led him to realize that a great many of the guests in his club, were literally falling over themselves to be in his company, especially so if the guests happened to be female. This was not his ego taking over, this was pure hard fact, for no matter how vehemently they may deny it, some women are incredibly attracted to danger. The gangster mystique – the image of an attractive guy who may be potentially dangerous – is a combination which makes bad guys irresistible to a great many women. Therefore, as the word got around that McGurn was affiliated with Capone, his female guests were getting around to getting him into their beds. Nevertheless, it seemed that none of them could turn his head long enough to get that far…until one night. As he sat at his usual table, a showgirl appeared on stage to perform a solo dance number. Her name was Louise Rolfe.

McGurn had already known Louise for a few months, having met her when she came to audition for a job as a showgirl at the club. He had immediately found her attractive indeed, she was certainly his kind of woman, or rather the kind of woman he had recently become fond of. Whereas Helena was a deep brunette with perfect olive skin, McGurn had grown desirous of women of a fairer complexion, like Elvira Callahan. Louise was tall, extremely slender, with platinum blonde hair styled into a fashionable bob, yet despite being struck by her beauty the very moment he laid eyes on her, his will to remain devoted to Helena had restrained him from making any advances. Now however, that will had dissipated to the point of extinction, and as he watched her dancing on the stage, her knee length sequined dress made her shimmer, like some divine vision in what otherwise felt like a desolate void. Without stopping to consider the consequences of his actions, he sent a note to her dressing room to say that she would be welcome at his table should she wish to join him for a drink. His invitation was accepted, and as they sat together, McGurn found that Louise was just as enchanting to talk to as she was to look at; she was funny, intelligent and, like most of the other women, was excited by McGurn's aura of danger. The word that McGurn was in some way connected with Capone, had not failed to reach the ears of Louise and for her, to be brought into the realm of the gangster mystique was an enticing prospect. Entranced by his charm and generosity, Louise soon fell under McGurn's spell and despite having heard what he purportedly did for a living, she found upon meeting him, that the rumours were difficult to believe. How could such a warm, charming and handsome man possibly be a killer? Nevertheless, the possibility was there and as such, so was the exhilaration. It was the era when to be a gangster was to be a celebrity and Louise was honoured to be in the unadulterated company of such a man. Whilst McGurn was without doubt a dangerous man, a man who had killed both personally and professionally, the majority of the public would be enthralled by his presence and would relish the feeling of unbridled pleasure: Louise was no exception.

Over the next couple of months, a relationship began to develop between Jack and Louise and it was not long before they could regularly be found sharing a hotel room. McGurn found Louise both sensual and sexual and so had acted upon the words of Oscar Wilde and yielded to his temptation. Jack and Louise enjoyed a fantastic sex life, forever dreaming up new and different ideas with which to tantalize each other. This was once demonstrated by the testimony of a maid at the Hawthorne Hotel, who told of the day when she had discovered handcuffs, chains and lingerie strewn across the couple's hotel room.

In spite of his falling completely head over heels for Louise, McGurn was as careful as ever to keep her as far away as possible from his work; in his line of business, complications were extremely unhealthy. Should McGurn show any point of weakness, no matter what form it may take, he would be giving any enemies an exploitative edge. Just as Helena had been kept in the dark, so too was Louise, although by now, Helena had put two and two together of who exactly her husband's employer was. Despite the fact that Louise knew that McGurn was involved in some way with Capone, had anyone asked her what his exact employment was, she would have been unable to answer. As far as his professional life was concerned, all she had to go on were rumours and stories.

It was not long before Jack and Louise realized that they had fallen in love with each other. Jack even toyed with the possibility of leaving Helena, but decided that this was impossible. Not only would such a move once again display a weakness, but the rest of the Outfit would take a very dim view of the situation. No matter what they chose to do, the majority of the Outfit's members held dear the values of their Latinate upbringing. Notwithstanding the fact that many members had mistresses themselves, the idea of leaving their wives was one that did not even enter their heads. Stability was the mainstay of the gangster life; emotional turbulence could be professionally destructive. Therefore, Helena and Louise were kept secret from each other, whilst the killings that McGurn had committed and would continue to commit, would be kept secret from them both.

CHAPTER FOURTEEN

THE ENTERTAINER

It was April 4, 1927, when Capone received some news that made his day, if not his year; Vincent 'Schemer' Drucci – an integral player in the North Side gang – had been killed. Surprisingly however, he had died not at the hands of any rival gang member, but of a police detective. Drucci had been picked up by Detective Daniel Healy, who was attempting to execute a warrant for the arrest of the North Side leaders on a charge of robbery. It was whilst driving around the North Side, that Detective Healy caught sight of Drucci, exiting the Hotel Bellaire. Pulling his car to a halt outside the hotel, Detective Healy rushed up the front steps and immediately apprehended Drucci, who appeared to take instant chagrin at his arrest, verbally abusing Healy as his hands were cuffed in front of him. Though still only in his mid twenties, Healy was a highly skilled Detective, and having already killed a man during a stand off following a hold up, was hardly perturbed by Drucci's verbal onslaught. Detective Healy's statement – contained in the Chicago Police Homicide Records – told that the verbal abuse continued in the car, with Drucci threatening the detective that he would wait on his doorstep for him so that he could *'fix him.'* Repeatedly Detective Healy told him to keep quiet, yet true to the Drucci style, he steadfastly ignored the warnings and continued by challenging Healy to take off his gun and have a fight. He then took to taunting Healy, charging that he was not so tough without a gun and that he could *'kick the hell out of the kid copper.'* Healy's statement continues that after that, Drucci got up on one leg and kicked out with the other, catching the young detective in the side of the head. By this time they were outside the police headquarters, and as Healy stepped out of the car, Drucci made his move and lunged for Healy's gun. Healy fought back, trying to protect his gun which had now been released from its holster. When Drucci grabbed hold of Healy's left arm and tried to prise his gun from his hand, Healy shot him four times; Drucci was hit once in the arm and leg and twice in the abdomen. A squad car was immediately ordered to drive the two men to the Cook County Hospital, but Drucci – aged just twenty-seven – was dead before they could even reach the hospital gates.

Privately, Capone and McGurn, together with the rest of the Outfit, were ecstatic at the news. Despite the enduring peace accord, the Outfit still maintained a suspicious and bitter hatred of the North Siders – and vice versa. Now, should the peace accord happen to break down, there would be one less of the enemy to deal with. Publicly however, it was a different story. Capone waxed lyrical over how sad he was that his old friend had been killed and that his death had been such a waste of life. Not that anyone actually took his comments to heart…the vicious and bloody war between the Outfit and the North Siders was still too fresh in the memory for that.

★ ★ ★

By now, Jack McGurn had developed into an archetypal movie star gangster, a man whom James Cagney or Edward G. Robinson would gladly have brought to the silver screen. He had a character that boasted an intoxicating blend of components including – but not exclusive to – that of a killer, a charmer, a lover, a public benefactor, an athletic dancer who could achieve full-to-the-floor splits better than any flapper, a deft ukulele player, skilled sportsman and doting father. McGurn truly was a man of total contradiction, yet one who presented an apodictic image. As a journalist at the time wrote *'McGurn was a really nice guy. If you didn't know who he was, you would want him to be your friend;'* everybody who came into contact with him adored him.

At the outset of his career, he had felt that the world was his oyster with which he could do as he pleased. Now, four years after joining Capone, and as his name became more and more known throughout Chicago, he felt that he was unstoppable. The knowledge that he was in charge of the entire hit crew and bodyguard entourage, allowed his ego to gorge itself on ideas of total domination, until the perception of grandeur left it inflated and distended. Whilst he knew that to the men under his command, his word was fiat, his now amplified self importance yielded the belief that the same was also true amongst those outside the Outfit. He took to asserting his authority within The Green Mill, personally overseeing the hiring and firing of employees and exhibiting exorbitant arrogance in his position of club owner. The mantle of club owner meant that he now held Outfit membership status, a detail which gave him immense egotistical pride. No longer was he merely a $300 a week bodyguard. He was now the man, chief honcho, king of all he surveyed. The quiet, mild mannered boy who held the utmost respect for women had vanished, replaced by a man who operated a casting couch system for showgirls; it was certainly no coincidence that all of the girls whose applications were successful were preferentially blonde.

However, in spite of all this brash vulgarity, he was extremely careful to employ that magical McGurn charm whenever and wherever possible. McGurn found it incredibly easy to be charming without the slightest hint of patronization, a priceless asset in both his professional and personal life. Yet at no time did any of this appear to be an act, indeed it was as if he had always affected such a debonair style. McGurn soon realized the potential that his magical charisma held when it came to signing new and big name stars to appear at The Green Mill. Frightfully few stars could resist having their egos massaged and the catering to their every whim, and as the star studded guest list grew and grew, there were even less names that could resist the offer of performing at such a prestigious nightspot. One such performer to fall under the McGurn spell was the comedian, Joe E. Lewis.

Born Joseph Klewan on January 12, 1902, Joe E. Lewis had just begun to make a name for himself as a comedian/singer. A regular feature at various cabarets all over Chicago, Lewis's attraction was so great that a club owner could virtually guarantee a sell out each and every night. It was hardly surprising therefore when, at the end of May 1927, Lewis received an offer from McGurn to perform at The Green Mill at $650 a week for six months. McGurn's debonair charisma and the promise of a massive salary was a potent mixture, against which Lewis was rendered helpless. As soon as the contract was signed, opening night was set for June 2, 1927.

May that year was not just an important time in the lives of McGurn and Lewis, it was also of massive significance for every man, woman and child in America, if not the world. For it was on May 21, that the news broke that Charles A. Lindbergh and his plane *The Spirit of St. Louis* had touched down in Paris, after successfully completing the first non stop, solo flight across the Atlantic. The news was greeted with awe and admiration, not least in the Midwest from where Lindbergh hailed. Upon his return to the United States, he was given a hero's welcome and was promptly declared a living saint of the Midwest. Amidst the euphoria of the celebrations, no one would have guessed that just five years later his name would once again make headline news, though for altogether more sinister reasons.

On opening night – as expected – The Green Mill was packed to the rafters. It was just as McGurn had dreamed it would be, with his club finally recognized as the most happening entertainment spot in Chicago. The finest quality champagne, beer and of course, the newly acquired Real McCoy, flowed freely throughout the evening and Lewis went down a storm. The crowd could not get enough of him, and at the end of the evening when McGurn took to the stage to thank the audience for their presence as his guests, they loved him too. Each subsequent night was just like opening night; the club was always full, with a perpetual line of guests waiting to be allowed inside. As surely as a river flows to the sea, so an endless tide of money was flowing into McGurn's coffers. However, a dark North Side cloud soon loomed ominously on the golden horizon.

Like most performers, the façade which Joe E. Lewis presented on stage was not his real persona. The reality behind his joviality was that he was a drinker – and a heavy one at that. Following the culmination of his act, the jesters mask was removed to reveal a face full of Pierrot melancholia. As Lewis was earning upwards of $650 a week, the general assumption was that he was a wealthy individual, yet the truth could not have been further removed. The majority of his earnings were blown primarily on booze and secondly on gambling. Anything left over after that, he spent on prostitutes. It came to a point where Lewis was struggling to support his habits, indeed it was arguable that he was actually performing at The Green Mill free of charge. This conclusion is brought about by the fact that he spent his salary drinking in the club's ground floor speakeasy, gambling on the first floor, and once his thirst was sated and his pockets virtually emptied, he inevitably visited one of the many Outfit owned brothels. Whatever he shelled out on Lewis, McGurn could be sure to recoup it from the man himself within a few hours.

Then came the news that another club called the Rendezvous, had just opened up on the border between the North and South Side. The club's owner decided that he too would like to have big name acts appearing at his venue, and so attempted to lure Lewis away from The Green Mill. Needless to say, McGurn was less than impressed when he was told of the rival bid, yet when he learned just who the owner of the Rendezvous actually was, his mood soon turned from mere annoyance to that of seething rage. The man who was attempting to poach McGurn's prize asset was none other than George Moran. McGurn countered the North Side offer by offering Lewis an extension to his contract, an increase in his salary to $1,000 a week, together with a share of the club's profits. In hindsight, it was something of a foolish miscalculation on the part of Lewis when he chose to reject McGurn's improved offer, for the rivalry between Moran and the Outfit was nothing short of common knowledge. Lewis accepted the rival bid from Moran, causing McGurn to fly into a rage; he had been wronged and his temperamental Sicilian anger, like a sleeping dragon, was suddenly awakened. Legend has it that as Lewis walked out of The Green Mill, McGurn uttered the words *"You'll never live to open."* Believing that he had misheard what McGurn had said, Lewis meekly replied *"I'll leave tickets for you at the door,"* thus adding insult to injury and throwing fuel on McGurn's already smouldering temper.

In the heat of the moment, many people make remarks that are not intended to be taken literally, often retracting their impassioned state-ment once the confrontation has abated. Therefore, even if Lewis had not believed that he had misheard McGurn and his words had actually registered within his psyche, he may not have been inclined to take the threat all that seriously anyway. Yet he would have been well advised to take the threat extremely seriously, for McGurn was a man of conviction and had never been known to make such a flippant remark. Nevertheless, McGurn was fond of Lewis and so decided to give him another chance. Contacting the Cicero Precinct, he requested that an officer on the Outfit's payroll be assigned to take a message to Lewis. The message was that McGurn was willing to forgive the insult, and that his generous offer of $1,000 a week was still on the table. Should Lewis still remain undecided about his future, the police officer was to urge him to return to The Green Mill and inform him that he would live a great deal longer if he did so. The message was subsequently delivered and a few hours later, the police officer returned with a response; unbelievably, not only had Lewis once again declined to accept the offer, but he was also adamant that his show would open at the Rendezvous as planned, on November 2, 1927.

Joe E. Lewis did indeed open as planned, although as he was accompanied by a bodyguard, it was obvious that he now regarded McGurn's threat as a sincere one. The Rendezvous was – as expected – packed for the entertainer's opening night. The crowd bubbled with excited anticipation, waited with bated breath, and finally erupted into a crescendo of delight when Lewis finally appeared on stage. After thrilling the audience with a one hour performance, he returned cautiously to his dressing room where his bodyguard was keeping watch. To his relief however, the whole evening passed off rather uneventfully, as did each subsequent night. For the next week, Lewis continued to play to the packed club, and whilst every night saw him arrive at the venue in the company of a bodyguard, nothing even remotely suspicious occurred. By the end of the week, Lewis believed that he had played down the threat of McGurn, convincing himself that if he was going to make a move, he surely would have done so by now. He reasoned that three months had passed since he left The Green Mill and that if McGurn had indeed intended to strike, he would undoubtedly have done so whilst the iron was hot. Secure in his belief, he took the decision to allow his bodyguard to stand down. Whilst Lewis knew a great deal about the intricacies of a stage performance, he obviously knew very little about the machinations of the mind of Jack McGurn.

For convenience, Lewis was residing at the Commonwealth Hotel, just a stone's throw from the Rendezvous on Pine Grove Avenue. On November

8, following his appearance on stage, he returned to his hotel room and after several drinks too many, promptly fell into a drunken slumber. He was awoken early the next morning by a knock at the door. Feeling somewhat worse for wear due to the effects of the morning-after-the-night-before, he groggily crossed the room to answer the call. Despite the fact that he had dismissed the thought of any possible threat, he was still careful to use the door chain as he opened the door. No sooner was it opened however, than three armed men burst in, breaking the chain and forcing Lewis back into the room. Suddenly awake, Lewis fought valiantly to fend off his attackers, but was soon overpowered after the briefest of struggles. Brandishing a revolver, the lead man began to viciously pistol whip Lewis with the butt of his gun, before the second man – also wielding a gun – joined in the attack. Lewis endured a sustained assault, as the two men rained blow after blow down onto his skull until the entertainer slumped unconscious to the floor. The third man who had, until this point, simply been watching, now took over the brutal attack. Armed with a hunting knife, he plunged the blade up to the hilt into Lewis's jaw, just below his ear. Pulling the knife half way out, he then proceeded to drag the blade across his neck to slit his throat, before slashing violently, yet methodically at Lewis's face and tongue, making sure that the wounds were as close together as possible in order to make them difficult to heal. By now, the pallid Pierrot visage had been all but destroyed, with grotesque swathes of blood pulsing from his body with each and every heartbeat. Their mission completed, the three men then left the room, being careful to close the door behind them.

Around fifteen minutes later, the cleaning maid came to tidy the room and found the now conscious Lewis still slumped on the floor, crying out in agony as blood poured from his hideous wounds. Screaming, she ran into the hallway, the noise grabbing the attention of the other guests and hotel staff. Immediately, an ambulance was called and Lewis was swiftly trans-ported to the Colombus Memorial Hospital, where a team of surgeons spent eight hours attempting to rebuild him.

The entire episode had been carefully and expertly orchestrated. There was no doubt that it was McGurn who had ordered the assault, though he had reconsidered his original plan of having Lewis killed. Instead, he had decided that it would be far more beneficial to have Lewis serve as a warning to any other recalcitrant performers who harboured ideas of defection. The hired assailant's *modus operandi* was proof that they were experienced in this kind of assault, a further indication of McGurn's methodical and meticulous nature.

The following day, The Chicago Tribune carried a report of the brutal attack on a well loved comedian. The report declared that the assault had been so incredibly violent, that Lewis had been robbed of the power of speech. Thus, when the police were allowed in to question him, he was only able to answer their questions by either nodding or shaking his head. He was asked whether he knew who may responsible for either ordering or carrying out the attack, to which he nodded in the affirmative. However, when the questioning officer produced a piece of paper and a pencil so that he could write down a name, the pain from his wounds combined with a sudden bout of Chicago amnesia, rendered him unable to do so. Joe E. Lewis was to remain in hospital for several weeks, during which time he was guarded day and night by North Side gunmen. The Chicago Tribune had certainly not exaggerated the ferocity of the attack, for it would be a full year before Lewis would be able to speak once more.

A few days after the attack on Lewis, Jack McGurn was summoned to Capone's suite at the Hawthorne Hotel. By this time, every national and local paper was carrying the story that it had been an Outfit orchestrated attack, much to the consternation of Capone who despised bad publicity. Capone demanded an explanation of McGurn's actions, reminding him that such unilateral behaviour was unacceptable without proper permission. This was not simply to be a symbolic dressing down of his protégé, for it was a matter of pride for Capone that McGurn had failed to even consult with him over the problem, to seek his advice and request his forthright intervention. Capone also knew that various other high ranking Outfit members such as Frank Nitti, would be reviewing these proceedings with a keen eye, secretly hoping that he would mercilessly aver his authority.

As soon as McGurn arrived at the hotel suite, he was immediately asked for full and frank explanation of his disregard for the protocol. This he did, and in doing so revealed that the attack was not merely in retaliation for Lewis's defection to the North Side. There had been another problem in that, whilst Lewis had been performing at The Green Mill, he had gained a reputation as something of a ladies man. McGurn explained that he had considered this to be little more than harmless, flirtatious fun…until Lewis began to make moves towards Louise Rolfe. According to Louise, she had politely informed Lewis that she was Jack's girl, at which point, most would be suitors would have gotten the message and taken their affections elsewhere. Lewis however, was apparently not that smart and had continued in his pursuit. Eventually, Louise felt that she had no other option but to tell Jack that Lewis was bothering her. This explanation appeared to change Capone's whole perspective on the situation. He knew that many men, including himself, are notoriously sensitive about unwanted advances towards their girlfriends, especially when a friendly warning to leave well alone fails to have any effect. Whilst Capone still harboured a slight disappointment that McGurn had failed to seek his advice, he refrained from handing down the expected stern reprimand, and merely stated that under the circumstances, his actions were extreme but understandable. To the chagrin of certain members, Capone's favourite was off the hook.

The remainder of 1927, passed off without incident. With William 'Big Bill' Thompson in the mayoral seat, prohibition raids had all but dried up, whilst those that did take place were little more than exercises in public relations. Police departments across the city were receiving so much money from the Outfit that financially, they would have been cutting their own throats had they chosen to really close down the clubs and speakeasies. For example, Chicago Police Captain John Stege was on the Capone payroll at $5,000 a month, in return for information as to where and when a raid would take place, in addition to information on the activities of rival gangs. Speakeasies, gambling joints, saloons and cafés all operated with impunity; the Joe E. Lewis incident was swept under the carpet and both The Green Mill and the Rendezvous continued to pull in the crowds. McGurn's plan to make The Green Mill a success by offering better booze and entertainment than anyone else appeared to be working, as its reputation as the best night-club in town spread rapidly along the Chicago grapevine. Before long everyone knew that if it was high class flappers, beautiful dancing girls and supreme quality liquor you were looking for, The Green Mill was the place to be. One night a week was reserved solely for gentlemen, a night when the dancing girls would be replaced by exotic strippers who were more than adept at keeping the men *'entertained.'*

By now McGurn was pulling in around $14,000 a week from The Green Mill, the majority of which was kicked back to Capone, although he kept around $3,000 for himself, in addition to his $300 a week body-guard salary. A large portion of this money was spent on Louise, in whom Jack delighted in showering with extravagant gifts of fur coats and stoles, diamonds, exquisite custom designed clothes, plus money to spend on make-up and hair. He also made sure that Helena financially wanted for nothing, ensuring that she had ample money for both herself and Helen. Emotionally however, it was a different story, as their relationship continued to deteriorate still further. Rumours abounded that Jack had been seen with another woman on his arm, rumours from which Helena could not shield herself and which prompted her to constantly question her husband as to whom this woman was. On his part, Jack could neither admit the truth that there was indeed another love in his life, nor the saddening reality that he now loved Helena purely because she was the mother of his child, and that that was as far as his feelings for her could go. Louise had shown him more excitement within the past couple of months than he had ever had with Helena, whilst his time at The Green Mill had brought him to realize that there was just too much bootleg hooch to be served and too many girls to have fun with; he could not turn his back on all that just to play out the charade that he was a born again family man. Jack and Helena were fast approaching the end of the line, yet neither of them had either the strength or the will to halt their calamitous course.

In addition to all these distractions, Capone was beginning to increas-ingly rely on McGurn. In spite of the fact that there were plenty of able bodied and able minded men within the Outfit, Capone always requested McGurn. It was as if McGurn's youth and enthusiasm for the job were somehow reflected onto Capone. Not that Capone was old, indeed he was still only twenty-eight, yet in gangland terms, he had already far exceeded his life expectancy. Capone viewed McGurn as something of a paragon and treated him as a father would treat his favourite son, tutoring him through his life and hoping that his own dreams and ambitions may be borne out in him. To McGurn, Capone was a close friend and he often felt that he had known him all his life. He took his job as bodyguard extremely seriously, performing his duties not because he was being paid to, but because he wanted to. The two men enjoyed a relationship not often seen in the realms of gangland, one of implicit trust and absolute loyalty. As long as Capone was around, McGurn was untouchable and vice versa, and it was precisely this relationship which the enemy would soon come to exploit.

One evening, in late 1927, McGurn was in The Green Mill, sitting at a corner table in the company of Louise Rolfe. In between laughing and chatting with his paramour, McGurn kept a cautious eye on the door, taking a mental note of all those entering and leaving the club. As the evening wound to a close, McGurn spotted a man named Joseph Goldberg entering the club. Goldberg was a Cicero Police Captain on the Outfit payroll, and as McGurn knew him to be disinclined to frequent establishments such as this, he knew that the visit must be due to some kind of business. As Goldberg approached the table, he asked if he could speak to McGurn alone and after taking him to one side, promptly informed him that someone had fired several shots at McGurn's home; Goldberg was quick to point out that despite being in the house at the time, both Helena and Helen were unharmed. Whilst Goldberg was effectively an Outfit employee, McGurn had, over the years, realized that in this game it pays to be suspicious. It was not unheard of for an enemy to employ such a ruse simply to force their intended victim out into the open and into the path of a waiting assassin. He therefore called home first and, once he was satisfied that the story related by Goldberg was indeed true, McGurn immediately left the club and headed home.

On arrival at his home on Edgemont Avenue, McGurn found the façade of the house peppered with bullet holes, whilst gouged chunks of masonry littered the floor. Inside, he found Helena and Helen badly shaken, but otherwise completely unharmed. McGurn was sure that the people responsible for the attack were either headed by, or working for Moran, for it was against Outfit rules to involve or strike at any non-combatants, such as wives and especially children; the non-Italian North Siders were not party to any such rule. Helena was distraught, though not because she herself had been placed in danger, but that their only daughter had been placed in the same peril and her father had not been there to protect or comfort her. Curiously however, in spite of the fact that she now had solid evidence that her husband most definitely did not work in a regular nine-to-five job, Helena still did not even entertain the thought of leaving him. Was it possible that she herself was aroused by the gangster mystique? That she found the thought of her husband being such a volatile and dangerous man impossible to resist? Or was it more the case that despite feeling repulsed at the notion that her husband, the man she thought she knew, was in fact a gangster, she could not escape the reality that she was still completely and madly in love with him? The latter is of course the most romantic, though whether or not it was the most accurate reason for her action, or rather inaction, is a point over which psychologists could endlessly argue.

The following morning, McGurn left the house and headed for the Hawthorne Hotel. He informed Capone as to what had happened and was less than surprised when he replied that he already knew. Capone suggested that McGurn move his family from the house and that they all reside in a nearby Outfit owned hotel called the McCormick. McGurn agreed, and later that day returned home to inform Helena of the impending move.

Rather than putting her at ease, the news only served to rattle her nerves still further, for she now realized that they were all in grave danger. She also saw that she was now in the somewhat perverse situation whereby the only way any of them was to remain safe, was for her to put her complete faith and trust in the one man who had created this situation in the first place. Worried that Moran gunmen may still be watching the house, Jack told his wife not to pack anything; he did not want to give the impression that they were leaving, for not only would it send out clear signals of fear, but any observer could easily pursue them to their new location. Because of this, it was under cover of darkness when McGurn moved his family out of their home at 1522 Edgemont Avenue and into the McCormick Hotel, Suite 1100. McGurn checked them in as Mr. and Mrs. Vincent D'Oro, an alias designed to thwart the inquiries of any potential enemy.

Aside from the profound effect upon McGurn's family, the attack also had a distressing effect on the wider family of gangland. As rumours spread that it was indeed Moran who had ordered the attack, the realization that he had struck out in an attempt not only to kill another gang member, but also that member's family, sent a clear and unsettling message rippling through the streets of Chicago: the fragile peace and ceasefire had been broken.

In the ensuing days, Capone was forced to use all his powers of reason, call on every element of their friendship to restrain McGurn from retaliating against Moran. His reasoning for such restraint was perfectly clear and justifiable. Firstly, all they had were mere rumours – albeit from reliable sources – that it was indeed a Moran led attack, and it would be foolish to act on conjecture. This in turn led on to the second reason, whereby should McGurn retaliate, Moran could always plead innocence and thus claim that it was the Outfit who had broken the peace. McGurn listened intently to what Capone had to say before grudgingly accepting his mentor's advice. He was learning yet another important lesson, that sometimes, even when pressed to breaking point, it is far more beneficial in terms of warfare to hold fire, to unsettle your enemy with complete inaction and thus force him to inadvertently reveal what he has up his sleeve.

Capone also had his own selfish reasons for his placation of McGurn. He needed McGurn to be on hand instead of running over to the North Side, for he was now planning a move of his own. The Outfit's expanding operations, together with Capone's desire for grandeur, had outgrown the confines of the Hawthorne Hotel and so they were changing location to the nearby Lexington Hotel. The Lexington was indeed grand for its time, with the interior providing a true depiction of the roaring economy. Magnificence and opulence abounded, from the cut crystal chandeliers adorning the fabulously decorated ceiling, to the exquisitely polished black and white marble floor. Typically of a five star hotel, the rooms were extravagantly priced, so that only the real high fliers of the world of business and finance ever stayed there and then for only one night at a time. Capone and his entourage took over three entire floors, two of which were to be the residence of the core of bodyguards and hit men, whilst Capone would occupy the very top floor. Despite having just moved his family into the McCormick Hotel, McGurn would now be spending much of his time at the Lexington, as Capone now desired him to be by his side virtually twenty-four hours a day. It could be said that McGurn was being asked to act more as a *'consigliore'* or advisor, rather than in his original capacity. Being at the Lexington however, did have its advantages, for he was now able to move Louise Rolfe into one of the suites on the lower floors. This allowed him to give Helena the perfect excuse that he was working, when in actual fact, he was in the lap of luxury with the beautiful Louise.

It was in the beginning of 1928, when Jack McGurn realized that he did not know as much as he thought about the lovely Louise. As they lay on the bed in her opulent suite, a telephone call came through that there was someone at reception who wished to see him. When he arrived at the front desk, McGurn was confronted by a man who claimed that he had been told that his wife had regularly been seen in his company. A little perplexed, McGurn asked as to the identity of his wife, to which he replied Louise Boex. Truthfully, McGurn rejoined that he knew no one by that name, and that whoever told him such a thing was obviously mistaken. The man then said that his wife was a dancer and that as a stage name, she often used her maiden name of Rolfe. Naturally, McGurn was more than a little surprised that his supposedly single girlfriend was actually married, yet he remained defiant in his stance that he knew no one by that name. Realizing that he was getting nowhere fast, his inquisitor left the hotel, leaving McGurn to confront Louise.

Upstairs in the suite, McGurn demanded a full and frank explanation from Louise, reminding her that he did not like being lied to. Louise quickly told Jack that she had been married for about a year when she met him; a carpenter by trade, her husband was a Dutch immigrant by the name of Johan Boex. When they had first met, he was extremely hardworking and seemed determined to build a life for them both however, six or seven months into their marriage, he had become lazy, preferring to go out drinking with friends rather than working and leaving her alone both day and night. It was for these reasons, and the fact that she desperately needed excitement, that she had applied for a job in The Green Mill. Time and again she insisted that she had not intended to lie, but that she had been forced to do something, if for no other reason than to sustain her sanity.

After hearing her story, Jack was far more sympathetic towards her. He said that he could not understand any man who refused to provide for his wife, either financially or emotionally. He undoubtedly failed to see the parallel between the actions of Johan Boex, and the way in which he was treating his own wife.

So much in love. Jack McGurn and his lover Louise Rolfe
pose happily for the camera.
(John Binder Collection)

McGurn's boss and mentor, the infamous 'Scarface' Al Capone.
(John Binder Collection)

Outfit Headquarters: The Lexington Hotel at
2135 South Michigan Avenue and Cermak Road.
(John Binder Collection)

Capone and his son enjoy a baseball game at Comiskey Park, as the
ever present Jack McGurn and Philip D'Andrea (2nd row) keep watch.
(Chicagoi Historical Society – ICHI-23881)

Dion O'Banion with his wife Viola. Maniacal North Side leader who dared to double cross Capone.
(John Binder Collection)

Consequences of the double cross: O'Banion's monument and gravestone in Mount Carmel Cemetery. (Author's Collection)

Even the sacred steps of the Holy Name Cathedral failed to prevent
McGurn from executing his murderous assignment.
(Author's Collection)

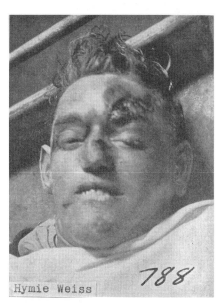

The face of death: Hymie
Weiss lies in the morgue.
(Chicago Historical Society –
ICHi-26693)

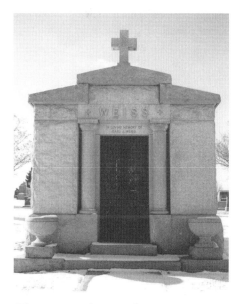

The mausoleum of Hymie Weiss
in Mount Carmel Cemetery.
(Author's Collection)

Frank 'The Enforcer' Nitti. Capone's debt collector and future Outfit leader.
(John Binder Collection)

The Genna Mausoleum in Mount Carmel Cemetery.
(Author's Collection)

George 'Bugs' Moran, leader of the North Siders and primary target of the St. Valentine's Day Massacre.
(John Binder Collection)

A rare golfing photograph of 'Machine Gun' Jack and his younger brother, Anthony. Jack would later go on to be an accomplished professional.
(John Binder Collection)

CHAPTER FIFTEEN

DEATH OF DARKNESS

February, 1928, and Jack McGurn had a problem: his shipment of The Real McCoy from New York had failed to arrive as expected. He immediately reported the matter to Capone who announced that his liquor had also failed to be delivered. Capone ordered his brother Ralph, who was employed by the Outfit as the liquor manager, to investigate what had gone wrong. This he did, and later that day, Ralph reported that the entire shipment had been hijacked en route to Chicago. In light of the agreement that had been struck with Frankie Yale, this news was puzzling to say the least. Capone placed a call to Yale, who vocally shared the concern of his *paisan*. After a lengthy discussion, Yale proffered the explanation that it must have been local hoods who had hijacked the shipment, unaware as to whom it actually belonged. Capone and McGurn agreed with Yale that this was indeed the most likely explanation, especially so given the proliferation of low level gangs, all vying for a slice of the prohibition pie. Yale gave his assurance that the next shipment would leave New York on schedule and that he would personally put out the word that all trucks heading for Chicago were strictly off limits. Capone expressed his relief at the swift resolution of the matter and told Yale that he looked forward to taking receipt of the shipment the following month.

Privately however, Capone and the Outfit were unconvinced. Local hoods would probably be capable of taking one or two trucks, three at the most, but to take an entire shipment of twelve trucks took some intense planning and organization, not to mention manpower, qualities which were generally scarce amongst small time hoodlums. Despite drawing their own conclusions over what had happened to their liquor, Capone and McGurn decided to bide their time and to wait and see what happened next month; should the delivery arrive in tact and on time, then Yale was obviously telling the truth.

The following month proved to be identical to the month previous, with both Capone's and McGurn's deliveries once again failing to arrive. Again Ralph investigated, and as expected, the news came back that this consignment had also been hijacked – on exactly the same stretch of road where the last shipment had been appropriated. A second call was placed to Yale, who gave his assurance that all twelve trucks had safely left the New York Harbour and that he had, as promised, personally put out the word that these were his trucks and were not to be touched. Everyone knew that in New York, Yale's word was fiat; the notion that anyone would dare to incur his wrath by such blatant disobedience was inconceivable. Nevertheless, it was the only explanation that Yale could muster and as such, the one which Capone and McGurn had no option but to accept…on the surface at least.

In reality, they were having great difficulty in accepting Yale's exegesis, resulting in an urgent meeting between Ralph, Capone and McGurn. The three men all agreed that unless someone had developed a serious problem with living, or had acquired a sudden death wish, then the idea that they would seize a Capone-Yale shipment on two successive occasions was implausible to the extreme. McGurn then remembered Eddie Lynch, the former White Hander who had so successfully betrayed Pegleg Lonergan, and who now worked for Yale. There was a slim chance that having already proved himself a turncoat in one gang, he may be persuaded to do the same in another, especially if the reward on offer was a lucrative job in the Outfit. The three men agreed that this was the best option, for aside from travelling to New York and personally confronting Yale, they had very few viable alternatives.

It soon became apparent that Eddie Lynch was only too willing to betray his new boss. Following the Adonis Club murders, Yale had told Lynch that he would be rewarded with a piece of a New York club however, thus far he had been given little more than odd jobs here and there, with Yale treating him more as a dispensable errand boy than valuable member. Lynch gave his word that he would attempt to learn what misfortune had befell the trucks. Had he not chosen a life of crime, Lynch would have made an excellent government spy, for he seemed to have a curious talent for working his way into the right situations at the right times. It was with this gift that he managed to persuade Yale to allow him to be the driver of one of the trucks in the Chicago consignment. Lynch immediately called Capone to inform him of the development, and promised that should anything happen, he would call with the details.

The day after the delivery was due to arrive, Lynch called to say that the consignment had indeed been hijacked, apparently confirming Yale's story. However, there was a sinister twist to this seemingly benign tale, for the hijackers were Yale's own men. Lynch continued that the hijackers had pulled the trucks over – as would happen on a regular hijacking – but instead of forcing the drivers out of the cabs and driving the trucks away themselves, the drivers had been ordered back to Yale's own warehouses. The scam meant that Yale was winning on all fronts, for he was still receiving the monthly payment for the liquor, though by failing to deliver the goods, he was free to resell it as returned stock at a discount price and still make a handsome profit. Lynch promised that he would try to discover the names of the hijackers and that he would report back to Capone the next day. For Lynch however, the next day would never come. Buoyed by his own success, he had been a little too blasé over who may be listening to his phone conversations and a few days later, the Outfit received word that Lynch had been assassinated whilst making a call from a public phone booth. Merely a pawn in the deadly game of gangland chess, it was doubtful that Lynch would have ever made it to Chicago in order to take up employment there, especially as he had twice proven to hold a traitorous streak. Nevertheless, the Outfit had the all the information it needed: the only question now was what to do about it?

Fear and power are extremely puissant emotions, functioning hand in hand and complimenting each other perfectly. Within the animal kingdom, there are those creatures of which every other creature is afraid and consequently, since they have no natural predators, will be around for a long time. The same rule follows with humans, and it is precisely this which allows gangsters to survive. They are perfectly aware that the majority of the populace is afraid, not of who they are, or what they have done, but rather what they perceive them to be capable of. Therefore, these individuals who have the power to do as they please, will undoubtedly be around for a long time to come.

Frankie Yale was certainly no exception to this rule. Throughout his meteoric rise to power, he had constantly exploited the fear and power factors to breaking point. It was no secret that the people of New York were fearful of him, after all, he had not acquired the nickname *'The Prince of Darkness'* by playing the nice guy. His problem however, was that he had grown so accustomed to the fear factor, that not once did he contemplate the possibility of being faced with someone who was not afraid, indeed someone who held an equal amount of fear and power over his own people. He therefore thought nothing of betraying his old friend, Al Capone, rationalizing that Capone was miles away in Chicago and so even should the perfidy be discovered, there was little that could be done. This blasé approach went so far as to lead him to believe that Capone may never find out, for he would never knowingly suspect such a good friend as Yale. On this point, Yale was absolutely correct, for never would Capone have expected such a low down double cross to emanate from Yale's direction. In fact, when he sanctioned the employment of Eddie Lynch, Capone rather expected to discover Yale's men operating behind his back. To discover that the man he held in such high esteem could so flagrantly disregard their friendship, was a disappointing blow indeed. Perhaps on this point, Capone was guilty of being a touch insouciant, for experience should have told him that amongst the majority of hoodlums, friendship is only ever present on the surface. Notwithstanding this fact however, there was no room for reflection or sentiment. This was gangland, a land whose laws decreed that there was only one way to deal with such a situation.

Ordering the death of Frankie Yale was one of the most difficult decisions that Capone had ever had to make, yet make it he must, and in his mind, there was only one man for the job. He had no qualms whatsoever about handing the contract to McGurn; the hard part was deciding who should accompany him. Yale was a canny and dangerous man. Should he discover the plot, then the hunters would quickly become the hunted. The final call was left to McGurn himself, for although Capone personally knew the many and varied members of the hit crew, it was McGurn who knew their strengths and, more importantly, their weaknesses. Eventually, the selected team consisted of Albert Anselmi and John Scalise, Fred 'Killer' Burke, who hailed from the Circus Gang, a powerful Outfit ally in St. Louis and of course, McGurn himself.

With his team established, the next task was to procure the weapons, one which Capone took on personally. He contacted Parker Henderson in Miami, a hopelessly gullible man who was completely overawed by the gangster mystique. The manager of the Ponce de Leon Hotel, named after the Spanish explorer and conquistador, Henderson was also a close aide of Mayor Loomis of Miami, not his son as other criminology publications have suggested. Capone informed him that he believed his life to be in immediate danger and that he would be most grateful if he could obtain some weapons for his bodyguards. Naturally, Henderson was only too willing to oblige and a few days later, McGurn, Burke, Scalise and Anselmi, arrived at the Ponce de Leon Hotel to take possession of six Tommy Guns and six of McGurn's favourite weapon – the .38 revolver. After taking charge of the weapons, the men then rented a car from the Florida Motor Sales Company, the manager of which was a personal acquaintance of Capone. From there, the quartet drove to the Jacksonville Rail Terminal, where they boarded a train bound for Philadelphia, before catching a connecting train to New York.

Upon arrival in the *'Big Apple,'* the four men immediately purchased a black Buick, which would be used in their surveillance of Yale. The reasons for such complicated maneuvers are a little vague, though it is possible that they were designed to either foil the attempts of any uniformed police officers wishing to earn themselves and extra stripe or two, or indeed to fool any spies employed by a perhaps overly suspicious Yale.

McGurn wanted some background on Yale, to find out what his movements were and to discover whether or not he was a creature of habit. Although no firm date had been set for the hit, McGurn believed that given enough information, they would know when the time was right. It was almost the end of June, 1928, the long days seemingly tailor made to facilitate unimpeded surveillance of their prey. They watched Yale in the mornings as he left his house, kissing his wife Lucy goodbye before departing to his *'office.'* They watched as he went about town, who he met with and whether he met them alone. They watched as he returned home in the evenings, observing that his wife was ready and waiting at the door. They soon discovered that he was totally besotted with, and devoted to his wife, a factor which gave the team the idea of how a trap could be sprung. On

Thursday June 28, 1928, the team was, as always, watching as Yale took possession of a brand new, dark brown Lincoln complete with bullet proof bodywork. It was then that they decided on the date for the hit.

Three days later, Sunday July 1, the four men were watching and waiting outside Yale's home. He emerged just as expected, ready to take his new Lincoln for a spin on the quiet Sunday roads. As he pulled away, he did not appear to notice the black Buick which fell in behind him at a discreet distance. Yale toured the streets, testing and enjoying his newly acquired toy, unaware that these few precious moments of pleasure would be the last in which he would ever indulge. After a few miles, Yale's Lincoln slowed to a halt outside The Sunrise Bar, on Sixty-Fifth Street and Fourteenth Avenue. McGurn and his men pulled their car to the curb on the opposite side of the street and watched as Yale entered the drinking establishment. There they waited for about one hour, enough time to allow Yale to get comfortable at the bar, before McGurn instructed Burke to go to the phone booth just down the street and make a pre-arranged phone call to the bar. Burke was to ask the bartender whether or not Frankie Yale was there, and once this was confirmed, would ask to speak to him urgently. When Yale came to the phone, Burke would tell him that he must come home immediately because something was wrong with Lucy, after which he would hang up.

The phone call went according to plan and Burke had only just stepped back inside the Buick, when the four men saw Yale come tearing out of the bar, jump into his Lincoln and speed off down Fourteenth Avenue. The black Buick followed suit, though this time at not such a discreet distance. At some indeterminate point in time, Yale noticed the pursuing Buick in his rear view mirror; witnesses stated that the Lincoln suddenly accelerated and began careering erratically down the city streets, before turning onto the heavily residential Forty-Fourth Street. On this street – at number 923 – a noble Jewish couple named Solomon and Bertha Kaufman were standing in their front garden, entertaining friends in honour of their only son's Bar Mitzvah. Suddenly, the jovial atmosphere was punctuated by a distinctive, yet unfamiliar noise; it sounded like gunfire, but with the shots coming in unbelievably quick succession. What they were hearing was in fact the sound of machine gun fire, though the Kaufman's can be somewhat excused for their ignorance, for this was the first time that the Thompson submachine gun had been used on the streets of New York. The bullet proof bodywork of Yale's Lincoln held up well against the incessant fusillade, however unfortunately for Yale, the windows were not constructed of bullet proof glass and it was not long before a machine gun slug blasted through the rear window and buried itself into Yale's left shoulder. The Lincoln now appeared to be completely out of control, as an incapacitated Yale struggled to keep hold of the wheel. Eventually, the car mounted the curb, careering along the pavement for a short distance, before smashing heavily into and destroying the Kaufman's front wall. As the Lincoln struck the brickwork, the now dazed and injured Yale fell limply from the driver's side. Realizing that Yale was going nowhere, the pursuing Buick slowed to a halt just behind the carnage, allowing McGurn to vault from the car, and in full view of the stunned onlookers, emptied his revolver into the head and neck of New York's underworld czar. Leaping back into the Buick, McGurn and his murderous colleagues, sped away down Forty-Fourth Street, before turning west onto Tenth Avenue. As the car disappeared out of sight, a cautious Solomon Kaufman nervously ventured forth to see if there was anything that could be done for the injured Yale. However, the blood which poured from his neck wounds and the gaping holes where flesh and bone should have been, made it gorily apparent that the *'Prince of Darkness'* was dead.

Yale's funeral was the most magnificent event that gangland had ever seen, far surpassing Dion O'Banion's revue *in memorandum* some four years earlier. His shattered body was encased in a $15,000 solid silver casket, which was paraded through the streets of New York in a flower laden hearse. The hearse itself was followed by a procession of one-hundred and forty-two cars, one-hundred and four of which carried the mourners, whilst the remaining thirty-eight were filled with flowers and wreaths. The streets were choked with obsequies chic obsessed onlookers, all straining to catch a glimpse of the man about whom they had heard so much, yet who most had never seen. Many of the bouquets and wreaths had been sent by gangsters from all over the country, the size of their display apparently demonstrating the level of their affection. However, by far the most extravagant and the one to cause the most whispers amongst the crowd, was a huge heart made entirely of red roses, pierced by a floral dagger. The entire ensemble was enclosed with blue and white violets fashioned into, a clock, the hands of which pointed to the time that Yale was killed. There was no card to accompany this arrangement, merely a ribbon upon which was printed *'we'll see them kid.'* Exactly who sent this remarkable floral display remains a mystery to this day, though the suspects are as numerous as they are varied. The most likely explanation is that it was sent by one or more of Yale's allies, who felt more than a little aggrieved at the sudden loss of their friend, though theories also abound that it was sent by the Outfit, knowing just how to leave false clues for both the police and public alike. Still another theory suggests that the sender was someone whom Yale had perhaps never met, but who nevertheless took the murder as a personal insult. The reasoning behind this theory is that a heart pierced by a dagger is a traditional Sicilian symbol of revenge.

In the ensuing investigation, the finger of suspicion inevitably pointed at Capone and the Outfit. Capone went public with his grief over the loss of his friend and effected outrage at the notion that he would either kill, or have killed, a man for whom he held nothing but affection. The police then turned their attention to McGurn, who of course knew nothing about the man they mentioned, and who claimed that he had been with his girlfriend in Chicago on the day that the killing took place. Both pleas of innocence were almost proven to be false when the police traced one of the revolvers found in the abandoned Buick to one Peter Von Frantzius, an arms dealer who held the dubious distinction of being the major weapons supplier of Illinois gangland. However, this piece of evidence was at best circumstantial and could in no way be expected to bring about a charge of murder; the fact that the gun came from Von Frantzius merely showed that the killers could have been from, or had connections with, any one of Illinois numerous gangs. McGurn's charmed life continued, and once again, as he had done on many previous occasions, proved that he was fully adept at getting away with murder.

Eventually, the furor over the death of Yale died down, and like all the other killings which preceded it, the public forgot about it and got on with their own daily lives. Perhaps society was now in the same mind-set as Captain William Shoemaker, in that if the gangsters were going to kill anyone, then they may as well be killing each other. After all, if they carried on the way they were going, there would soon be none left to worry about anyway.

CHAPTER SIXTEEN

PRELUDE TO DEATH

The Unione Siciliana was now headed by Capone associate and ally, Antonio Lombardo, the man who had chaired the Hotel Sherman meeting on Capone's behalf. The benefit of having an ally in such a respected position was certainly a factor that was not lost on Capone, for now, after many frustratingly failed attempts, he had succeeded in placing one of his oldest friends in the envied and influential seat of power. Despite his position as a respected individual, Lombardo's relationship with the Outfit had brought him many enemies, one of whom was Joe Aiello. The eldest of three brothers, Aiello had been a close and personal friend of Dion O'Banion, and had continued to maintain close ties with the North Siders. Aiello had long since made his feelings perfectly clear on the subject of a Capone man being the head of the Unione, though his judgment was based primarily on jealousy rather than business. This was adequately displayed when the question arose as to whom he would rather see heading the Unione Siciliana instead of Lombardo, to which he promptly named himself. Everyone except the North Siders found this idea highly amusing, yet Aiello's ambitions and visions of glory were as wild as O'Banion's, whilst his trigger happy temperament rivalled even that of Weiss.

On September 6, 1928, Aiello launched an audacious attack on Antonio Lombardo and Capone. The two men, accompanied by bodyguards, exited the Hawthorne Smoke Shop, a cigar store owned by old corruption stalwart, Michael 'Hinky Dink' Kenna, and situated a few doors away from the Hawthorne Restaurant. Capone was flanked by McGurn and Philip D'Andrea, whilst Lombardo was under the protection of an unknown bodyguard. Unbeknown to all of them, they were being watched by George Moran and Joe Aiello, who were ensconced in a second floor apartment across the street. The first realization of this clandestine surveillance was when the retort of gunfire reverberated around the buildings. As the first shot rang out, McGurn and D'Andrea threw Capone to the floor, D'Andrea covering Capone with his own body whilst McGurn peered upwards from the doorway, scanning the building opposite for any signs of life. A second shot rang out and hit Lombardo in the chest, piercing his heart and killing him instantly. Had his bodyguard been as proficient as McGurn and D'Andrea, he may well have survived, but it was not to be. Apparently satisfied with the one hit, the gunfire ceased and the gunmen fled. Once again, the North Siders had failed to get Capone, although they had succeeded in eliminating one of his most omnipotent affiliates from the equation.

Like many gangsters before him, Antonio Lombardo was laid to rest in Mount Carmel Cemetery. The day after his killing, September 7, was the day when all Italians celebrated the feast of *'Our Lady of Loreto,'* a festival in which a statue of the Virgin Mary is carried through the streets of Little Italy as a symbol of protection and hope for the community. Devastated by the ceaseless and senseless violence, Father Louis M. Giambastiano, the priest of the Church of San Filippo Benizi of Italy, posted a sign of sorrow and reflection on the door of the church. It read:

FRATELLI

Per rispetto a dio in cui credete per onore della patria e dell'umanita – Pregate perche cessi l'indegna strage che disonora il nome Italiano dinazi mondo civile.

This translates as:

BROTHERS

For the respect you owe in god in whom you believe and the honour of your country and humanity – Pray for an end to the horrid slaughter that has dishonoured the Italian name before the civilized world.

The good people of Little Italy obeyed their priest, and prayed to their god that the death and disgrace would end, and that peaceful equilibrium would return. Nevertheless, in spite of the hundreds of prayers that were said over the course of the feast and indeed over the course of the following days, the

Italian name would continue to be dishonoured before the civilized world. Men would continue to plot the death of their fellow men and it would be a long time yet before the slaughter would end.

Satisfied as they were with the death of Antonio Lombardo, George Moran and Joe Aiello still maintained an unquenchable thirst for blood. Amazingly, Moran and Aiello still held dear the fantastical vision of Hymie Weiss, to take out Capone and take over the Outfit. Many people would have undoubtedly seen a lethal pattern emerging as a result of the pursuit of such an unrealistic and hare-brained scheme, as both men who had previously attempted to oust Capone, now perpetually resided in the grounds of Mount Carmel Cemetery. However, with a touch of pathos, Moran and Aiello continued to delude both themselves and their followers that this was not only a realistic goal, but an achievable one. They knew that the first obstacle to overcome in order to realize their dream, was to get rid of Capone, yet this had already been proven to be a near on impossible task. Upon reflection, Moran noticed a common denominator, a single point at which all their best efforts were thwarted. Moran told himself that the elimination of this factor would afford them a clear shot at Capone and as such, decided that it was time for a tactical change, one which meant that the North Siders homicidal gaze now fell onto Jack McGurn.

McGurn still maintained his residence at the McCormick Hotel, and despite the alias, he knew that should anyone wish to discover this information, they would certainly not find it an arduous task. Indeed, no matter where he chose to live, anyone could discover the address with ease. As such, the Aiello-Moran partnership found few obstacles in the way of their pursuit. So cautious was McGurn however, that the real task was figuring out exactly how to get a good shot at him, for he was always in the company of others, either protecting Capone or with friends and acquaintances. This meant that at no time would they be afforded a clear shot. Having found their quarry, it seemed that there was little more they could do other than to watch and wait. It was Aiello who eventually realized that, as it was nearing Christmas time, McGurn would, at one point or another, undoubtedly venture out alone in order to purchase Christmas gifts for his friends and family, not to mention his girlfriend. Aiello suggested that this could be their window of opportunity.

The gunmen that Moran and Aiello decided on were Frank and Pete Gusenberg, brothers who were renowned as the best *'torpedoes'* or triggermen that the North Siders had at their disposal. Legend has it that the brothers were so close in every way and had worked together on so many hits, that they could actually predict what the other would do in any given situation; it was also said that they would often finish each others sentences during a conversation. The North Siders knew that with the brothers on McGurn's trail, a successful hit was almost inevitable.

Finally, after weeks of surveillance, Frank and Pete saw their window of opportunity, almost an exact replica of the moment when John Torrio was gunned down. The day was December 18, 1928, and McGurn – just as Aiello had predicted – had been indulging in a Christmas shopping trip and had returned to the McCormick with his car laden down with gifts. As he stepped from his car onto the street, he merely glanced at the black Lincoln which was parked opposite. Leaning down into his car, McGurn picked up an armful of exquisitely wrapped gifts and proceeded to walk to the door of his hotel. He had taken no more than a few steps away from the car, when the Gusenberg brothers saw that they had an unimpeded line of fire. Levelling their Thompson submachine guns (chosen with regard to their victim's sobriquet) at their prey, the two men opened fire, hitting McGurn five times in the left arm and shoulder. With his survival instincts overriding the intense pain, McGurn fell like lead onto the street, as the rattle of machine gun fire reverberated around him. It is a certainty that had the Tommy Gun been a more accurate weapon over distance, then McGurn would surely have been killed; as it was, it was all his assailants could do to keep aim. With blood pouring from his gaping wounds, McGurn crawled back to where his car was parked. He knew that the bodywork was not bullet proof, and so resisted the temptation to prop himself against the doors, instead lying flat on the sidewalk. With nothing but the dark winter air to aim at, and panicked by their target's sudden disappearance, the Gusenberg brothers screeched their Lincoln away from the scene.

As soon as the gunfire had ceased and the Lincoln had disappeared around the corner, witnesses began to emerge from the sanctuary of side streets and doorways, and rushed over to aid the injured McGurn. Staff from the hotel called for an ambulance and within minutes – again in almost an exact replica of the Torrio hit – McGurn was rushed to the Jackson Park Memorial Hospital. There, surgeon Doctor Byrne removed the five bullets from McGurn's arm and shoulder, before patching up the damaged tissue and sewing up the wound.

When Helena heard the shots outside the hotel, she was naturally alarmed, though not for a second did she suspect that the bullets which were being sprayed across the street were intended for her husband. Only when a member of staff called on her to inform her of what had happened, did she realize the enormity of the situation. Following the shooting outside their home, Helena had convinced herself that it had been a mistake, and that whoever had fired the shots had merely mistook their home for that of another. She now knew that this was not the case and that the only error the assailants had made that evening, was their failure to kill or injure anyone. Now her husband lay in hospital, dying for all she knew, and all she could think of was how to get to his bedside as quickly as possible. When she did arrive at the hospital, she found Jack in a private room with armed men guarding the door. She instantly recognized one of the men as Philip D'Andrea, a fact which is significant for two reasons. Firstly, the Outfit obviously still believed that McGurn's life was in grave danger and secondly, Capone clearly thought so highly of McGurn and cared for him so deeply, that he had sent McGurn's own second in command to protect him. In situations such as these, it is customary for lower ranking members of the bodyguard command to be detailed, thus leaving the higher ranking members free to protect the chief. Therefore, to have such a high ranking member as D'Andrea assigned to the ward was highly unusual and speaks volumes for the relationship between the crime czar and his protégé. D'Andrea recognized Helena immediately, allowing her to enter so that she could be with her husband. Helena found Jack heavily sedated, however Doctor Byrne reassured her that he looked far worse than he actually was.

After just a few days, McGurn was allowed to leave the confines of the hospital. Doctor Byrne was duly impressed by the speed of his recovery, although he readily admitted that his youth, good health and physical fitness had undoubtedly contributed a great deal. Upon his release, Capone insisted that McGurn move his family into the Lexington Hotel; unsurprisingly, he no longer considered the McCormick to be a safe residence for his most trusted hit man, bodyguard and companion. Within a matter of hours, Jack, Helena and little Helen had moved into Suite 230, situated on the third floor of the Lexington, just one floor below Capone. In this room, McGurn spent the next two weeks in convalescence, with Helena and the hotel staff tending to his every need.

During this time, Louise desperately wanted to see her sweetheart. Throughout his hospital stay she had been unable to visit him, as Helena had constantly been by his side. Now that he was home, she was still unable to see him as Helena refused to go out, terrified to leave her husband alone for fear that something awful might happen whilst she was away. Louise tried to tell herself to be patient, but it was no use; until she saw the condition of her lover with her own eyes, she was inconsolable. She managed to convince herself that he was close to death and that she would never be able to hold him close to her ever again. Finally, after constantly pleading with and beseeching to Philip D'Andrea, a plan was hatched which would allow her to visit her beloved. D'Andrea persuaded Helena to take Helen for a walk in a nearby park, telling her that he would send someone to accompany them and that he would remain at the hotel to guard Jack. At first Helena refused, but capitulated when told that it was in the best interests of Helen. It was not good for a little girl to be placed under so much stress and kept in the confines of a hotel suite. They would take her to the park where she could play on some swings, run around in the snow and generally blow off a little steam: it would do them both good.

As soon as they had left the hotel, D'Andrea swiftly transported Louise from the nearby McCormick to the Lexington and into McGurn's suite. The relief that she felt as she realized that her paramour truly was alive and well was too much to bear, and she broke down, sobbing uncontrollably in her lover's arms. They stayed together only for a short while, enjoying each other until they were informed that Helena and Helen were on their way back to the room. However, those few brief moments were to be some of the most important in McGurn's life, for it was whilst holding Louise in his arms that he admitted to himself for the first time that he no longer loved Helena.

On January 16, 1929, McGurn returned to the Jackson Park Memorial Hospital to have his bandages removed for good. Aside from the heavy scarring, his arm and shoulder had healed remarkably well, though it was uncertain whether he could still handle a Tommy Gun with the same level of deftness and accuracy. He himself was convinced that he could, however, the other Outfit members were not so sure. Nevertheless, one thing they were sure of was the fact that the attempt on McGurn's life had added ever more credence to his apt sobriquet, for 'Machine Gun' Jack McGurn had actually been hit by machine gun fire and had lived to tell the tale.

The following day, January 17, was Capone's birthday, and McGurn chose this day of celebration to request a private conference with his friend and mentor. The subject which was on his mind was the familiar topic of revenge, a need to get even for everything, a need that was tinged with a certain sense of urgency. McGurn had long since realized that the North Siders would not stop until they had succeeded in their goal of killing either Capone, himself, or indeed, both of them. He had also seen the emergence of an alarming trend, one which had its genesis in the murder of Dion O'Banion. For no sooner was one North Side leader eliminated, than a plethora of power hungry disciples were vying to take the lead, each one more dangerously maniacal than the last. He therefore met with Capone in order to secure his approval for the plan which was currently forming in his mind, a plan that would prove to be the most extravagantly outrageous piece of homicidal architecture of which any gangster had ever conceived, and which would ensure that the streets of Chicago were perpetually blood-stained. McGurn did not yet know it, but his murderous machinations would live on, not only in the minds of native Chicagoans, but of people the whole world over.

CHAPTER SEVENTEEN

THE ST. VALENTINE'S DAY MASSACRE

'Before anyone could make answer, the whole world seemed to explode around them. Dashes of flame cut through the gloom of the place. The terrific roar of shotguns and the mad scream of a machine gun ripped and shattered the silence. Flenger fell in his tracks. Mitchell reeled back between the glowing headlights of the truck, spreading his arms over the radiator in an effort to keep himself on his feet, then groaned and sagged to the floor. Baer whirled uncertainly, sank to his knees with a curse and hurled the remnants of a whiskey bottle in the general direction of the last flash he had seen. It was Slenk who stood longest against the barrage of the rum killers.

A shadowy figure started around the end of the second truck. In his hands he carried a baby machine gun. A hoarse laugh crossed his lips. Calmly while Slenk watched him, terror in his eyes, the man lifted the gun, trained it upon him and again, the wild scream of 1,500 shots a minute tore at the walls of the garage.'

So reads an excerpt from *'Hooch,'* a fictional tale which appeared in the Saturday Evening Post on February 2, 1929. Written by Charles Francis Coe, the story dealt with the activities of gangsters and corrupt politicians, culminating in the quartet of murders detailed above. The readers of the evening newspaper found themselves transfixed by the vivid and often horrific detail of the plot. Little did they realize however, that in less than two weeks, the city of Chicago would prove once and for all that the real world of gangland is far more brutal and even more bizarre than any work of fiction.

THE CRIME

The failed attempt on the life of Jack McGurn meant that the Gusenberg brothers had, in effect, signed their own death warrant. They – indeed anyone who had cause to cross his path – undoubtedly knew that to leave McGurn alive was *the* fatal mistake. With his unquestionable retribution over the death of his father, McGurn had proved that murder came easily to him, especially when the reason was as evocative as revenge. Yet when McGurn realized that the threat posed by the North Siders endangered not only himself, but also Capone and everything he and the Outfit had been working towards, he began to think of vengeance on a much grander scale. The executions perpetrated by him personally, both before and after he joined the Outfit, would pale into insignificance compared with the idea over which he was now deliberating. McGurn was not merely contemplating hitting the Gusenberg's, nor was he thinking of solely taking out Moran; what he was actually mulling over was the extermination of the entire North Side gang, from leader to low level skivvy.

This was indeed a fantastical idea, one which was enhanced by the fact that he did not even know just how many men were directly involved with Moran. He knew that the numbers were nowhere near comparable with that of the Outfit, though it was certain to be significant. Needless to say, Capone was markedly impressed with the plan, though his admiration was tinged with more than a slight hint of apprehension. It was one thing to take on a rival gang, one, or even two at a time, but to eliminate an entire crew in one fell swoop, was to jump onto a higher level entirely. McGurn was told in no uncertain terms that should he be adamant in following this plan through, then the management, the recruitment of manpower, the acquisition of weapons, the whole shebang would be entirely his own. Should he require advice or verbal assistance he could count on Capone, but that was where his involvement would end. McGurn accepted that this was his show – wholly and exclusively – and that succeed or fail, he and he alone would have to live with the consequences or die because of them.

The first part of McGurn's plan was to discover exactly how many men were directly affiliated with Moran, and of those, what percentage did business with him on a daily basis. The location of Moran's headquarters was common knowledge throughout Chicago; just as Dion O'Banion and Hymie Weiss had held court in the back room of Schofield's, Moran used the cover of another legitimate business to front his dodgy dealings. The new North Side HQ was located at 2122 North Clark Street, in the dank and dimly lit garage of S. M. C. Cartage Company. Here, every week, the Moran crew would gather in order to take charge of liquor shipments, discuss delivery routes, air their views and complaints over insubordinate speakeasy managers and of course, figuratively sign death warrants. Across the street from the garage, at 2127 North Clark Street, stood a rooming house owned by Mrs. Jeanette Landesman. It was to this rooming house that Jack McGurn dispatched a man named James Bolton, a member of the infamous Alvin 'Creepy' Karpis and George 'Red' Barker gang. Bolton's instructions were to rent a room, not just any room, but one which had a clear and unadulterated view of both North Clark Street and the garage of S. M. C. Cartage Company. Bolton followed McGurn's instructions precisely, taking a room and paying Mrs. Landesman one month's rent, cash in advance.

With the perfect observation post secured, McGurn enlisted the help of two members of the Circus Gang, a group of close Outfit allies who had previously supplied McGurn with the services of Fred 'Killer' Burke for the hit on Frankie Yale. Operating out of St. Louis, the Circus Gang – so called because their headquarters was the Circus Café – was headed by long time Capone stalwart, Claude Maddox. Maddox was only too willing to offer his services to one of Capone's boys, after all, he and Capone went back a long way. McGurn requested two trustworthy men who would be required to live in the recently rented room, and whose principal task would be to observe the daily routine and occupational habits of the North Side gang. McGurn needed to know at what time all the members arrived at the garage. On which day or days did their meetings take place? How many men generally attended? Was Moran always present at these meetings, or were there times when a deputy would be left in charge? All of these factors were of vital importance to the plan, and McGurn enthusiastically stressed that he needed men who could be trusted to watch the premises twenty-four hours a day, seven days a week, soaking up every nuance of the enemy's behaviour. After some thought, Maddox replied that he had the perfect men for the job. Their names were James McCrussen and James 'Jimmy The Swede' Morand. Maddox gave his personal assurance that these men were the best surveillance team that gangland had to offer, adding that if these men could not take on the task then nobody could. Taking him at his word, McGurn ordered that the two men be immediately dispatched to Chicago, and on January 20, McCrussen and Morand moved into the room overlooking the garage of S. M. C. Cartage Company.

The remaining installments of the plan now went on hold until McGurn's surveillance team had reported back with their findings. McGurn was hopeful that their information would reveal the correct course of action, and that the North Siders themselves would inadvertently provide him with the perfect setup. He was not to be disappointed. As promised, McCrussen and Morand proved their proficiency in underworld espionage by providing McGurn with all the information he had requested and more. They revealed that George Moran held court practically every day, with the meetings usually taking place in the mornings at around nine or ten o'clock. The duo also disclosed that at these meetings – besides Moran – there were normally around four or five other persons present. McCrussen and Morand could not identify these attendees, save for the Gusenberg brothers, whom they claimed were in constant attendance. Their intelligence went further still, stating that liquor trucks delivered booze shipments almost every day, with the size of the shipment appearing to vary wildly from one or two trucks, to an entire consignment of ten or twelve. Delighted as he was by the intelligence gleaned thus far, McGurn knew that given more time, his spies could no doubt discover even more about his enemy's activities, though he was ready to accept that there was only so much to be learned from distant observation. In a perfect world, he would have placed a spy in the midst of the Moran crew, yet as Eddie Lynch had proved, to successfully pull off such an infidelity was a risk which was often not worth taking. Content with the information received, McGurn dispatched McCrussen and Morand, along with their payment of $1,200 each, back to St. Louis. A grateful telephone call together with a cash bonus of $2,000 to Claude Maddox himself, made sure that the cogs of collusion remained well oiled.

On January 26, 1929, McGurn, fearful of the possibility of a mole within the Outfit and that his plan may somehow be relayed to Moran, decided to take Louise on a short vacation to Miami, Florida. Capone himself already owned a home in the area – an expansive property located on a private estate in the center of Palm Island – so McGurn thought it a good idea to take time out, relax with his boss and indulge his girlfriend's expensive tastes, whilst clandestinely planning to teach George Moran the true meaning of nemesis.

Two days later, Pullman train number 2896, carrying Jack and Louise, pulled into Miami station, and while Jack headed straight for the Palm Island retreat, Louise headed for the Dallas Park Hotel. Checking Jack and herself into the hotel under the name of Mr. and Mrs. Vincent D'Oro from Havana, Cuba, she informed the desk clerk that her husband would be joining her later that day, at which point she was allocated room number 72, a double suite on the second floor of the hotel. A few hours later – just as Louise had stated he would – Jack arrived at the hotel, appearing at the entrance driving a cream coloured, long wheel base Packard Roadster, which later investigation showed had been rented for him by Capone from the Florida Motor Sales Company, 1220 Biscayne Boulevard (McGurn had had previous dealings with this particular company, when procuring a vehicle during the planning of the Frankie Yale hit.) Upon arrival at the hotel, McGurn informed the clerk that he and his wife would be staying until January 31, before stunning the hotel staff by not only paying in advance for the three days, but also by unfurling a roll of bills in order to pay the $225 in cash.

The following day, while Louise partook in a little retail therapy with Capone's wife Mae, Jack set about procuring weapons for the intended hit. He had already decided on his contact, the distinction going to Capone's old friend Parker Henderson who was, as always, only too willing to oblige. Following McGurn's instructions precisely, Henderson contacted Peter Von Frantzius in Chicago, and asked him to supply four Thompson submachine guns, two shotguns, plus four-thousand rounds of ammunition. Henderson was also instructed to have the weapons delivered to the Ponce de Leon Hotel, rather than any of the Outfit's hangouts, thus removing one firm source of evidence from the inevitable investigation. Precautions such as this were of the highest priority for McGurn, for should the police discover any evidence which linked the crime to the Outfit, it was one hundred percent guaranteed that Capone would take the fall. As Capone's close friend and chief protector, there was no way that McGurn would ever allow that to happen, a fact he had made clear during his acceptance of sole responsibility for the entire hit.

On January 31, Jack McGurn and Louise Rolfe checked out of the Dallas Park Hotel and headed back to Chicago, once again taking the luxurious Pullman Train along the Atlantic Coast Line Railroad. Before they left, McGurn consulted with Capone once more at his Palm Island villa and instructed him – for his own security – to avoid contact with Chicago at all costs; that meant no telephone calls, no telegrams, no communication in any way whatsoever. In doing so, McGurn was attempting to remove the possibility of the police trying to prove that Capone had directed the whole episode from Miami. McGurn would also put this distancing technique into effect with the rest of the Outfit, save of course for those members whose assistance may be required. He knew that to remain aloof may not only thwart any investigation, but it would also protect Capone and his underlings. This was a significant element of McGurn's plan, for he knew that should one other Outfit member be proven to have prior knowledge of the hit, a charge of conspiracy would be levelled at the Outfit and ultimately, Capone would take the rap. Therefore, upon arrival in Chicago, Jack and Louise headed not to the Lexington, but to the Stevens Hotel, a large multi-storey establishment in the heart of the Loop. This was certainly a strategic location, far enough away from the Lexington so as to create the illusion of detachment, yet prominent enough to show that he had nothing to hide. For all intents and purposes, McGurn was merely indulging in a romantic break with his girlfriend in the run up to St. Valentine's Day. As if to add even more credence to the story, the couple checked in as Mr. and Mrs. Vincent Gibaldi.

The next installment of McGurn's plan was to choose the men who would be capable of carrying out such a massive hit. The requirements were that they must be experienced machine gunners, so therefore must be relatively strong and well built. However, whoever he chose had to also be from out of town, men who had either never before set foot in Chicago, or if they had, were unknown to the North Siders. For two reasons this specification was of vital importance. Firstly, should the hit fail and any North Side members be left alive, there would be little chance that they could identify their assailants. Secondly, following the event, the perpetrators could simply disappear back to their home state with no trace that they had ever been in Chicago. The third and final requirement was that all the participants must have the ability to remain cool, to be devoid of emotion no matter what the circumstances. Finding one person who would fit all these criteria was difficult enough, but McGurn needed an entire hit squad of four men.

To help him find the right men for the job, McGurn once again turned to staunch stalwart, Claude Maddox who, after a few hours, came up with four names. They were Fred 'Killer' Burke, the experienced St. Louis hit man who had participated in the murder of Frankie Yale, Byron Bolton, an ex Navy machine gunner and the brother of James Bolton who had rented the room across from the Moran garage, Pasqualino Lolordo, whose brother Giuseppe had been murdered in a hit sanctioned and abetted by Moran, and finally Gus Winkler, a vicious yet degenerate gambler. McGurn liked the idea of Fred Burke and Byron Bolton, but he believed that Lolordo and Winkler could be liabilities; this could certainly be true of Lolordo, whose sentiment and emotional impartiality may serve to cloud his judgment. In their place, McGurn decided on the pitiless Outfit duo of John Scalise and Albert Anselmi, men who despite being known in Chicago were visually unknown to the Moran gang. Via Maddox, McGurn arranged for a safe house for them in St. Louis where they could hole up for a short while after the event, just until the furor had died down. Now that McGurn had his crew, all he needed was a setup.

Paul Morton was a professional hijacker, whose territory covered quite literally anywhere in the United States. Whilst there were many hijackers during that period of time, the vast majority went about their business rather haphazardly, not really knowing what the appropriated vehicle contained until they opened up the back. Morton was different, in that he specialized exclusively in hijacking beer and liquor trucks. His favourite hold-up spot was up in Idaho, on a small road not far from the Canadian border; since prohibition laws only applied to America, there was nothing to stop the big brewing companies from moving their operations over the border in order to continue production. Of course, the transportation of the brewed liquor into the United States was still illegal, yet the breweries made sure that independent delivery drivers took all those risks for them. Considering the fact that the breweries got paid no matter what, and that most of those trucks wound up in the hands of people like Paul Morton, it is clear that the link between brewer and hijacker was a perfect, if rather bizarre, working relationship.

Morton had been a friend of Capone's for quite some time, ever since his brother James had been killed in a shootout involving Moran. The shock over his brother's death was enhanced by the fact that James had not been the intended target, nor was he the member of any gang – he was merely an innocent passer-by caught in the crossfire. In the aftermath, Capone took Paul under his wing, giving him money for both himself and his mother and telling him that should he ever need anything, all he had to do was ask. Paul had never forgotten the kindness he had been shown and in return, told Capone that he would be willing to help him, or any of his men at any time. Jack McGurn was now ready to call in that favour.

McGurn's idea was that Morton would be supplied with a consignment of Old Log Cabin whiskey, a desirable commodity indeed, one which was often described as one of the finest and smoothest whiskeys on the market. Morton was to approach Moran with the consignment, telling him that it was a freshly hijacked load, and that he was willing to sell it to him for the unbelievably low price of $5,000. McGurn knew that Moran would check out his story, and so made sure that the consignment on offer had indeed been hijacked – not only that, but it had been hijacked in the middle of a busy street in front of dozens of witnesses. There were a hundred cases of whiskey on the truck, meaning that Morton would be offering the consign-ment to Moran at $50 per case. McGurn knew that Moran could easily sell one bottle to a speakeasy for $30 and as such, hoped that he would be swayed by the incongruously large profit margin. Morton had been further instructed that, should Moran buy the first load, he was to tell him that he had information to suggest that another shipment would be leaving the brewery the next day and that he was prepared to give Moran first refusal. Blinded by the dollar signs dancing before his eyes, Moran took the bait, buying the entire truckload there and then, and ordering the next consign-ment as soon as it came available. As soon as Morton left the Moran HQ, he headed straight to McGurn to inform him that another appointment had been made. The second shipment was due to be delivered in three days time, on Thursday February 14, 1929, at 10.40am.

With the date set, McGurn once again contacted James McCrussen and James Morand for further surveillance work. Informing them that the room in Mrs. Landesman's rooming house was still reserved, their job was to occupy that room during the evening of February 13, and the morning of February 14, during which time they would again note the comings and goings of the North Siders. The purpose of this vigilance was to ascertain exactly when George Moran entered the garage in order to attend the pre-arranged meeting with Paul Morton. Once his presence had been noted, McCrussen and Morand would send a coded message to the hit crew, informing them that their prime target had arrived. With the setup complete, all McGurn could do now was to wait and hope that the pieces of his criminal masterpiece would fall neatly into place.

Even before the first morning light of February 14, the city of Chicago had witnessed its first killings. At 5am, at an address on the far West Side, husband and wife Harriet and Rockford Carlson got into a conjugal spat, the kind that most married couples have at one time or another. However, instead of the argument ending with the couple kissing and making up, the row would only cease when Rockford killed his wife with a single blast from his shotgun, before going into the basement of their house and taking his own life. As Chicago's early risers read the initial reports of this story in their first edition papers, they were blissfully unaware that the bloodshed was set to continue, and that before the day was over, they would have witnessed the blackest and bloodiest day of their city's history.

Later that morning, McCrussen and Morand watched as members of the North Side gang filed one by one into the garage of S. M. C. Cartage Company. Exactly who arrived first and last is unclear, suffice to say that a total of seven men arrived at the premises. The motley crew comprised: ALBERT KACHELLEK a. k. a JAMES CLARK, born in Germany in 1889, and brought to Chicago around 1895/6. By 1905, he had spent four months in the workhouse for robbery, before later being sentenced to four years for burglary. It is not known at what point in his colourful life that he became involved with the North Siders, though he now served as Moran's business manager.

ADAM HEYER a. k. a. ARTHUR HEYES a. k. a. FRANK SNYDER. Also born in 1889, Heyer was twenty-two years old before he spent his first time in jail, thus being regarded by the criminal fraternity as something of a late starter. Upon his release from jail, he made a short lived attempt to go straight by enrolling on an accountancy course, before serving time again in 1923, for a confidence game conviction. In 1929, his accountancy training paid off, and he now served as the financial consultant for a Moran owned dog track.

JOHN MAY, a thirty-five year old mechanic and father of seven. As with the previous characters, he too had a colourful past, having been a failed safecracker and twice charged with robbery and larceny. He began his career with Moran working as a liquor truck driver, though that job had ended two months previous, when Moran had changed his duties to include the maintenance of the trucks themselves. May arrived at the garage with his German Shepherd dog, Highball, who once inside, was habitually chained to a pipe.

ALBERT WEINSHENKER a. k. a. ALBERT WEINSHANK. At the age of just twenty-six, he was the youngest member of the gang, although he was already the sole proprietor of his own speakeasy. Despite his youth, Weinshenker was a brilliant businessman, and was currently attempting to assist Moran in his efforts to infiltrate the cleaning and dyeing business.

Next came PETER and FRANK GUSENBURG, the brothers who had failed so spectacularly in their attempt to assassinate McGurn. At age forty, Peter was the eldest, whilst Frank was four years his junior. Later, an associate of theirs described them as *'Tough sons of bitches, who wanted the whole world to know it.'* Peter had previously been convicted on a mail robbery charge, resulting in his incarceration in Leavenworth Federal Penitentiary. Frank on the other hand, had beaten every charge that had been thrown at him, including one count of murder. Later that day, the two were due to meet their kid brother Jimmy, at which time all three of them would drive up to Detroit to pick up another batch of bootleg hooch.

The last member of this heterogeneous group was REINHARDT H. SCHWIMMER. Initially, police believed him to be an innocent victim, an unfortunate case of being in the wrong place at the wrong time, and it is easy to see how this conclusion was reached. A qualified optometrist, Schwimmer was the proprietor of a small surgery in the Loop and with no criminal convictions whatsoever, he appeared to be as clean as they come.

However, looks can be deceiving. For Schwimmer – an obviously well educated man who really ought to have known better – was totally enraptured by the gangster chic and could not resist the thrill of hanging around with gangsters. Indeed, he had once even boasted to a friend that he could have anyone killed whenever he wanted. Surely, there will never be a clearer illustration of the vast difference between education and wisdom.

The notable absence from this list is George Moran himself, the man declared the number one target of Jack McGurn, and for whom this entire charade had been orchestrated. Yet surprisingly, McCrussen and Morand failed to notice this apparently conspicuous omission and gave the signal to the quartet of assassins that the North Siders, *including* Moran, were inside the garage. How was it possible that two surveillance men, men who were obviously held in such high regard, could make such a horrendous mistake? Upon further analysis of the situation, the error becomes perfectly understandable, for Albert Weinshenker bore an uncanny resemblance to Moran, so much so that he had once been arrested by detectives sent to arrest Moran, and was only released when his wife arrived to prove his identity. Nevertheless, the signal had been given and there was now no way to retract it.

At 10.35am, just a few moments after the signal had been relayed, a police squad car pulled into the curb outside the garage of S. M. C. Cartage Company. The doors opened and out stepped four men, comprising two uniformed officers and two plainclothes detectives, who to the untrained eye, could possibly have been prohibition agents. This law enforcement quartet was in fact McGurn's hired assassins, with Fred Burke and Byron Bolton playing the roles of the uniformed officers, whilst Albert Anselmi and John Scalise – complete with heavy winter overcoats – took the role of the detectives. The four men stepped boldly towards the garage entrance, pushed open the door and went inside.

Immediately they found themselves in what was, in essence, a small office, complete with desk, chair, telephone and '*in*' and '*out*' filing trays. Behind the desk was a partitioning wall, in the center of which was a door leading through into the rear of the building. Stepping through this door, the murderous ensemble found themselves in the actual garage area, the place where all the meetings were held, and where John May serviced the liquor trucks. In this area, the men discovered five wooden chairs standing near the left hand wall, a small work-bench directly facing the doorway, and a large liquor truck which took up the majority of the right hand side of the room. The seven North Side gang members milled around, idly passing the time whilst they waited for the arrival of Paul Morton and George Moran. The unknowing victims were at first slightly perturbed at the sight of four strangers entering their inner sanctum, yet when they realized that the intruders were in fact only cops, they inevitably relaxed. To the majority of citizens who freeze at the very moment that they are presented with the image of police officers, the notion that these men would actually relax no doubt seems somewhat bizarre however, during the era of prohibition, gangsters had become accustomed to token raids and had come to realize that they would simply be arrested, taken down to the police station and released as soon as their lawyers arrived. To these guys, it really was no big deal.

McGurn's police officers and detectives barked out their commands, ordering the seven men to line up with their backs to the officers and their hands against the rear wall. Proving that they had completely bought the setup, the seven men duly complied, adopting the required stance and allowing one of the officers to step forward and relieve them of their weapons. Scalise and Anselmi then stepped forward, before unlimbering their Tommy Guns which had, up until this point, been hidden beneath their heavy winter coats. A few seconds later, the deafening roar of machine gun fire filled the room, reverberating around the bare brick walls as they raked the backs of their victims with hot lead. One by one, the seven bodies jerked and danced with demented puppetry, as bullet after bullet tore at their soft flesh. Fired from such close range, many of the bullets ploughed straight through their victims and would later be found embedded within the masonry. Almost in sequence, the men buckled under the onslaught and slumped lifelessly to the concrete floor, blood pouring from each of their innumerable wounds. Frank and Pete Gusenberg fell side by side at the left hand end of the line, with Weinshenker, Heyer, May and Schwimmer falling in order alongside them. Clark, who had been standing next to Frank Gusenberg, slumped sideways along the wall, his body falling across the feet of the others. Seventeen bullets had reduced the body of John May to little more than a sickly, bleeding mass, yet unbelievably, Burke held the notion that he still showed signs of life. Stepping forward, he stood over the body and proceeded to obliterate the entire left side of May's head with a single shotgun round. Confident that their mission had been successfully completed, McGurn's murderous quartet calmly stepped back through the partitioning door and proceeded to leave the horrific and bloody scene. It had all taken little more than a matter of minutes, yet the St. Valentine's Day Massacre would be forever remembered in the legend and folklore of gangland as one of the worst crimes ever to be perpetrated.

George Moran was a man who was habitually late for everything; the event nor the occasion mattered, for he simply could not adapt his mind to the principle of punctuality. The morning of February 14, was no exception. Having risen from his bed at around 9.30am, Moran was partaking in a leisurely breakfast with Ted Newberry – another North Side hood – while McGurn's hit men entered his place of business. With their appetites sated, the pair then proceeded towards the garage however, as they rounded the corner of North Clark Street, Moran spotted the police squad car parked directly outside his HQ. Deciding that neither of them was in the mood to be arrested that morning, Moran and Newberry turned on their heels and headed in the opposite direction, unaware that for them, the saying *'he will be late for his own funeral'* was chillingly accurate.

Had Moran and Newberry hung around, they would have witnessed the final, elaborate scene in this already intricate play. Before the hit man quartet left the building proper, they swapped weapons, with Scalise and Anselmi now concealing the shotguns beneath their overcoats. The pair then raised their hands above their heads, before stepping out into the street ahead of Burke and Bolton, who now trained their Tommy Guns at their colleagues' backs. As the police at that time also used Tommy Guns, to any potential witnesses it appeared that the police had entered the premises for the purpose of a prohibition raid, during which a shootout had occurred and now two suspects were being led away. The four men then re-entered their waiting automobile and within seconds, were making their getaway back down North Clark Street.

The genius of the crime was accented by the sheer virtuosity of the getaway plan. Burke, Bolton, Scalise and Anselmi had been instructed to drive their police squad car to a remote garage on the outskirts of Chicago. Here, Claude Maddox would be waiting with a separate car which the four men would then use to drive to St. Louis, Missouri, where arrangements had been made for them to hide out with members of the Circus Gang until the heat died down. Maddox would also supply them with a change of clothes, with the ones they were wearing being left behind to be destroyed. The guns they had used would travel with them to St. Louis, the assumption being that no one would think to look for the murder weapons so far out of town. Maddox had already arranged for the car and the clothes to be burned, meaning that no clothes, weapons or vehicle would be found with which to provide evidence which could be linked with the crime. If everyone played their part and if everything went according to plan, Jack McGurn and his associates would have planned and executed the perfect crime, one which would never be solved.

THE INVESTIGATION

It is difficult to imagine the horrendous cavalcade of thoughts and emotions which assaulted the police officers at the very moment they were confronted with the scene of carnage that lay in the rear of the building at 2122 North Clark Street. Police Lieutenant Thomas Loftus and Sergeant Clarence Sweeney, were responding to reports of a disturbance at that particular address, and having found the office in the forepart of the building to be empty, had proceeded through the partitioning door and on into the garage itself. There they found the massacre that McGurn's police had left in their wake, the seven lifeless, blood soaked bodies, and the pooling blood which had now begun to flow along the inclined floor and into the drains. They also found Highball, the German Shepherd, howling and barking insanely at the death of his owner. Steeling themselves, the two officers stepped apprehensively towards the bodies, knowing that it was imperative to discover their identities, whilst trying to override their basic instinct to flee.

Suddenly, Loftus realized that not all of the seven men were actually dead. He had twenty-two bullets lodged within his body, yet Frank Gusenberg was still alive, albeit barely. An ambulance was immediately called and whilst Loftus continued with the job of identifying the victims,

Sergeant Sweeney accompanied Gusenberg to the Alexian Brothers Hospital. There, doctors declared that there was little they could do; he had lost an immense amount of blood and was now far too weak to undergo surgery. Gusenberg was placed in a private room, where Sweeney attempted to glean as much information from him as possible before it was too late. The following transcript is taken from the subsequent report which was filed by Sweeney himself.

Sweeney: *Do you know me, Frank?*
Gusenberg: *Yes.*
Sweeney: *Who shot you?*
Gusenberg: *No one…nobody shot me.*
Sweeney: *Frank, Pete's dead and you're in a bad way. Who shot you?*
Gusenberg: *No one.*
Sweeney: *Want a preacher, Frank?*
Gusenberg: *No. I'm cold Sarge, awful cold.*
Sweeney: *Who was it, Frank?*

Sergeant Sweeney never did get his answer. At 1.35pm, less than three hours after being shot, Frank Gusenberg died, taking with him the names of those who had perpetrated this heinous crime.

Inevitably, the name of Capone was linked to the crime and indeed, within hours of the grim discovery, the police had converged on the Lexington Hotel, full of questions regarding the whereabouts of Capone on that day and the preceding days. They were however, set to be disappointed, for Capone had followed McGurn's instructions over remaining in Miami and avoiding all contact with Chicago until after the event. As such, there were no telephone calls, no letters, not even so much as a telegram that could link Capone with the crime. Indeed, Capone's alibi was rock solid, for as the killings were taking place, he was sitting in the office of Dade County Solicitor Robert Taylor, answering questions that were being put to him by Assistant States Attorney Louis Goldstein, who had been charged with the investigation of his tax affairs. Even the Chicago Chief of Police William Russell couldn't argue with that.

The St. Valentine's Day Massacre was obviously front page news for the city and national media alike. There was hardly a single broadsheet or tabloid which did not inform citizens of the awful events which had unfolded that day. The headlines below are just a sample of those published on February 14, and 15, 1929.

CHICAGO DAILY JOURNAL
GANG 'FIRING SQUAD' KILLS 7

HERALD & EXAMINER
FIRING SQUAD KILLS 7 IN BIG GANGLAND MASSACRE
Gangland Garbs Its Executioners In Police Uniforms
Massacre Wipes Out Last Of Powerful O'Banion Gang

EVANSVILLE JOURNAL
GANG EXECUTES SEVEN MEN
MACHINE GUNS SPRAY DEATH IN HEADQUARTERS

CHICAGO DAILY NEWS
MASSACRE OF 7 MORAN GANG
VICTIMS ARE LINED AGAINST WALL
ONE VOLLEY KILLS ALL

CHICAGO DAILY TRIBUNE
GANG SLAY DOCTOR IN MASSACRE

"Only Capone kills like that" are the now infamous words uttered by George 'Bugs' Moran upon hearing the news that his entire crew had been wiped out. That single statement, more than any other, branded itself into the consciousness of William Russell. From the very moment that the crime had been reported, deep in his soul he knew that Capone – if not the man himself then certainly the Outfit – was responsible for what people were now calling *'The Massacre.'* Realizing that Capone's alibi was virtually bombproof, Russell ordered his men to delve into the backgrounds of every Outfit member, both past and present. For two weeks the investigators scoured the records, searching for any clue, no matter how insignificant,

that may at the very least give them a motive. Time and again their efforts proved fruitless. Just as they were giving up hope, one of the investigating officers happened upon the name of Jack McGurn. He found evidence of his meteoric rise through the Outfit's ranks, his love of the spotlight, his flash suits and cars, not to mention his penchant for blonde, fur clad women. Whilst none of this triviality was of any consequence to William Russell, his attention was nevertheless grasped by the newly uncovered evidence of McGurn's close encounter with the Gusenberg brothers.

On February 27, 1929, police officers once again entered the Lexington Hotel and arrested Jack McGurn and Louise Rolfe on charges of murder and accessory to murder, respectively. The pair was taken to the Cicero Police Headquarters, where William Russell insisted on interrogating them personally. Beginning with McGurn, he questioned him as to his whereabouts on the morning of February 14, to which McGurn replied – in all honesty – that he had been with his girlfriend Louise Rolfe in room 1919A at the Stevens Hotel. He went on to say that they had retired to their room in the hotel on February 13, and had only left it on the morning of February 15, and that from the time they had entered the room until the time they left, they had not been out of each others sight. Russell then skeptically asked what they had done about food or drink. Once again, in all honesty, McGurn rejoined that they had had all their meals and drinks, plus daily papers, sent up to their room. Louise, McGurn claimed, had wanted a romantic St. Valentine's Day and that was exactly what he had given her. Realizing that this could very well be an alibi which could be substantiated, Russell then probed into McGurn's feelings towards the Gusenberg brothers, it being a notable fact that it was they who had attempted to kill him. With the brothers, and indeed most of the North Side gang out of the way, McGurn was able to temporarily turn off his hatred for his enemy and replied that until Russell mentioned their names, he had had no idea who had shot him that day.

Feeling as though he was doing little more than banging his head against a brick wall, Russell decided to turn his attention to Louise Rolfe. He reasoned that should it be put to her that she could go to prison as an accessory to murder before, during and after the fact, she may very well capitulate and tell the true version of events. Louise however, proved far stronger than she looked, backing up McGurn's story to the hilt (for it was essentially true) whilst taking time to add that he had given her the most wonderful Valentine's Day she had ever known. Russell then put it to her that she may have become bored and left the hotel room for a moment, after all, forty-eight hours was an awfully long time to remain in one room. Looking him straight in the eye, Louise fluttered her eyelashes before innocently replying *"Officer, when you're with Jack, you're never bored."*

Despite their corroborating stories, Russell remained convinced that McGurn was involved in the massacre, though he could not prove that he may have been one of the actual killers. Later that day, just a few hours after being arrested, McGurn was charged with the only crime that Russell could realistically throw at him, that of conspiracy to commit murder. He was arraigned at the Cook County Court before Judge Schwarba, who set bail at $15,000. Casually, McGurn reached into the pocket of his immaculate suit jacket and pulled out a roll of bills which an onlooker later described as being *'big enough to choke an ox.'* After peeling off the required amount, Jack McGurn and Louise Rolfe (the police had decided not to prosecute her) walked free from court.

The police investigation into the massacre began to peter out almost as soon as it had begun, mainly due to the fact that the investigating officers actually cared very little that seven gangsters had been murdered. Indeed for many of them, the only grievance was that they could no longer take backhanders from the North Siders. For William Russell however, there was the problem of clearing the name of the entire Chicago police force, for Mrs. Jeanette Landesman, who had seen the charade before and after the massacre, had claimed that the perpetrators were the police themselves. Yet there was very little that Russell could do, for with no suspects – save for McGurn – no murder weapons and no motive, he knew that it was unlikely that this investigation would ever have a satisfactory outcome.

February 23, 1929, saw the opening of the Coroner's Inquiry, from which the police, media, and ordinary citizens alike hoped answers would emerge. However, an endless stream of reluctant witnesses armed with only the vaguest of memories, meant that the Cook County Coroner could not even reach a verdict. In fact, the sole piece of hard evidence to be presented was the pathologist's report, which only served to tell people what they already knew, that the victims had all died from multiple gunshot wounds. Whilst they did not yet know it, the entire investigation was about to get a break. From the haze of intrigue and suspicion came a man who would describe himself as *'a gun crank since childhood.'* His name was Colonel Calvin Goddard.

Born and raised in New York, Goddard had been in love with firearms for as long as he could remember. There was not a single type or make of gun that he did not know the smallest detail about. As soon as he was old enough, he enlisted himself in the New York Police Department, eventually serving with the firearms division. The advent of The Great War brought with it his call up papers, and from then until its conclusion, he served as an ordinance officer. After the war, he found that his interest was moving on to the actual science of the firearms themselves and before long, had developed a theory that every gun leaves its own unique *'fingerprint.'* This discovery made Goddard the first man to promote the existence of ballistic science.

Now in 1929, Goddard was renowned as *the* authority on firearms and weaponry and therefore, as a last gasp effort, the coroner ordered that all the bullets that had been removed from the scene of the massacre, including those taken from the bodies, be handed over to Goddard for examination. After two weeks, Goddard reported back with his findings. He told the inquiry that two Thompson submachine guns and one pump action shotgun had been used in the attack. The shotgun had fired one shot only, whilst the two machine guns had fired two-hundred and twenty, and two-hundred and fifty rounds respectively. Goddard was then told of the numerous theories which surrounded the massacre, in particular the theories which suggested that the attack was perpetrated by the police. In order to quell or confirm these theories, Goddard was asked to examine every gun, both past and present, used by the Chicago Police Department. After many weeks of waiting with bated breath, the police could breathe a sigh of relief, as Goddard reported that not a single gun used by the force matched the bullets taken from the garage. However, Goddard was quick to point out that should any suspicious weaponry come to the knowledge of the police, he could easily determine or refute its involvement in the massacre. The trouble with that was, that could be a never ending story, as no one could even take an educated guess as to where the guns were likely to be, if they still existed at all.

Late in the evening of Saturday December 14, 1929, two cars collided outside the City Hall of St. Joseph, Michigan. The accident could never be regarded as serious, with the entire damage consisting of a broken rear tail light, coming to a grand total of $5. Despite this however, the two drivers entered into a furious and heated argument and eventually, a concerned witness decided to call the police. Policeman Charles Skelly was first on the scene, and upon realizing that the situation would not be readily resolved, demanded that the two motorists accompany him to the local police station in order to ascertain who was to blame. However, as Skelly hauled himself up onto the running board of one of the cars, the driver shot him three times with a pistol; Skelly died three hours later in hospital after never regaining consciousness. In a frantic attempt to flee the scene, the driver crashed his car into a telegraph pole, this time, managing to break a wheel. Beset by sheer panic, he then abandoned his own car and hijacked another before he was able to escape. Had the killer not been careless enough to leave papers containing the initials FRB, together with an address in his abandoned vehicle, that most certainly would have been the end of the matter. As it was, police immediately searched the address, a search which uncovered two machine guns, numerous revolvers, two bullet proof vests, enough ammunition to supply an entire army and $319,000 in cash. The occupants of the house were subsequently arrested and at the time, gave their names as Frederick and Viola Dane, names which were completely unknown to the police. There was however, still the matter of the initials FRB which were found on the paperwork inside the abandoned car. Before long, the connection was made, for FRB were in fact the true initials of Frederick Dane, Dane being an alias for one Fred R. Burke.

Until this point in time, Burke's name had never been mentioned in connection with the massacre, so therefore it was purely because of the fact that the weapons' seized from his home were deemed suspicious, that they were sent to Colonel Goddard for analysis. Goddard matched one of the machine guns with bullets removed from the body of John May, and the second machine gun to those taken from the body of Reinhardt Schwimmer. Goddard knew that he need not test any further, for these guns had undeniably been used in the massacre. The fact that Burke was in possession of the guns however, did not prove that he had a hand in the actual killings; indeed, when investigators probed his background, they found no evidence whatsoever that he had ever worked in conjunction with the Chicago Outfit. Lack of evidence and motive had once again thwarted the best efforts of law enforcement. Eventually, Burke was tried and convicted of the murder of Policeman Charles Skelly, with no charges relating to the massacre ever being brought.

Goddard's unsurpassable knowledge of firearms then gave the police their next lead. He knew that very few sporting goods stores sold Thompson machine guns and so, by process of elimination, it should be possible to trace where the weapons came from. It did not take long for the retailer, Peter Von Frantzius, to be discovered and to be immediately ordered to appear before the Coroner's Committee in order to give evidence. His initial equivocation was soon eradicated by the reminder that he was under oath, at which point he testified that he did remember selling the guns though surprisingly, he could not remember to whom he had sold them. Even mug shots of various suspects failed to jog his memory. Frantzius was then asked whether he had ever knowingly sold guns to *'unsavoury characters or suspected gangsters,'* to which he replied that he had. In 1929, knowingly supplying criminals with weapons was not deemed to be a crime indeed, the only law that Frantzius had violated was the Statute of Illinois, which stated that all firearms retailers were required to keep records of a customers name and address. Just as in the case of Fred Burke, no charges were ever able to be brought, and Peter Von Frantzius was free to continue in business.

Twelve days before Burke's arrest, Jack McGurn and Louise Rolfe – now dubbed by the media as *'the blonde alibi'* – appeared at the Cook County Court to hear declaration that the state was ready to have McGurn stand trial for his alleged involvement in the St. Valentine's Day Massacre. McGurn had appeared in court on four separate occasions and in each case, Assistant States Attorney Harry Ditchburne, had been forced to admit that the State was not yet ready to present its case. On this occasion, Judge Barnes asked if the State was ready to present its prosecution, to which Harry Ditchburne replied that they were not and requested a further delay.

Judge Barnes reminded Ditchburne that Illinois State Law required that, if after four delays the State was not ready to prosecute, cases must be dismissed. Therefore, as four delays had already been granted and with a request for a fifth formally given, Judge Barnes had no option but to declare the case *Nolle Prossed* or *'dismissed.'* It seemed that McGurn's charmed life was staying true to form, for having personally masterminded *the* worst atrocity in gangland history, he had nevertheless evaded the law indeed, never again would he be subject to any prosecution regarding the massacre.

Aside from the seven dead, the St. Valentine's Day Massacre claimed one further victim…McGurn's marriage. Upon hearing reports that her husband had been arrested and charged in connection with mass murder, Helena finally began to wonder why she was still choosing to remain steadfast in her support of him. She told herself that there was the chance that he was innocent, although reality forced that thought to be tempered by the rationale that the police had not simply plucked his name from thin air. Nevertheless, Helena would have stayed had McGurn not used Louise Rolfe as his alibi. Helena had now effectively heard from her husband's own lips that her suspicions were well grounded, and that he did indeed have someone else. Whilst she was fully prepared to stand by him and defend him against the allegations which were being laid against his name, she would not compete against, nor would she share him with another woman. She cursed at Jack for backing her into a corner, for forcing her to make the heartbreaking decision that no spouse would ever want to make. She immediately packed a few clothes for Helen and herself, before writing a note to inform Jack that she was leaving for good. As the door to their suite in the Lexington Hotel closed behind her, so did the most remarkable and emotional chapter of her life.

It should have all been so different, and had the massacre taken place in today's society, it undoubtedly would have been. Once the murder weapons had been uncovered, it would generally be assumed that piece by piece, the case would simply begin to come together. As it was however, the discovery of the guns and the revelation that they had originated from the outlet of Peter Von Frantzius, were the last true facts ever to emerge from gangland history's most notorious event. Since the failed investigations into Fred Burke, Von Frantzius and Jack McGurn, no one has ever been questioned over the deaths of the seven men in the garage of George Moran. In 1962, the FBI, whilst still choosing to maintain a permanent file on the atrocity, declared the case of the St. Valentine's Day Massacre closed. To this day, more than seventy years on, gangland's most infamous and bloody crimes remains formally unsolved.

ALTERNATIVE THEORIES

When a major crime takes place, very often the only thing which can be one hundred percent guaranteed, is that there will be an infinite number of theories and explanations as to whom, what, why, where and when. Even when a crime has been formally solved and the perpetrator or perpetrators, locked securely behind bars, there are those members of society who simply refuse to believe the verdict. The St. Valentine's Day Massacre was, indeed still is, no exception, and the conspiracy theorists' imaginations continue to be fuelled by the fact that the crime remains unsolved. There is some kind of cover up…isn't there? These alternative theories range from the very plausible to the categorically ridiculous, yet in order to truly study the crime, it is impossible to ignore them completely.

Immediately following the massacre, rumours abounded that Jack McGurn himself was a part of the murder squad and that he had personally fired one of the Tommy Guns. If true, this would indeed be the most captivating detail, and would serve to add even more romance to his already intriguing life. Sadly however, this version runs into one major flaw, in that Frank and Peter Gusenberg knew McGurn by sight. The very moment that they saw him enter garage, they would have known that something was wrong and quite probably, the only one to be killed that day would have been McGurn himself. The theory is still further flawed by the fact that, just under three months prior to the massacre taking place, McGurn had undergone surgery to remove five bullets from his arm and shoulder. It is highly unlikely that he would have sufficiently recovered enough strength to fire a Tommy Gun at a sustained rate, which would be needed if he were to take part.

On January 28, 1935, a letter addressed to J. Edgar Hoover, arrived at the FBI Headquarters in Washington, D.C. The sender was Frank F. Farrell, a Junior Highway Engineer with the State of Illinois. Farrell's letter stated that on November 28, or 29, 1928, Albert Kachelleck, James Clark, John May, Albert Weinshank and Reinhardt Schwimmer, took a young man by the name of William Darren Jr., the son of a Philadelphia police officer, for a *'ride.'* After shooting him in the car, they threw him out at the corner of Rush and State Streets. Darren died in Henrotin Hospital on December 29, or 30, 1928, but not before he had told his cousin – a known hoodlum named 'Three Fingered' Jack White – who had shot him. In retaliation for the death of his cousin, White orchestrated a bank payroll hold-up, in which he would be assisted by the five men responsible. The plan was that they were to come to the garage at North Clark Street in order to receive their final instructions, whereby White planned to kill them all. However, at the last moment, Frank and Pete Gusenberg had walked in and demanded that they be part of the deal. Not wishing to leave living witnesses, White agreed that they could be in on the hold-up, before ordering them to line up with the others. That, claimed Farrell, was why seven men had been killed instead of five. Whilst this is certainly an extremely plausible theory, there is one small point that appears to discredit Farrell's story. 'Three Fingered' Jack White was a known hoodlum in the Outfit indeed, not long before the date in question, White had been released from Leavenworth Penitentiary after serving a two year term for manslaughter. The main question which arises therefore, is why would a known Outfit member enlist the help of the North Siders? Also, the chances of an Outfit member being allowed to get within striking distance, let alone inside their inner sanctum, are considerably remote. In addition to all of these impeding factors, White would have needed Capone's permission to go ahead with the hit. The possibility of permission being granted to someone who was not only a low ranking member, but also one who was most definitely being watched by the police, is at best unlikely. In any event, the atmosphere which hung over Chicago at that point in time meant that had White so much as set foot on the North Side, Moran would have known about it.

Another theory concerned the purported confession of Byron Bolton, one of the four killers, and the brother of the man who had initially rented the room at Mrs. Landesman's rooming house. He apparently confessed to the FBI that he was one of the four hit men who had carried out the crime, naming Murray 'The Camel' Humphreys, Fred 'Killer' Burke and Fred

Goetz and his murder squad cohorts. These names totally contradicted the official police theory as to who the culprits were indeed, upon reading the confession, Police Captain William Russell – a man who would have been more than delighted to declare the case solved – made a statement to the newspapers that there *'was not a word of truth in it.'* Even the FBI agents were divided as to whether it was fact or fiction. The niggling question however, was why would anyone make a confession to the FBI, knowing that the consequences would be death either at the hands of the Outfit, or in the electric chair? The answer, it seems, is that the confession had been composed by the Outfit themselves. After all, what better way to deflect attention from the real miscreants, than to hand the police a complete fabrication? It was later discovered that Bolton was already a walking dead man, having swindled the Circus Gang out of $20,000 and it was obviously far more appealing to die in the electric chair, than to lose his life at the hands of Claude Maddox. At least with the State, Bolton could plead for leniency. Eventually, evidence was uncovered to the effect that Murray Humphreys was serving a six month sentence in the Cook County Jail at the time the massacre took place. Bolton was subsequently released without charge, only to be rearrested a few months later in connection with a bank hold-up organized by the infamous Karpis-Barker Gang.

There is one final alternative, one for the die hard conspiracy theorists. It is possible that the St. Valentine's Day Massacre was not the work of any member of the Outfit, nor of any member of any major gang in Chicago. It could be that the crime was indeed the work of the police themselves, carried out in order to frame Capone and have him – with a little luck – sent to the electric chair for mass murder. The result would have been that in one fell swoop, they would have successfully gotten rid of a painful thorn in their side, as well as the entire North Side gang. Of course, Calvin Goddard had proved that none of the weapons used by the police had been used in the massacre, yet it would not have been too difficult for the police to have used previously confiscated guns, only to plant them at the home of Fred Burke who was at that time, under arrest for the murder of a policeman. Naturally, the police would angrily deem this theory to be the product of an over active imagination, yet history has proven time and time again that gangsters are not the only members of society capable of getting away with murder.

CHAPTER EIGHTEEN

TREACHERY

Despite the fact that the St. Valentine's Day Massacre had failed to permanently eliminate the prime target, it nevertheless effected his disappearance from the Chicago gangland. In one swift movement, Moran had seen almost his entire gang wiped out, and whilst a handful of men still remained ready and willing to follow the Moran call, the question that hung permanently on their lips was, what was the point? Time and again it had been proven, with staggeringly violent efficiency, that Moran and his original band of North Side disciples was no match for the Outfit, so how then could he even hope to compete with only a smattering of support? It must have been a question which Moran had been asking himself, for a couple of days after the massacre he held a press conference in his hotel room, announcing to the media that he was retiring from the rackets. He had, he said, decided to quit whilst he still had his life, adding that he had made more money than he ever could have hoped for, and that whilst many thousands of dollars were still waiting to be made, the risks now far outweighed the rewards. The media, indeed the city as a whole, could have been forgiven for believing that this emotional rhetoric was little more than a counter charade, designed to lull Capone into a false sense of security, for Dion O'Banion had uttered almost precisely those self same words five years earlier. Unlike O'Banion however, Moran soon proved his sincerity and evanesced from the Chicago scene.

For Jack McGurn, it was a case of a job well done. True, Moran had not been killed, but he had nevertheless been forced out, leaving McGurn in the enviable position of being the chief bodyguard, principal hit man and close friend of the undisputed king of Chicago. At this very moment in time, Capone was *the* most powerful gangster ever to control the city indeed, not even the great 'Big Jim' Colosimo wielded the same puissance which

Capone now held. Capone himself knew that he owed a great part of his success to McGurn, for without his foresight, combined with a cool head and vengeance ridden nature, the outcome of his battle for supremacy could have been very different; without a doubt, history would not be as we know it today.

The St. Valentine's Day Massacre served to bond the two men ever closer, in fact so often were they seen together that people began to joke – albeit not to their faces – that the two were conjoined. Capone began to rely increasingly heavily on his protégé, regarding him as the most valuable asset to the Outfit, and treating him ever more as a close friend rather than an employee. For his part, McGurn revelled in the affectionate glow of his master, adopting the persona of a spoilt teacher's pet. The rest of the Outfit however, was less than enthralled by the ever deepening friendship. As with any large corporation, the lesser members of the workforce sought to ingratiate themselves with the hierarchy, in the vain hope that this would catapult their careers to the forefront of the business. Of course, this tactic very rarely worked and the sight of McGurn, who had never intentionally sought Capone's affection, being mollycoddled by *'The Big Fellow'* was more than some could bear. The situation was hardly helped by the fact that on numerous occasions, Capone had informed members along the chain of command that they could all learn from McGurn, and that he wished he had a hundred men just like him. Fuelled by jealousy, a wildfire of rumours that Capone was going soft began to spread throughout the Outfit, whilst many believed that no strong leader should ever allow himself to grow so close to an underling, and that he was no longer able to take on the job at hand. Members like Frank Nitti, who had been in the Outfit since Capone first came to Chicago, began to feel that they would undoubtedly be passed over for promotion when the time came. Like distant thunder, the rumblings of a coup began slowly rolling in.

April, 1929, – two months after the massacre had taken place – and the Outfit sent word to St. Louis that the furor and heat had sufficiently subsided, and that it was now safe for John Scalise and Albert Anselmi to return to Chicago. The two men came back to a heroes welcome, being greeted by the entire Outfit as though they were brave soldiers returning from war. In order to celebrate their safe return – not to mention the demise of the troublesome North Siders – Capone threw a massive party in the ballroom of the Lexington Hotel. Over the years, Outfit parties had become steeped in legend, with the revelry often continuing until six or seven o'clock in the morning, and this party was set to be no different. There was however, one factor which set this party apart from all those which had gone before, for it was at this party that Scalise and Anselmi met Joseph 'Hop Toad' Guinta. Guinta was Outfit small fry, more of an odd job man than a regular employee, one who would never achieve membership status. This subordinate treatment had forever piqued his pride, for he believed himself to be more than capable of holding his own within the higher ranks. Unfortunately for Guinta however, no one else could see this hidden potential, due in no small part to the fact that he had the will, but lacked the skill. The three men talked and talked, and as the evening wore on and the merriment caroused around them, they discovered that there was one common denominator which linked all three of them together; they all believed that good old Al was growing increasingly weak as a leader and that it was high time that someone put him out of his misery. By the time the final guests were leaving the ballroom, Scalise, Anselmi and Guinta had decided that it was they who would orchestrate the removal of Capone.

Before the Outfit began to consider the problem of when Scalise and Anselmi could safely return, Jack McGurn discovered that he had a problem of his own, a problem which presented itself in the form of Louise's estranged husband. In 1929, adultery was considered illegal and as such, a night of extra-marital passion could result in one or both parties being arrested and astonishingly, facing the possibility of jail. Now, angered by the fact that the woman he loved would never again reciprocate his affection, Frederick Boex had reported his wife's disloyalty to the police. It was March 2, 1929, and McGurn had just arrived at The Green Mill, when he received a telephone call from a tearful Louise. Sobbing, she told him that she had been arrested and that she needed him to come down to the police station to bail her out. No sooner had he placed the receiver back in its cradle, than he was on his way over to the Cook County Precinct, where upon arrival, he paid the $500 bail to secure her release. Once they had left the building and were sitting in McGurn's car, he persuaded Louise to tell him what had happened. This took quite a bit of coaxing and once she had told the story, it was easy to see why. Frederick Boex had not only reported Louise's infidelity to the police, but had also demanded that she be prosecuted to the full extent of the law. Louise was terrified of telling Jack, for she knew his temper and was rightly fearful that he may decide to teach Frederick a lesson; everyone could still remember the example he had made out of Joe E. Lewis. For once though, Louise was surprised, as the expected rage which she was sure would begin to manifest itself, never materialized. Instead, Jack hugged her and told her that everything would be alright, before driving her back to the Lexington.

Later that evening, a messenger was dispatched to the home of Frederick Boex. The messenger was in possession of a letter, which he had been instructed to hand to Boex personally. The letter bore no outward threat and was written in language that could in no way be described as intimidating. It read along the lines that Louise was now considered to be the girlfriend of Jack McGurn, that he loved her, and therefore did not wish to ever see her as upset as she was today. The letter ended with the statement that should Mr. Boex wish to know more about Jack McGurn, then he could by all means ask around about him, or he was welcome to visit his club, where all questions would gladly be answered. Not a dim-witted man, Boex obviously fully understood this sugar coated message, for two days later the adultery accusation was dropped.

McGurn was not lying when he said that he loved Louise. As he had realized when she visited his suite during his recuperation, he felt more for her than he did for Helena, and whilst he was slightly embarrassed at the fact that Helena had now left him, the feeling was nevertheless tempered with relief that he could now court Louise openly. The truth was that Helena had in fact done him a huge favour, though it was doubtful that he would ever admit to that.

★   ★   ★

It was not too long before rumours of a possible coup reached the ears of McGurn. At first he dismissed them as nonsense, for over the years there had been many such rumours, most of which were nothing more than the idle dreams of self important wannabe's. However, the distant rumblings

soon began to get louder and louder until eventually, McGurn was sufficiently concerned to mention the problem to his second in command,
Philip D'Andrea. He too dismissed the rumours, after all, who on earth
would even contemplate a coup on the Outfit after the fate which had
befallen the North Siders? Nevertheless, McGurn took little comfort from
D'Andrea's words of wisdom, and before long, was finding it increasingly
difficult to allay his fears and suspicions. He decided to begin a covert
surveillance operation on those whom he believed to be the prime suspects;
he observed their behaviour, watching for any tell tale signs that may just
give them away, whilst simultaneously cataloguing any change in their
habits or normal routine. If there was a plot, sooner or later the conspirators
would slip up and betray their disloyal thoughts.

The surveillance eventually paid off, when he overheard a discussion
between Scalise and Anselmi, a conversation which appeared to be on the
subject of where and how to get rid of Capone, and how to divide up the
assets. McGurn was furious with himself for not suspecting them sooner. A
few years earlier, when he discovered that they had once been allied with
Tropea, his trust in them had been all but eroded. Since then however, that
trust had been somewhat regained, to the point where he now curiously
found himself almost liking them, especially as they had appeared to be as
loyal to the Outfit as he himself. McGurn immediately brought the
discovery to the attention of Capone, though breaking the news that two of
the most trusted and competent hit men were planning to assassinate
Chicago's criminal overlord, is certainly an unenviable task. Despite the
revelation, McGurn was disappointed, for Capone blankly refused to
believe that two faithful and dedicated stalwarts – such as Scalise and
Anselmi were – could be guilty of such treachery. Yet so convinced was
McGurn, that he told Capone he believed he could prove that they were the
instigators of the plot against him. If he was correct, then immediate and
direct action should be taken however, if he were proved wrong, then he
would step down from his position with immediate effect. Capone knew
that McGurn would never make such an irrevocable statement without
having due cause, and besides which, his instinct had never let him down
before. On the basis of these primary factors, Capone accepted the deal.

The next day, Scalise and Anselmi were summoned to Capone's suite to receive orders for an urgent hit. When the duo arrived, they discovered quite a remarkable scene in progress. McGurn and Capone were having a furious argument, with the two men yelling at each other just inches away from each other's faces. They could hardly believe the way in which McGurn was talking to Capone, indeed, they were sure that if Capone were armed, his life was in serious danger. Disbelief soon turned to total astonishment, when McGurn slapped Capone across the face and shouted that a Sicilian could never trust a Napolitan (Capone's parents had emigrated from Naples) before storming out of the suite. The entire scene had of course been a total set up from the start, nothing more than a ruse to grab Scalise's and Anselmi's attention. Now all McGurn had to do was wait and see if the fish would take the bait.

The following afternoon, McGurn sat at his corner table in The Green Mill, when he was visited by the two conspirators, together with Joseph 'Hop Toad' Guinta. Scalise and Anselmi spoke enthusiastically over how greatly impressed they were by McGurn's show of bravado, after all, very few men would even *dare* to speak to Capone that way. They had relayed the news of the altercation to Guinta, and the three of them had decided to make McGurn an offer: the chance to join them in their plan to permanently terminate Capone's reign and jointly take over the Outfit. Fighting the urge to whack all three of them there and then, McGurn agreed to come in on their plot, feeding them the story that he had grown increasingly weary over Capone's belief that he was the ultimate ruler, and that he would like nothing more than to be rid of him. In any case, he went on, he knew that he had overstepped the mark by talking to Capone that way and that now, it was undoubtedly he or Capone who would have to go. Believing that they had won over Capone's most trusted companion, the three men left, but not before agreeing to meet again in a few days time to finalize their plans. McGurn now had all the proof he needed that Capone was in serious danger, and as head of security, it was his job to eradicate that threat.

The news that two trusted and competent members of his crew, along with the totally incompetent Guinta, were indeed planning to assassinate him, came as a real body blow to Capone. He knew that McGurn would never invent such a story and that what he was being told must be the truth, yet he never imagined that such a serious threat could come from within his own ranks. The question which now posed itself was how to deal with the problem. The penalty for such treachery was unquestionably death, but that was not the issue; the challenge at hand was how and where to mete out the punishment. After some discussion, Capone came up with the perfect solution, one which would deliver the rightful punishment, whilst simultaneously setting an example that such behaviour would not be tolerated.

To Honour Albert Anselmi, John Scalise and Joseph Guinta
for their loyalty and service
Your presence is requested at a gala dinner
to be held in the ballroom of the
Lexington Hotel, on May 8, 1929,
at 8.00pm

So read the invitation received by Philip D'Andrea, Orchell DeGrazio, Rocco De Grazia, Charlie Fischetti, Louis 'Little New York' Campagna, James 'King of the Bombers' Belcastro, Capone's younger brother Ralph, Jake 'Greasy Thumb' Guzik, the Outfit's principal whoremaster and accountant, Frank 'The Enforcer' Nitti, the Outfit's debt collector, and Jack McGurn. These men represented the inner sanctum of the Outfit, the men closest to Capone, with the first six names representing the bodyguard and hit man entourage. The three guests of honour had each been privately informed about the dinner to be held in their favour, to celebrate their unquestioning and loyal service to the Outfit. Needless to say, they were overwhelmed by such acclaim, firmly believing that they now had Capone's implicit trust and as such, their plans for a coup would never be suspected. The three men agreed that they would never enjoy another party such as this.

The evening of the party arrived and the guests began to arrive for the dinner. The majority of those invited did not have far to travel, residing as they did in the Lexington itself. Indeed, it was Jake Guzik who had the furthest to travel, with his residence being a few miles away in Stickney, the heart of the Outfit's vice empire. As they entered the ballroom, each guest was asked to hand in his weapon. No one had a problem with this as for them, this was almost like a family get together, where there really was no need to be armed; even McGurn allowed his revolver to be taken. When all of the guests were seated, Capone led in the three guests of honour. All were met by rapturous applause, an ovation which continued until they too had been disarmed and had taken their seats. Capone promised the assembled guests a grandiose evening, before telling everyone to relax and have a good time.

The exact menu for the dinner is not known, yet it is fair to assume that as all but one of the guests was either Italian or Sicilian, the fare would have been in a corresponding style. Once the final course had been consumed and the guests were preparing to devour their coffee and liqueurs, Capone rose from his seat, and after ensuring that every man had a full glass of wine, proposed a toast to the three honouree's. The cheers rang out *"Salute Anselmi, Salute Scalise, Salute Guinta"* as each man stood in turn and bowed in acceptance of the accolades being poured onto them.

With the toasts given, the gathering listened intently as Capone began a speech about loyalty, and whilst the exact wording has been lost in the annals of criminal history, it is known that he reached a piece regarding trust. As he did so, he casually removed a baseball bat from underneath the table. Continuing with his speech, he walked around the table, slowly passing each man until he arrived behind the three honoured guests. Without warning, Capone brought the bat down full force onto the head of Scalise, the force of which sent him lurching forward across the table. So unexpected was the attack, that the other guests jumped in their seats; even McGurn flinched, though more through surprise than fear. The blow caused a dull noise to ripple around the room, a sickening thud, like a cabbage landing on concrete. A second and third blow of similar magnitude rained down, only this time the noise was more subtle, muffled even, as Scalise's skull cracked and yielded under the force of the blows and blood began to seep out onto the pristine white tablecloth. The other guests were stunned, awestruck in their horror and aware that Capone had now moved to Anselmi, who seemed oblivious to the lethal presence which now hovered behind him. Anselmi met the same fate as his friend, as Capone brought the bat crashing down, cracking open his head like a coconut. Anselmi pitched forward, his face smashing into his as yet untouched coffee cup, as another two lethal blows shattered his already fractured skull. By now, Guinta had undoubtedly realized the emerging pattern, yet before he could move from his seat, Capone slammed the now bloodied bat into the side of his head. Just as with his two conspiratorial counterparts, Guinta was shown no mercy, as once more, two full force blows reduced his head to a bloody pulp.

So horrific was Capone's display of might, that no one noticed Jack McGurn rise from his seat in order to cross the room to retrieve his revolver. The now breathless Capone moved aside to allow McGurn to take his place behind the three loyal servants. Moving from one man to the next, McGurn fired two shots into each of their heads, thus extinguishing any life which may have remained. Only now did anyone else react, as Orchell De Grazio and James Belcastro, who had been sitting next to John Scalise and Joseph Guinta respectively, inched their chairs aside so as to prevent any of the pooling blood from soiling their immaculate suits. Having been virtually born together in Sicily, fleeing their homeland together, and living and working through their violent lives together, it is somehow fitting that John Scalise and Albert Anselmi should have died so violently together.

Unlike their fallen compatriots, Scalise, Anselmi and Guinta were denied the traditional gangland funeral, complete with obsequies chic. Neither were they laid to rest in Mount Carmel Cemetery, nor indeed any cemetery for that matter, for after their killings, the bodies simply disappeared. To this day, whilst official homicide records exist for the triumvirate of conspirators who dared to overthrow Capone, the final line is chilling in its ambiguity: *'location of bodies unknown.'*

It is quite possible that Jack McGurn felt a certain sense of satisfaction in the killing of his fellow Sicilians. Indeed, it was almost as though he had finally exorcised an old ghost, in that the only other known men allied to his father's murderer had at last met their justified fate. It is this angle which affords the possibility to make further sense of the theory that McGurn had both a father and step-father. As has been previously mentioned, this theory states that his father was murdered in New York, and goes on to say that once he came of age, the young Vincenzo (McGurn) travelled to New York to kill the two men who had slain his father, before returning to Chicago to exact the same revenge on his step-father's killers. This means that by the time he joined the Outfit, he would have killed five men instead of three. If however,

McGurn did indeed believe that the killing of Scalise and Anselmi meant that he finally had closure on this part of his life, then it is possible to see how many criminologists arrive at the idea of his killing five men.

By this point in time, a few of the Outfit's members had come to look upon the relationship between Capone and McGurn with increasing jealousy, though none of them viewed McGurn with quite so much contempt as Frank 'The Enforcer' Nitti. Born Francesco Nitto, Frank Nitti had been brought to America when he was just five years old. Like so many of their counterparts, he and his family settled into the claustrophobic conurbation of New York's Little Italy, and it was here that the young Francesco fell in with his first street gang, The Five Points Juniors. In time, he eventually became a fully fledged member of The Five Points Gang, where he was subsequently introduced to Al Capone. The pair became firm friends, and when Capone began assisting John Torrio with the running of operations in Chicago, he sent for Nitti, installing him as a debt collector, or enforcer within the Outfit. As the relationship continued, Nitti became convinced that he was Capone's closest friend and for a while, this was most certainly true. Therefore, the moment that McGurn joined the Outfit, both he and Nitti entered into an amicable yet frosty working association. Nevertheless, the two men put their feelings down to little more than a clash of personalities, however, Nitti soon began to feel that the more Capone warmed to McGurn, the more he himself was being pushed aside. By now, his feelings went deeper than mere jealousy, for he had begun to believe that when the time came it would be McGurn and not he who would ascend to Capone's position as chief. The structure and organization of the Outfit meant that this would never have happened, for as close as McGurn was to Capone, he was on the security, rather than the administrative echelon and as such, could never attain to the role of boss; likewise, Nitti would never be asked to protect Capone, for the simple reason that that was not his job. This was the constitution of the Outfit; every man had his specific role to play, with no crossover permissible, thus allowing for maximum efficiency. When McGurn was handed The Green Mill, it was a move which tested Nitti's powers of restraint to the limit, for he could not understand why such a relatively new Outfit member should be given everything, whilst he was given nothing in return for all the years of loyal service. Still, the fact remained that McGurn was now Capone's closest friend and as such, so long as Capone was around, there was little that Nitti could do about the situation.

★   ★   ★

It was on May 17, 1929, when the legal system managed to do what the Chicago gangs had been trying to do for years, and rendered the Outfit leaderless. The situation arose when Capone took a trip to Philadelphia, on the premise of attending a meeting with a few of the Outfit's East Coast allies. According to Capone's statement, following the meeting, he and his buddies had decided to take in a movie at the downtown cinema; he had a few hours to kill prior to heading back to Chicago. When they emerged from the cinema a couple of hours later, they found themselves surrounded by uniformed Philadelphia police officers, including the Philadelphia Chief of Police. The Chief questioned Capone as to what he was doing in the city, to which Capone replied, that he had merely been to visit a few of his friends. He was then asked whether he, or any of his friends were armed, something which Capone answered by retrieving his revolver from the back of his waistband and gently laying it down on the ground. Capone was immediately arrested on the grounds of *being a suspicious looking character and of carrying a concealed weapon*' and taken to the central precinct. The subsequent series of events were so extraordinary as to still be the subject of rumour and conjecture, for within sixteen hours, Capone had been charged with carrying a concealed weapon, arraigned, and sentenced to one year in the Philadelphia Penitentiary. Word was immediately sent to Chicago, whereupon the Outfit attempted to digest the earth shattering news.

Over the next few days, rumours abounded as to why Capone had been incarcerated in such expedient fashion. Frank Loesch, the septuagenarian head of the Chicago Crime Commission, charged that the Outfit itself had orchestrated the entire episode, so as to save Capone from the wrath of rival gang members in the aftermath of the St. Valentine's Day Massacre. This is unlikely to be the case, as it would undoubtedly have been easier to get to Capone in jail than it would be on the street. Whatever the reason however, the fact still remained that many of those outside the realm of gangland actually cared very little; to them, Capone was out of Chicago, and whilst his absence was only temporary, that was all that mattered.

In Capone's absence, it was Outfit enforcer Frank Nitti who assumed overall control. Whilst the majority of the Outfit was more than happy to see Nitti at the helm, Jack McGurn could be forgiven for refraining from jumping for joy. He knew that – given Nitti's feelings towards him – he was in for a rough ride and that so long as Capone was away, he would have to watch his back. He was not worried about being physically harmed, for such a move would require a legitimate reason, not to mention permission from Capone himself. However, emotional, or indeed professional suffering was another matter entirely, and it was from precisely this angle which Nitti now chose to work.

A few days after his succession, Frank Nitti called McGurn into his Lexington suite to inform him that he was demoting him to the position of lookout man with immediate effect. McGurn took this rebuff as an affront to his professional capabilities, for the job of lookout man entailed nothing more arduous than sitting in the lobby of the Lexington and looking out for suspicious looking characters. Nevertheless, he believed that this was merely a token move, little more than professional posturing on Nitti's part and as such, accepted his demotion with relatively little complaint. However, as time went on and the situation failed to improve, McGurn felt that he had no option but to confront Nitti about the issue. Unsurprisingly, Nitti bluntly told McGurn that he did not like him and that whilst he was in charge, McGurn would carry out his assigned duties or face the consequences. He went on to say that once Capone was back in the driving seat, he could take the matter up with him, though right now, he was merely acting as he saw fit; save from whacking Nitti – a move which would place his own life in danger – there was very little that McGurn could do.

Finally, in mid June, McGurn could take no more, and so requested a few days leave in order for him to cool his boiling temper and thus prevent him from making a potentially catastrophic decision. Of course, Nitti was only too happy to grant the leave, if for no other reason than to have a thorn temporarily removed from his side.

★　★　★

Title 18:Section 2421 of the United States Code states that *'Whoever know-ingly transports any individual in interstate or foreign commerce, or in any Territory or Possession of the United States, with the intent that such individual engage in prostitution, or in any sexual activity for which any person can be charged with a criminal offense, or attempts to do so, shall be fined under this title or imprisoned not more than 10 years, or both.'* Known as the Mann Act – so named after its author James Robert Mann – the Bill had been passed through the House of Representatives in 1910, though it had been used as Illinois State Law since 1904, when the City of Chicago sought to close Kenna and Coughlin's Levee after two-hundred and seventy-eight instances of enforced prostitution. James Robert Mann had drafted the law after viewing law enforcement figures, which detailed the startling rise in the number of complaints by women that they had been transported across state lines in order to work at various houses of ill repute. Now however, it was under the provisions of this law that the FBI had, for some months, been collecting evidence against Jack McGurn and Louise Rolfe.

On June 20, 1929, McGurn and Rolfe checked into the Stevens Hotel in the Loop, the spot where they had spent many happy hours wrapped in each others arms, whilst the entire North Side mob were being annihilated. This time however, the couple was not on vacation, rather they simply found living at the Lexington whilst Nitti was in charge to be a terrible strain. The pair remained there until June 25, when two Federal agents arrived at the hotel brandishing warrants for their arrest. The couple was informed that they were being arrested for violation of the Mann Act, and in the ensuing interrogations, it emerged that the investigation stemmed from the couple's trips to Miami, Florida. During the decade of the 20's, and indeed on into the 30's, it was generally assumed that girls who danced in chorus lines, or who were actively employed as strippers, were not obliged to refuse should a customer offer her money for a little extra *'private fun.'* Therefore, because Louise Rolfe had previously been employed as a stripper at The Green Mill, it was assumed that she was also a prostitute. Furthermore, as she was actively engaged in a relationship with a known hoodlum, it was alleged that they had visited Miami in order that she work with clients there. Of course, this was not only completely erro-neous, but it was also the only time that McGurn had been arrested over something of which he was totally innocent. The perverse side of the case is that the true reason for the Miami trip was to conspire to commit murder, a crime which is undoubtedly far more serious than prostitution. McGurn and Rolfe were charged and held in custody until the following morning, when they were arraigned before United States Commissioner E. K. Walker, who, upon hearing the couple entering pleas of *'Not Guilty,'* set bail at $5,000 each. It seemed that this could be the point where McGurn's luck ran out, for without calling Al and Mae Capone as witnesses, there was very little that either of them could do to prove their innocence. The federal government's reason for bringing such a charge is hardly complex, for its pride had been wounded and its patience frustrated in its inability to prose-cute McGurn over his involvement in the St. Valentine's Day Massacre. As many people are only too aware, it is a very rare occurrence that one is allowed to make a fool of law enforcement and get away with it.

CHAPTER NINETEEN

THE UNITED STATES VERSUS JACK GIBALDI

It appears ironic that the entire investigation into Jack McGurn and his *inamorata*, Louise, should stem from the alibi given by McGurn in the aftermath of the St. Valentines Day Massacre. The local police, in addition to the FBI, had of course visited the Stevens Hotel in order to verify their stories, and upon being informed that the couple had indeed spent a few nights there, requested access to the hotel register. It was at that point that they discovered they had falsely registered themselves as man and wife, which in itself was an actionable offence. However, the agents knew that this charge alone would, in all probability, never even make it to court, let alone secure a conviction, and so they kept digging, until they struck gold with evidence of their recent sojourns to Florida. Whilst much has so far been said regarding McGurn's criminal intelligence, it appears that in an effort to provide a watertight alibi for himself, his ideas had proved to be far too clever by half.

As soon as the bail bonds had been posted, Jack McGurn and Louise Rolfe were allowed to leave the courtroom. This should have meant the end of their ordeal – for a short while at least – for they could be sure that although the federal authorities had enough evidence with which to charge them, they had hardly any which would secure a conviction. In any case the trial, should there ever be one, would only take place in a matter of months or even years. Even so, the federal government had one card still to play, and as the couple left the courthouse, the FBI, in collusion with the Illinois state government, showed its full hand. McGurn and Rolfe were met outside by Special Agent in Charge E. J. Connally, who was accompanied by the United States Deputy Marshal (whose name is currently withheld under the Privacy Act Section of the Freedom of Information Act.) The US

Deputy Marshal informed them that a warrant had been issued for their arrest on a charge of fornication, whereupon the two were once again taken into custody and brought before Judge Francis Borrelli, sitting at The Court of Domestic Relations in the City of Chicago. Once again the couple entered pleas of *'Not Guilty'*, at which point bail was granted, with both being released on the same $5,000 bonds.

Frank Nitti meanwhile was suffering with problems of his own. Having not benefited, as Capone had, from the years of apprenticeship under the influential guidance of John Torrio, he was fast discovering that negotiating with politicians and rival gangs was hardly as easy as it may have first appeared. Unlike Capone, he was not equipped with the necessary bargaining skills needed in order to keep everyone in their place, whilst equally ensuring that all parties remained content. Within the first two months of his taking charge, there were five attempts on his life, each one originating from a different gang, who saw that without Capone at the helm, the Outfit was decidedly weak. The assassination attempts had a knock on effect in his relationship with the other members of the Outfit. He blamed his bodyguards for allowing the enemy to get too close, and they in turn blamed him for placing himself and those around him in unnecessary danger. Nitti soon realized that he had to take action, if Capone was to return to something which closely resembled the Outfit he had left. Indeed, given the current gangland climate, action would need to be taken if Capone was to return to Chicago in one piece. Eating a huge piece of humble pie, Nitti authorized Philip D'Andrea to contact McGurn at the Stevens Hotel, in order that he return to the Lexington and resume his normal duties as head of security. Resisting the obvious temptation to gloat, the obeisant request was accepted, and McGurn and Rolfe moved back into the Lexington later that day. Had anyone begun to doubt that the guardian angel, who had so far bestowed pitcher after pail of luck upon the life of Jack McGurn, was beginning to lose her patience, there was now no better proof that she was still dedicated to the task at hand and that his personal well of luck was far from dry.

The remainder of 1929, passed off without incident...with one exception. On November 1, a Federal Grand Jury sitting in Chicago and operating under the direction of Assistant United States Attorney Daniel

Anderson, returned an indictment on Jack McGurn and Louise Rolfe. McGurn, charged under the name of Jack Gibaldi, was charged with five counts of violations of the Mann Act, together with one count of conspiracy to violate the Mann Act. Louise Rolfe, charged under her married name of Boex, was charged with five counts of conspiracy to violate the Mann Act. This was indeed a blow, for it meant that the FBI had gathered together enough evidence for a Grand Jury to return an indictment, which in the normal workings of law meant that they had enough evidence to possibly secure a conviction.

The indictment, together with McGurn and Rolfe, was brought before Judge James H. Wilkerson that very same afternoon. Judge Wilkerson was a man of impeccable character, a reformist who prided himself on his knowledge of the law and on his incorruptibility. This knowledge and staunch reformist attitude would, as we will later see, have a detrimental effect on the entire future of the Outfit. After confirming their original pleas of 'Not Guilty,' McGurn and Rolfe were committed for trial, with proceedings set to begin on May 25, 1931.

★ ★ ★

March 17, 1930, and after serving ten months of his one year sentence, Al Capone was released from the Philadelphia Penitentiary. He returned to Chicago amid great pomp and circumstance, much to the chagrin of the Chicago reformists, who had rather hoped that they had seen the back of him. The very moment that Capone's car crossed the Illinois state line, Jack McGurn and Philip D'Andrea, together with a flivver of armoured cars, escorted Capone back to the Lexington. A huge ball had been planned for that evening, a party to eclipse all the Outfit parties that had gone before. In fact, according to reports released a few years later, the party began at around seven in the evening and was still going full tilt at nine the next morning. Further reports suggest that at around seven o'clock that morning, a call was placed by an unknown person to Ralph Capone, stating that Capone and McGurn had drank themselves into such a stupor, that they were currently in the process of wrecking one of their hotel suites. The caller then went on to say that assistance would be needed if they were to stand any chance of calming them down. These reports may of course be exaggerated, yet given the extravagance on which the Outfit sustained their existence, one is inclined – to a certain extent at least – to believe them.

Jack McGurn had been brought to the attention of not only the Chicago police department, but also to the countrywide forces. Just as the Chicago police were out to get McGurn, so were their nationwide counterparts. This fact was proven at the beginning of June, 1930, when McGurn, along with two of Capone's brothers, Albert and John, together with another Outfit lackey Louis Cowan, were enjoying a short vacation on Capone's Palm Island estate in Miami. The sojourn had been planned by Capone himself, though whether there was an exact reason for it remains unclear. On this particular day, Capone was not at the estate, having made a prior lunch engagement. Suddenly, and without warning, the Dade County Sheriff's Department descended onto the estate, arresting only McGurn and charging him with illegal possession of liquor. The same day, McGurn was arraigned at the Dade County Court however, the judge, possibly sensing a railroading, immediately dismissed the case.

A few days later, the Dade County Sheriff's Department again arrested McGurn, this time while he was partaking in his new found love of golf. As he was being dragged off the links, he inquired as to the reason for his apprehension, to which the Sheriff announced that he was being arrested on a charge of vagrancy. When one reads the description of what McGurn was wearing that particular day – white sports shoes, checked trousers, white shirt and grey waistcoat – it seems bizarre that he could be thought a vagrant. However, the police had the full legal right to arrest anyone on that charge, should the person in question fail to show any provable source of income. Whilst McGurn obviously had money, the fact that he held no official, or legal employment meant that he could not prove where he acquired it, and was therefore susceptible to the vagrancy charge. The police however dropped the charge before he could even be arraigned, a virtual admission that they were simply out to harass McGurn, in addition to politely informing him that he was not wanted in Miami.

Law enforcement, whether it be federal or state, and its ideological justice, is very often comparable to a runaway freight train. A great deal of power and effort is required to start the initial movement, yet once the wheels are in motion, one would be hard pushed to bring it to a halt. This was a lesson which McGurn was now learning the hard way. Up until the St. Valentine's Day Massacre, he had remained a rather inconspicuous character to the various law enforcement agencies. True, he had been arrested on numerous occasions in connection with one offence or another, yet these had been episodes when a number of gangsters were arrested at the same time, with his name being merely another on the list. Today however, it was a far different story, for he had now been arrested and charged in his own right, and his name was the *only* one on the list. The animal that is the justice system had its claws into him, and it would be a long time before it would be ready to retract them.

This fact was weighted with further evidence following events which took place on February 1, 1930. McGurn was walking in the Loop, when he was approached by a local police officer who, after asking his name, proceeded to search him. In McGurn's overcoat pocket, he discovered the .38 calibre revolver that habitually accompanied him wherever he went. McGurn was then arrested on the charge of carrying a concealed deadly weapon and brought before Judge K. I. Franchauser who, after recording his plea of *'Not Guilty,'* set the date of the trial for June 24, 1930. At the trial, McGurn admitted that he was indeed carrying a weapon that day, but that he had a valid reason for doing so. He told the court that in 1923, his father was murdered by Black Hand extortionists and that recently, he too had received threats. Given the past history, he held an inveterate belief that his life was in danger and therefore, he was carrying the revolver simply as a means of self defence, a basic constitutional right. The first part of his testimony, as we already know, is entirely true however, there is no evidence to support his statement that he too had received threats. His testimony also gives a certain amount of cause for concern, in that it appears that McGurn was willing to twist the murder of his father into an excuse for his carrying a concealed weapon. One wonders if it had been Vincenzo Gibaldi who was standing trial and not Jack McGurn, whether this would still have been the case. After all, so many facets of his personality had so far changed beyond all recognition, that one could quite reasonably view Vincenzo Gibaldi and Jack McGurn as two completely separate individuals. This argument is however, rather academic, for the jury failed to believe his story, and on

June 26, 1930, returned a verdict of guilty. McGurn's defence counsel immediately made a motion for a retrial, forcing Judge Franchauser to release McGurn on bail and defer sentencing until the Circuit Court of Appeals had made its decision.

On June 28, 1930, the Circuit Court of Appeals, denied McGurn's request for a retrial. Given the remarkable and dubious speed with which the case was heard, the decision was far from surprising. In fact, in anticipation of this decision, McGurn's counsel had drawn up a further petition which was to be immediately presented to the Illinois Supreme Court. It is probably correct to assume that almost everyone, including the lawyers themselves, believed that this appeal would also be rendered unsuccessful, after all the likelihood of the Illinois Supreme Court coming down on the side of a known hoodlum, had to be almost nil. Yet despite the serious misgivings, the judgment came as an immense shock for everyone concerned.

"The defendant's constitutional rights were violated beyond doubt. It is the opinion of the court that it is unconstitutional for a serving police officer to arrest any suspect in the absence of an arrest warrant in regards to the subject's apprehension. It is therefore the courts judgment that a retrial should be granted with immediate effect." So reads the final and crucial part of the judgment by Justices Peller, Ewan and Stracks of the Illinois Supreme Court, in regards to McGurn's conviction of carrying a concealed weapon. The honourable justices handed down their judgment on July 3, 1930, however a retrial never took place. Upon hearing their decision, Assistant US Attorney Daniel Anderson held a press conference, in which he stated that, given the State Supreme Court's stance on the matter, he would not be seeking further prosecution of McGurn. It was indeed a landmark decision, for the court had effectively brought a halt to the prosecution of a man who was not only a known gangster, but was known to be affiliated to Al Capone and who had been the prime suspect in the infamous St. Valentine's Day Massacre. One would be forgiven for thinking that any court would have welcomed the opportunity to put such a character behind bars, if indeed only for a short time.

The precise reason why the court made such a decision may never be known, although there are two schools of thought on the matter. The first is that the court was merely presenting its view on a point of law, and upholding the constitutional rights of a citizen of the United States. After all, no matter what crime a person is alleged to have committed, whether that person is an upstanding member of society or a known hoodlum, he is still entitled to the best defence of his personal and constitutional rights. Indeed, the Fourth Amendment to the US Constitution states that *"The right of the people to be secure in their persons, houses, papers and effects, against unreasonable searches and seizures, shall not be violated, and no warrants shall issue, but on probable cause, supported by oath or affirmation and particularly describing the place to be searched and the persons or things to be seized. An essential purpose of a warrant requirement is to protect privacy interests by assuring citizens subject to a search or seizure that such intrusions are not the random and arbitrary acts of government agents."* Therefore, the Supreme Court was perfectly correct on the point of law, given the fact that in this case no warrant had been issued, or indeed requested.

The second theory is altogether more cynical, in that it is impossible to view the court's decision without wondering whether the influence that Al Capone undoubtedly wielded over the legal and governmental institutions, reached as far as the State Supreme Court. There is no evidence that this is the case, though when dealing with a machine as powerful as the Outfit undeniably was, it is nevertheless a theory that must be considered. The theory is given increased weight, when McGurn's position within the Outfit and his relationship with Capone, is taken into account. Here was a man who was, without question Capone's favourite, a man whom he trusted with his life on account of the fact that he had saved it on so many prior occasions. It was an unquestionable fact that McGurn often acted in the role of *consigliore* or advisor to Capone – one only need look at the role which he played in protecting the Outfit from the North Side advances. When all this is combined with a later testament given by various federal witnesses, which lay claim to the fact that from the moment he entered the Outfit, Capone had been increasingly dependant on, and fawned over McGurn, is it so unlikely that Capone would have pulled out all the stops, stretched his influence as far as it would reach, in order to save his right hand man from a jail term?

As has been previously noted, Jack McGurn had, for a long time now, been the subject of a personality metamorphosis. So far, whilst the changes had been striking, they were nevertheless somewhat understandable, considering his rather dramatic change in circumstances. Now however, he began to demonstrate a part of this change which was altogether more worrying, an arresting aspect which was nonetheless well enough hidden to only become apparent when a study is made of the permanent file on Jack McGurn, held by the FBI. It was while the FBI were attempting to gather more evidence on McGurn, in order to present an even stronger case at his forthcoming trial, that they managed to track down his estranged wife Helena. They had spent many months attempting to find her, for no other reason than to get a background on McGurn, however, the more effort they put into trying to find her, the more effort she appeared to put into evading them.

Eventually, the agents did track her down, to 5202 Quincy Street, an address located in a remote corner of Chicago, whereupon she told of the reason for all her secrecy. It was, she said, because Jack had been sending her death threats, telling her that she should be careful she didn't have an accident, and that he had even sent someone round to their old house to threaten her. She said the reason was that he wished to divorce her so that he could marry his girlfriend Louise, but in order to obtain a quick divorce, he needed Helena to say that they had been separated – that is not living together – for more than five years. This was not the case, and so Helena had refused to lie. Besides which, as she informed the agents, she did not want to get divorced from Jack as she still loved him very deeply, and that she had only left him after he had been implicated in the St. Valentine's Day Massacre. She also asked the agents whether it was possible to drop the charges against Jack, as she felt sorry for him and did not want to see him prosecuted, especially if it meant that he could spend time in jail. Helena also divulged information to suggest that in the time when she and Jack were living together, he was a wonderful husband and doting father to little Helen. But, she said, since they had been separated, he appeared to have lost all interest in Helen, though up until they had gone into hiding, he had been making sure that they were both all right for money. What is worrying about this conversation is the fact that, if true, McGurn had been threatening the woman he once loved with all his heart, and the mother of his only child. Further studies reveal the reason why McGurn wished to marry Louise so desperately, though it is admittedly far from romantic. Having been told by his lawyers, Charles O'Rundall and Ferre C. Watkins that under American law a wife cannot be forced to testify against her husband, McGurn believed that should he marry Louise, the government prosecutors would then be unable to put her on the witness stand. Therefore, one wonders whether the behaviour which McGurn was now displaying in the threats to his estranged wife, were merely the result of sheer desperation, or whether it was the fact that his mentality was now so corrupt, that he was prepared to destroy anything and anyone who got in his way. It also forces the question as to whether or not he would have actually carried out his threat, for he must have realized that to do so would not only result in his being ostracized from the Outfit under the *'non combatant'* rule, but would also have left his daughter a virtual orphan, for McGurn was in no fit profession, or state to bring up a child.

In the end it was Helena who capitulated, and towards the end of 1930, she gave testimony to the Circuit Court of Family Affairs to the effect that she and Jack had not lived together for more than five years, therefore granting him a divorce. It is not clear if she did this out of fear that further refusal may cause harm to befall her, or as she had admitted to the FBI agents, that she still loved Jack and so wished to try and help him in any way she could to secure an acquittal and avoid a prison sentence, even if that meant perjuring herself. All that now remained to be seen was whether or not the divorce would become final before the beginning of the trial.

If Jack McGurn was under any illusion as to the combined government and law enforcement drive to bring him to justice, either by fair means or foul, he was soon dealt a blow which brought him hurtling back to the reality of the situation. The Chicago Crime Commission, a well meaning organization devoted to the obliteration of crime in Chicago, was headed by a septuagenarian named Frank J. Loesch. In 1928, Loesch, a criminal lawyer, had been appointed as Illinois State Attorney, his main task being to investigate the startling rise in organized crime. Once he had been replaced in that position, he gathered together many of his wealthy, like minded associates to form the Chicago Crime Commission. Despite their good intentions, the entire organization was rife with racist and xenophobic overtones, a fact which was glaringly obvious in a speech that Loesch had recently given on crime, in which he stated that, *"The American people are not lawless people. It's the foreigners and the first generation of Jews and Italians who are the offenders, the Jews furnishing the brains and the Italians the brawn."* Whilst it was true that many organized criminals of the day were Italian and Jewish, to intimate that not a single offender was American, was ludicrous.

Nearing the end of 1930, Loesch decided to fight the gangsters using an altogether different tactic; rather than using violence or the judiciary against them, he would shame them and stigmatize them. After having studied a list of approximately one hundred murderers, known gangsters, and what he described as *"murderers which you and I know but can't prove,"* he whittled it down to a list of twenty eight of whom he considered to be the most dangerous, or as he described them, *'Public Enemies.'* Loesch then proceeded to furnish that list to every American newspaper, police department, law enforcement agency, in fact anyone with a vested interest in maintaining law and order. The first seven names on that list were: Alphonse Capone, Ralph Capone, Jack McGurn, Frank Rio, Jack Guzik, George 'Bugs' Moran and Joe Aiello. Naturally, no one appeared to point out to Loesch that George Moran was no longer active on the gangland scene on account of the St. Valentine's Day Massacre. Nevertheless, if any member of the public were unaware as to whom this Jack McGurn was, they were now in no doubt whatsoever, for it was all there in black and white that this former quiet youth from Little Sicily, was now a fully fledged member of Capone's Outfit, and ranked as the third most dangerous man in the entire United States.

The idea of the Public Enemies list continues to this day, albeit under a different guise. At the beginning of 1931, the youthful director of the FBI, J. Edgar Hoover, adopted the concept, renamed it *'America's Most Wanted'* and touted it as his own creation. Over the course of the many decades that have passed since the halcyon gangland days, the idea has been so widely recognized as Hoover's invention, that the name of Loesch has been all but discarded from the records.

The title of the third most dangerous man in America forced the media spotlight onto McGurn. The newspapers had been interested in him before, though he usually had to either commit, or be associated with a crime, in order for his name to be mentioned. Now however, his every move was apparently of public concern, and in every headline his name was perpetually prefixed by his previously unused *nom de guerre*, 'Machine Gun.' When he hosted a party for his friends and associates at The Green Mill, the media were there; they were there whenever he stepped out of the Lexington hotel; whenever he and Louise were seen in public together, photographs inevitably appeared in the following days tabloids. A local reporter, who managed to obtain a brief interview with McGurn on the pretext of inquiring as to his involvement in a recent murder, later gave her impression of the racketeer and murderer in her article published in the Chicago Tribune. *"He has a kind, olive face, set with sparkling eyes and thick black hair that is pomaded straight. His entire demeanor is overwhelmingly charming and it requires hardly any imagination at all to understand his success in his chosen occupation. If one were a total stranger, oblivious to his past, one would describe him as harmless as a puppy."* If any more proof were needed to illustrate Sigmund Freud's observation, that women have a great sympathy for villains, then one is at a loss as to where to find it.

In 1931, prohibition was entering its eleventh year, the depression was biting ever harder, and there was now a mere few months before the start of Jack McGurn and Louise Rolfe's Mann Act trial. His lawyers, Charles O'Rundall and Ferre C. Watkins, had informed him that no more delays would be allowed and that the trial must go ahead as planned on May 25, 1931. As both Louise and Jack knew, the main line of their defence – that they were simply lovers and not prostitute and pimp – would be useless lest they could prove that they were in fact a couple. Despite the fact that Helena had filed for a divorce, the papers so far had failed to come through. It appeared that time was running out. Finally, on April 19, 1931, the Circuit Court of Family Affairs issued the *decree nisi* and two weeks later on May 2, the *decree absolute* declared that Vincenzo Gibaldi and Helena DeMore, were, after ten years, no longer husband and wife.

In light of the divorce becoming final, Jack and Louise wasted no time in making arrangements to be married. In fact, it was the following day, Sunday, May 3, 1931, that the couple came before Justice of the Peace Walter Wright, sitting at Waukegan, Illinois. Emerging around an hour later, they appeared as Mr. and Mrs. Vincent Gibaldi. It proved to be a rare occasion, for the press failed to learn of the ceremony until three days later, when the New York Daily News heralded the joyous event.

'MACHINE GUN MCGURN MARRIES HIS ALIBI GIRL'

Chicago, May 6. Machine Gun Jack McGurn and Miss Louise Rolfe, who were arrested after the 1929, St. Valentines Day Massacre, were married last Sunday in Waukegan, Illinois, it was learned today. The ceremony was performed by Justice of the Peace Walter Wright, shortly after the license had been issued under the name Vincent Gibaldi, which the police say is McGurn's correct name, and Louise Boex. Justice Wright said that he did not recognize either of them. A government official said that the couple's marriage would not interfere with the prosecution of Mann Act charges pending against them. The case is to be tried May 25. McGurn was formally charged with the slaughter of the Moran gangsters - the only man to be so charged. The charges were later dropped.

Unbeknown to McGurn and Rolfe, and to the public at large for that matter, the impending Mann Act case was causing ripples of unrest between the judiciary and the FBI. Whilst Assistant US Attorney Daniel Anderson was officially in charge of the case, he was nevertheless beholden to his direct superior, the United States Attorney, George Emmerson Q. Johnson. (Incidentally, the Q actually did not stand for anything, he purely added it into his name in order to distinguish himself from all the other citizens with that particular surname) Johnson was the man who initiated the FBI investigation and the subsequent continuance of the proceedings. Every government official knew and regarded Johnson as someone who always got his man, a character who never gave up no matter how well the odds may be stacked against him, and it was for this fact that he was highly esteemed. He did however, have one adversary, in the form of the director of the FBI, John Edgar Hoover. Johnson may have believed, or indeed kidded himself, that the feeling between the two of them was nothing more than professional rivalry, yet for Hoover, it went far deeper than that. A megalomaniac, Hoover constantly sought attention and publicity, therefore the fact that the spotlight constantly fell onto Johnson, was a source of immense embarrassment. This feeling was demonstrated in two letters contained within the FBI's permanent file on Jack McGurn. The first letter, dated May 10, 1931, was written and signed by Hoover himself, and was addressed to George Johnson. It referred to Johnson's request that the bureau continue with its full investigation and gathering of evidence regarding the Mann Act case, up until the moment that a conviction had been secured. In the letter, Hoover assures Johnson that *"You can rely on the bureau to assign the most paramount importance to this case. I can assure you that this is our number one priority and that the Special Agents assigned to the case, are fully aware that we wish to see this man serving a lengthy sentence in the penitentiary."* The second letter, addressed to Hoover and written by Special Agent W. A. McSwain, is a summary of the evidence gathered thus far in the Mann Act case against McGurn. At the foot of the letter, Hoover has added his own annotation, stating that *"I marvel that he (Johnson) can find this thing worthwhile within the bureau. He appears to believe that this individual is the only criminal in America and that we at the bureau have little else to do."* It appears that Hoover, regardless of the many man hours involved in the gathering of evidence on the case, would have been overjoyed should the prosecution fail and McGurn be acquitted on all charges.

Despite the rumblings of discontent, the trial of McGurn and Rolfe for violation, and conspiracy to violate the Mann Act, began as scheduled, on May 25, 1931. The evidence was heard by the trial judge Walter C. Lindley alone, as there was to be no jury present. This may seem a startling fact, yet it appears that this practice was widely used under specific dispensations, though the practice is little used today. The prosecution called forth a variety of witnesses, including members of staff who were on duty at the Stevens Hotel, at the time the couple resided there in order to maintain their alibi regarding the St. Valentine's Day Massacre. The list of witnesses, including any names mentioned in the evidence they related to the court, is pursuant to the Privacy Act Section of the Freedom of Information Act, with the actual names of the witnesses themselves also being withheld.

The first three witnesses in the trial consisted of the manager, the desk clerk, and the bell boy of the Stevens Hotel. The manager confirmed that the hotel records showed that McGurn and Rolfe had registered at the hotel under the names of Mr. and Mrs. Vincent Gibaldi. The couple was assigned to Room 1919A, and that he had been informed by his staff that neither party had left the room until February 15, 1929. The desk clerk stated that he was on duty the day that McGurn and Rolfe registered at the hotel, and that he could confirm the manager's account that they had registered under the names of Mr. and Mrs. Vincent Gibaldi. The bell boy was the next witness to take the stand however, he proved rather less forthcoming than his work colleagues. He stated that he was on duty on February 14, 1929, and that he made deliveries of newspapers to various residents of the hotel. When he was asked whether he delivered newspapers to room 1919A, he stated that he could not remember. His memory failed to improve even after he was shown a sworn statement, signed by him, stating that he had in fact delivered papers to that room. Even the threat of a jail sentence for contempt of court could not jog his memory. This phenomenon has occurred on many previous occasions, whereby a witness in a gangster trial cannot remember where he or she was, or what he or she was doing, on the day in question. It happened so often in fact, that the media came to adopt the name given to the condition by Dion O'Banion: Chicago Amnesia

The next witnesses for the prosecution were members of staff at the Dallas Park Hotel, in Miami, Florida. The desk clerk stated that he distinctly remembered checking McGurn and Rolfe into the hotel under the name of Mr. and Mrs. Vincent D'Oro from Havana, Cuba. He said that the female defendant arrived first, and announced that her husband would be joining her later, and that later that day, the gentleman arrived at the hotel driving a cream or yellow Packard that he believed to be owned by Al Capone. The curious point in this testimony is the fact that he would never, could never have known that Capone owned the Packard, for it was a rental car, and therefore owned by the Florida Motor Sales Company and not Capone. It is therefore reasonable to assume that this information was either common knowledge throughout the Miami community, in that Capone had been seen driving the same car and so citizens believed him to be the owner or, that the information had been fed to him in order that he may testify to that effect in court, thereby inextricably linking McGurn to Capone.

Next came the bell boy employed at the same hotel. He testified that he saw the couple on several occasions, and that on one occasion in particular, he rode up to their room in the elevator in order to deliver a package. He stated that he let himself into the room and upon entering, he noticed a machine gun lying on the bed, and that curiosity then got the better of him and he began to look around the room. He went on to say that he opened the wardrobe, and in a bag, he noticed a thousand rounds of ammunition. It is not specified as to whether he was asked if he counted the ammunition, for if he did not – which indeed may be the case – it seems unlikely that he would have known at a glance how many rounds there were. Of course, he may have meant that he saw a lot of ammunition, and that a thousand was purely a number which came into his head.

The second day of the trial brought with it a revelation from the manager of the Dallas Park Hotel. He was due to take the stand in order to show the court the page of the hotel register signed by the defendants. However, he telephoned the Assistant US Attorney Daniel Anderson that morning, to inform him that his hotel room had been broken into the previous evening, and that the page in question had been stolen. When asked to elaborate on this fact, he said that he had gone to a bar the previous evening so that he could have a nightcap to help him sleep. He said that a few minutes after entering the bar, a man came over to his table and asked if he minded if he joined him, to which he replied that he did not. They talked for a few hours, during which time the man ordered several drinks, mainly top quality bourbon, and that when he informed the man that he had to leave and so wished to pay his share of the bill, the man replied that it had been taken care of. He stated that he believed this to be strange, for he had not seen the man move from the table in order to pay the bill, nor had he seen him hand any money to anyone. He then went on to state that upon returning to his hotel, he discovered that the door to his room was open, and the page from the hotel register was missing. When asked if anything else had been taken, he replied that his identification card containing his name and address had also been stolen. He then informed Anderson that he was now in fear of his life, and so would not be appearing at court that day, continuing that he did not care if he was charged with contempt of court: he would much rather lose his liberty than his life.

Once the court had been informed that the hotel manager would not be appearing that day, the next witness was called. The manager of the Florida Motor Sales Company, 1220 Biscayne Boulevard, Miami, Florida took the stand, and testified that in December of 1928, and January 1929, he rented several automobiles to Al Capone. One of these automobiles was a 1929, yellow Packard roadster, engine number 210429, serial number 210267, and that he later saw the defendant driving around Miami in the said automobile.

In their defence, O'Rundall and Watkins produced no witnesses whatsoever, save for McGurn himself, for to do so would have meant calling any number of the Outfit's members, including Capone. O'Rundall and Watkins presented to the court the certificate of McGurn and Rolfe's marriage, stating that this would prove that they were lovers, and that there was nothing more sinister to the matter. Charles O'Rundall stated that the trips which the couple took together were simple holidays, the kind taken by most couples all over America. He charged that *"The government seems to have picked these two out of a thousand who have violated the Mann Act. Theirs was a love affair. McGurn was trying to get a divorce at the time, the girl already had been divorced and they were only waiting for the first opportunity to get married."* He also went on to say that the prosecution was not particularly bothered as to whether Louise Rolfe was or was not a prostitute, rather that it was a source of immense disgust to US Attorney Johnson and Assistant US Attorney Daniel Anderson, that the two lovers were residing together out of wedlock, and therefore, there was no substance whatsoever to the prosecution's case.

When McGurn took the stand, he was asked by Assistant US Attorney Anderson, about the time he was charged with carrying a concealed weapon, though he failed to add onto that, the fact that the initial arrest had been deemed unconstitutional. McGurn stated, as he had done at the original trial, that in 1923, his father was murdered and that he had since received threats, *"that's why I carried the gun"* he said. However, he added that *"As for the machine gun and a thousand rounds of ammunition, that's all wrong."*

On May 28, Judge Lindley ordered both prosecution and defence attorneys to file their final summations, and upon reading and considering each in turn, he would then present his decision. That decision came two months later, on July 22, 1931. Judge Lindley found Jack McGurn and Louise Rolfe guilty on all five counts of violation, and conspiracy to violate the Mann

Act. He imposed an immediate sentence of four years for McGurn, the maximum sentence that could be imposed, to be served in Leavenworth penitentiary, and a minimum four months for Louise, to be served in the Cook County Jail. *"However, once the felon has served two years of the sentence"* Lindley announced in reference to McGurn, *"I shall recommend that he be considered eligible for parole."* Before passing sentence, Judge Lindley, in response to Charles O'Rundall's charge that this sort of behaviour goes on every day, said that *"If there are many similar violations, it is a sad commentary on our civilization. As long as we believe in the principles of monogamous marriage, I must find the defendants guilty. The marriage vows are the foundation of our moral laws. This is a serious crime. If our civilization is to amount to anything, we must observe the moral traditions and teachings that have been passed down to us. These things cannot go on."*

Charles O'Rundall and Ferre C. Watkins immediately filed a motion for a retrial, though rather unsurprisingly, this request was denied. Judge Lindley however, did grant the attorneys leave to appeal. An application for bail was then made, pending the outcome of the appeal. This request was granted, with both McGurn and Rolfe being released on bonds of $15,000 and $3,000 respectively.

As soon as the verdict was announced, the media machine sprang into action, only this time the couple found themselves adorning the front pages of virtually every newspaper in Chicago. The Chicago Herald & Examiner ran the headline:

MCGURN GUILTY
JUDGE CALLS FLORIDA TRIP GRAVE OFFENSE

———

Capone Gangster Sorry for
"Blonde Alibi"; Louise Says
'I'm as guilty as Jack is'

The Chicago Daily Tribune followed suit declaring:

MCGURN AND WIFE SENTENCED IN MANN ACT CASE
He Must Go To Prison, She To Jail

Whilst the Chicago Daily News carried the headline

MACHINE GUN JACK GETS TWO YEARS
BLOND ALIBI, FOUR MONTHS

---

90 DAYS FOR APPEAL

Even the New York Journal chimed in with its own:

KILLER MCGURN AND BLONDE GUILTY

A trivial, yet noteworthy fact, is that in today's American climate, the last headline would have held the paper open to a law suit, on the grounds that McGurn had never been convicted of any killings whatsoever.

The verdict sent McGurn's senses reeling. At no point in time had he ever considered that he or Louise would be found guilty. In fact, his emotions were heightened by the fact that both were indeed innocent of all the charges laid before them. The feelings of total injustice boiled within him, just as they would in anyone who had been convicted of a crime they did not commit. Moreover, he felt an immense sadness for Louise, for in spite of what anyone may have thought of their relationship, he did love her immensely. He knew that although he had married her in order that she would not be put on the witness stand, he would have married her one day anyway. To him, the prosecution had only served to make them marry sooner than they had planned. As they stepped into their dark Cadillac to make their way back to the Lexington from the courthouse, McGurn was unusually silent, lost in a tumultuous cavalcade of thoughts. Not since the death of his father had he felt such an overwhelming sense of anger, mixed with a loss of what to do next. His silence let Louise know what he was feeling, and whilst she would have been lying had she said that she was not frightened of the possibility of a jail term, her only thoughts were now for her husband. Nevertheless, there was little that either of them could do except sit and wait, and hope that their legal team knew what they were doing.

The guilty verdicts were undoubtedly a blow to McGurn's system, and once again it seemed as if his guardian angel had deserted him, only this time for good. The government, or rather the United States Attorney George E. Q. Johnson, could have been excused for feeling rather pleased with himself, for not only had he successfully targeted McGurn, but he had effectively issued a threat against McGurn's boss and mentor Al Capone. Unlike any gangland threats however, this was one caveat from which McGurn could not protect him.

Earlier in the year of 1931, a Federal Grand Jury had returned five indictments against Capone, charging him with federal income tax evasion between the years of 1924, to 1929. They charged that in those four years, Capone had enjoyed an income of $1,038,660.84, on all of which he had failed to pay a single cent in taxes. This meant that the government believed it was owed the grand total of $215,080.48 in back taxes. The Grand Jury also returned a separate indictment, charging him with conspiracy to violate the prohibition laws between the years 1922, and 1931. Thus far, Capone's able attorneys Vincent Giblin and Michael Ahern, had successfully managed to stall the inevitable trial on four separate occasions however, it now seemed that their time had finally run out.

McGurn had barely arrived back at the Lexington after hearing the guilty verdict against him, than Capone's lawyers arrived to inform their client that a pleas and directions hearing had been scheduled for July 30, and that there was nothing they could do to stall it. George Johnson however, proved that he had one more trick up his sleeve, for the very same day, Capone's lawyers returned bearing a plea bargain directly from the lips of the eminent US Attorney. If Capone would plead guilty to the tax evasion charges, Johnson would not only drop the conspiracy to violate the prohibition laws charge, but would also guarantee that the government would not press for the maximum sentence, in fact they would recommend a sentence of no more than two years. However, should he choose to plead not guilty and run a trial, the government would have no choice but to prosecute him to the full extent of the law. The final part of the message was that Johnson wanted an answer within two days. After forty eight hours of rumination, Capone sent an emissary to Johnson with his answer. He had a deal.

On July 30, 1931, Capone arrived at the Federal Court Building for his pleas and directions hearing, presided over by Judge James H. Wilkerson.

The hearing was technically a formality, for in accordance with the deal that had been struck between himself and the US Attorney, Capone would enter a plea of guilty, at which point the court would be adjourned until a later date, when sentencing would begin. However, Judge Wilkerson was set to prove that he was not the kind of man to effectively allow the most notorious gangster in Chicago, if not the world, to get away. As Capone took the stand, George Johnson announced that a deal had been done with the defendant, and that he was under the impression that a guilty plea would be entered. At this point, before Capone or Johnson could say anything else, Judge Wilkerson announced that he was not party to any deal, and that should the defendant choose to plead guilty, he should do so in the knowledge that no recommendation of a lighter sentence would be taken into account. Undoubtedly, both Johnson and Capone were stunned by Wilkerson's remarks, so much so that Johnson threw a glance in Capone's direction, indicating that the ball was now in his court. Realizing that he had been effectively backed into a corner, whilst being unsure as to whether Johnson's tendencious view had caused him to purposely create this subterfuge, Capone did what came naturally to him and retaliated. Following the reading of the charges, the question was asked as to how the defendant wished to plead. The reply was forthright and adamant, 'Not Guilty.' Whether this had indeed been the intended outcome, was a question which was now rendered rather academic, as Judge Wilkerson ordered Capone to return to court on October 6, 1931, at which point the trial would begin. There was now little which could be done to halt the impending battle between the gangster's machine gun and the sword of justice.

The St. Valentines Day Massacre. McGurn's machine gunners
left a scene of carnage never before seen on the streets
of prohibition era Chicago.
(John Binder Collection)

Crowds gather outside the S-M-C Cartage Company, headquarters of the North Side gang and scene of the St. Valentine's Day Massacre.
(John Binder Collection)

Long since demolished, the S-M-C Cartage Company building no longer remains. In a poignant reminder of life, seven small trees now stand where once the North side gang perished.
(Author's Collection)

Cook County Court Building where Jack McGurn would spend many
hours at war with the judiciary.
(Author's Collection)

1928, 'Machine Gun' Jack McGurn takes counsel with his attorney's
Charles O'Rundall (right) and Ferre C. Watkins (left).
(Chicago Historical Society – ICHi-26692)

Jack McGurn listens intently to proceedings, whilst his blonde alibi,
Louise Rolfe, glances to the camera.
(Chicago Historical Society – DN-0088601)

Joe Aiello, (right) was the
last of the North Siders. His
$50,000 open contract on
Capone ensured his swift
execution at the hands of
McGurn.
(Jonh Binder Collection)

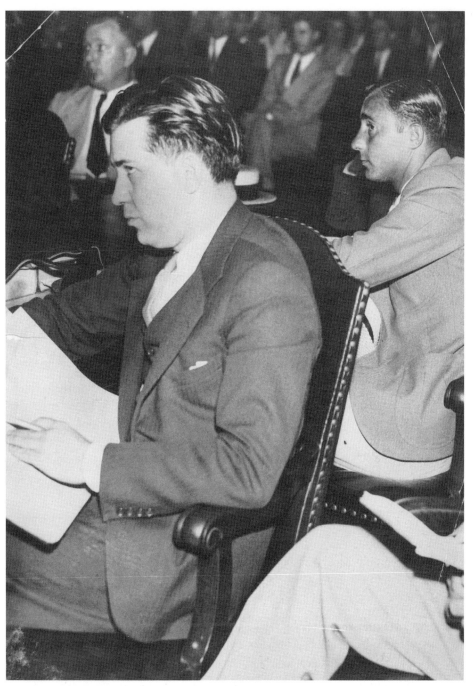

Jack Gebardi, alias Jack McGurn, fights his Mann Act case with attorney, Ben Feldman (left). His eventual exoneration by the U.S. Supreme Court was a consummate embarrassment to the government of the time.
(Chicago Historical Society – ICHi-26693)

McGurn tees off for another
round of his favourite sport.
(Jonh Binder Collection)

Jack and Louise take time out to
relax on the beach.
(Jonh Binder Collection)

A fine example of the luxurious
type of car favoured by McGurn,
a 1930, long wheel base,
Packard Roadster.
(Author's Collection)

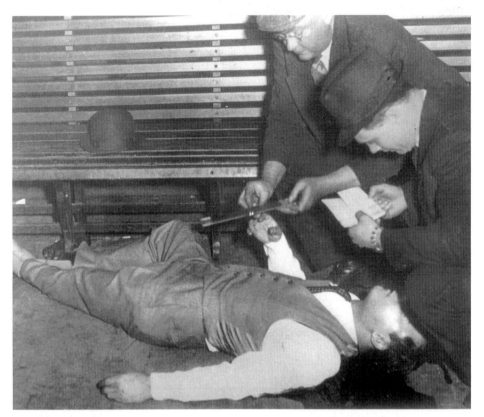

Poetic Justice: 'Machine Gun' Jack McGurn lies dead on the floor of the Avenue Recreation Rooms, gunned down in the same fashion as so many of his own victims.
(Jonh Binder Collection)

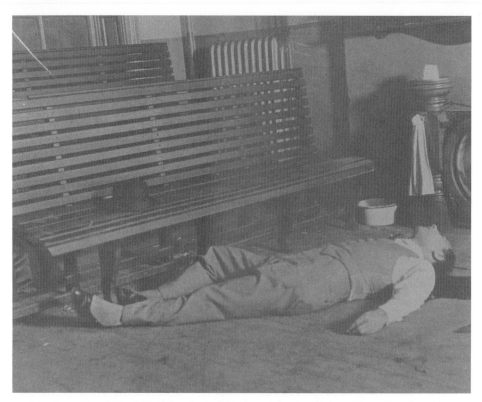

Having identified the body, officers step back to allow the baying
press photographers to have their fill.
(Jonh Binder Collection)

Jack's mother, Josephine died
just three years after her son's
death and now lies next to
him in Mount Carmel
Cemetery.
(Author's Collection)

Head Stone of Vincent Gebardi,
alias 'Machine Gun' Jack McGurn,
on a cold winter's day in Chicago's
Mount Carmel Cemetery.
(Author's Collection)

CHAPTER TWENTY

THE LAST OF THE NORTH SIDERS

Dante Alighieri, the great Italian play write and poet, in one of his greatest works, *Convivio*, wrote that '*The man must not forget the favours of a less important friend, when he becomes the friend of a more important one.*' This statement could have been written advice for a North Side pimp and political fixer named Jack Zuta. Zuta, a short, podgy man with a round face and mournful Basset Hound eyes that accented his soft bow-like mouth, had begun his career with Al Capone and John Torrio, during the formative years of their Chicago Empire. He was known as a man who could get you anything and at anytime, for the right price of course. In the aftermath of the North Siders assassination attempt on the life of John Torrio, Zuta mistakenly believed that there was about to be a change in the power structure, and promptly shifted his allegiance to the Weiss-Drucci-Moran faction. With them, he became the political fixer of the North Side, ensuring that business continued undisturbed by the appropriation of funds to the correct police officers and government officials. This convenient relationship continued until February 14, 1929, when Zuta suddenly discovered that he was now without an employer. In an effort to remain in employment, as well as wishing to prolong his time on earth, the podgy gangster turncoat scurried back to the Capone side of town, in order to beg forgiveness and to reapply for his old job.

Despite various protests from his aides and advisors, Capone agreed to readmit the reformed Judas, though he was informed that he could not resume his old duties as they were now in the control of the equally podgy Jack Guzik. He would have to start once again from the bottom of the ladder, and if he kept his nose clean and proved himself to be a good earner, promotion awaited him. This part of the story should have ended here, but the tale of gangland would hardly be regarded as quite so fascinating if it did.

The now defunct North Side suddenly discovered that it had a new leadership. It came in the form of the Aiello brothers, namely Giuseppe or Joe, Salvatore, known as Sam and Pietro or Pete. This emergence of power was not really new, rather just forgotten, for the Aiello brothers had initially fancied themselves as the successors to the old Genna territory. Following the demise of the infamous brothers, they briefly assumed control of Little Italy, in addition to their powerful positions in the North Side hierarchy, when the infamous massacre had taken place. In the aftermath of this event they had laid low, not daring to show their faces lest they were identified and dealt with as yet another Capone enemy. However, with the dust well and truly settled, they now foresaw that the time was right, that they could rear their heads and reassume control, not only over Little Italy, but over the entire North Side.

One could be forgiven for thinking that the brothers Aiello were more than a little thin on the intelligence side, for it soon became apparent that they also had designs on the Capone Empire. A brief look at the recent history would hardly have gone a miss; a bloody tale of disastrous conse-quences befalling anyone who even dared attempt a coup on the mighty Outfit. Indeed, their thinking was very much along the same lines as those North Siders who had gone before, in that each one considered themselves stronger and better prepared than their old comrades. Joe Aiello in partic-ular, wanted the head of Capone, still smarting as he was over the *'Big Fellow's'* continual blocking of his succession in the Unione Siciliana. Together, the brothers believed that with virtually no opposition to their reign, they were now the most powerful leadership that the North Side would ever have, and save from publishing a declaration of war in the Chicago Tribune, they announced that they were at war with the Outfit.

The tale of bad blood between the Aiello's and Capone would not be complete without elaboration over the point of the Unione Siciliana. Since the death of Michael Merlo, each subsequent leader of the Unione had been sponsored, either wholly or in part, by Capone. Thus, once in power, the leader had ultimately favoured Capone in all gangland negotiations, a source of tremendous chagrin to Joe Aiello, who fancied that one day he would sit that powerful seat. However, he knew that with Capone effectively ruling the city, his dream would never be realized. This was of course entirely correct, for Capone was determined that Aiello would never ascend to such high ranks, meaning that the power struggle between North and South was set to continue.

Throughout early months of 1930, the Aiello brothers made numerous assassination attempts, not on Capone, but rather on the lives of his immediate bodyguards. The Aiello's idea was simple – if not effective – in that if they could deplete the Outfit's security, Capone would be left unprotected and open to attack. Again, a short history lesson would have informed them that George Moran had held the same belief when he ordered Frank and Pete Gusenburg to take out McGurn, a move which resulted in the most catastrophic of consequences. Nevertheless, their campaign began in mid February, when Philip D'Andrea was hospitalized with an Aiello bullet lodged in his right shoulder, whilst a few days later Rocco De Grazia discovered too late that he was their next target. Despite taking six slugs in his arm and torso, he went on to make a full recovery.

Next it was McGurn's turn, though fortunately for him, he saw his would be attackers first, firing at them before they even had a chance to ready their arms. Fortunately for the Outfit – though unfortunately for the Aiello's – they proved to be just as accurate and proficient as any of the North Siders who had gone before them, with none of the hits ever really worrying the Outfit.

Nevertheless, one aspect of the Aiello's campaign did worry the Outfit, and that was the fact that the would-be assassins always appeared to know exactly where their quarry would be and when. This was proven in the case of McGurn, when his plans for that day changed from a day spent at the Lexington, to include an early trip to the Loop. He had just stepped from the foyer of the Lexington, when he noticed the two odd looking strangers waiting across the street. To any passer-by, they looked just like any other member of the public, but to McGurn, they looked strange. Whether it was that their overcoats or hats did not really match their faces, or if it was the fact that they were simply standing and staring, whilst all those around them bustled about, he could not be sure. The only thing he could be sure about was that something about those men just did not fit. Suddenly, he spotted one of the men making the movement to reach inside his overcoat, and in a reflex reaction, McGurn drew his own revolver and fired. The two strangers immediately fled, disappearing into the city's thronging crowd, a reaction which only served to heighten his already alerted suspicions. McGurn immediately went back inside and straight to Capone's suite. He now knew that there was a serious problem within the Outfit itself, for no other rival gang member could have known about his change of plans. All of this he related to Capone, ending his speech with a statement which shook his boss right down to his custom made shoes. There was no other explanation. The Outfit had a rat.

Greasing the wheels of the political and judicial machine, not only reaps the advantageous rewards of uninterrupted business, but at times also yields illuminating information. Such was the case on May 22, 1930, when a young police captain on duty at the detective bureau on West Washington Boulevard, telephoned Capone to inform him that Joe Aiello had been arrested whilst in the company of Jack Zuta. Suddenly, the pieces began to fall into place. The rat which McGurn had discovered now had a name, and the name was Zuta. McGurn and Capone now knew that he was the recalcitrant member who had been informing the Aiello's as to the whereabouts of their next target.

Within a few minutes of the phone call being received, a flivver of Cadillac's drew up outside the detective bureau and out stepped Jack McGurn, Philip D'Andrea, Orchell De Grazio, Charlie Fischetti, Louis Campagna and James Belcastro. This was the Outfit's entire security detail, with the exception of Rocco De Grazia, who was still recovering from his Aiello inflicted bullet wounds. Detective Hanlan, watching from the thirteenth story window, recalled later that he believed the men to be detectives escorting a prisoner inside. However, he then observed that the men, all except one, disappeared into shop doorways, alleyways and around street corners. The remaining man he suddenly identified as McGurn, and was alarmed to see him heading inside the bureau brandishing a revolver. McGurn barely made it through the door, before he was forcibly halted by a score of detectives literally landing on top of him. Immediately, he was taken before the desk sergeant where he was charged with illegal possession of a deadly weapon within a federal building. Given his already pressing legal troubles, it appears rather foolish, if not asinine to purposely place himself in a position which would invite further legal inconvenience. Once he had been charged, McGurn was placed in a cell to await the arrival of his lawyer, who would post bail and secure his client's release. It is at this point where it becomes apparent that this was yet another charade, for the only cell available happened to be the one right next door to the cell currently occupied by Jack Zuta. Both Zuta and McGurn hailed from Sicilian extraction and so now, through the adjoining cell bars, McGurn was able to speak to the traitor in his native dialect. It is a well known and well used warfare tactic that the mental demolition of ones enemy, facilitates their physical destruction. A duty patrolman, who was himself Sicilian, listened in on the ensuing conversation, before making a written report of what he had overheard. The following is taken from that report.

McGurn: *"You're dead, friend, you're dead. When you get out of here, you won't make it to the end of the street still walking."*

Zuta: *"Can't we settle this? Give me fourteen days. I'll sell my stores, my house, everything and quit Chicago for good. Can't we settle it? Think of my wife and baby."*

McGurn: *"You dirty rat. You've broken faith with us twice now. You started this. We'll finish it"*

Soon after, Zuta's lawyer arrived and secured his release on a writ of *habeas corpus* or wrongful imprisonment, though his client informed him that he did not dare venture into the street. Terrified, Zuta went straight to Police Chief O'Connor to request police protection on the grounds that his life was in immediate danger. Initially O'Connor refused, stating that the only time he would grant protection to any hoodlum, would be if they planned to head straight to New York and board the next available passenger ship bound for their native homeland. When Zuta's wife and six month old baby son arrived at the bureau however, O'Connor relented and detailed two police officers to escort them home. That night, Zuta kept his word, and together with his young family, left the city of Chicago, never to return. Notwithstanding this fact however, the Outfit was equally determined to keep their word, and within a matter of hours, allied informants both state and countrywide were put on alert to look out for Zuta.

* * *

Much has been said of the relationship between McGurn and Capone, how the two men complimented each other perfectly with a classic yin and yang partnership. Yet it would be inaccurate to say that theirs was a relationship based purely on a professional basis, for the two men had, over the years, become good friends with a shared interest in many various pastimes. One such interest was a love of sports, indeed as has been previously stated, Capone was in awe of McGurn over the fact that whatever sport he turned his hand to, it was as if he had been practicing his whole life. Whilst they enjoyed all sports, it was boxing which held the position as their sport of choice. Ever since he had fought as an amateur, McGurn had retained the love of the noble art, whilst Capone was also an avid fan and had been ever since his youth. Their love of boxing extended as far as to include close relationships between them and various boxers and their families, although it can be said that some of the relationships were rather less legitimate than others.

One of the most legitimate ones however, was the one that the two men held with a lady by the name of Temo Zilla Fitzsimmons. She was the widow of one of boxing's all time greats, Bob Fitzsimmons, the sports first triple World Champion, holding world titles at Middleweight, Light-Heavyweight and Heavyweight. It is a known fact that both Capone and McGurn paid great attention to her, purely for the fact that they so much admired what her late husband had achieved. There is no evidence to support any theory that the men were in any way involved with Fitzsimmons himself, or indeed with any of his fights. In fact, since Bob Fitzsimmons passed away in Chicago in 1917, three years before Torrio or Capone had set foot in the city, the likelihood of his ever associating with the Outfit as it is known today is rather remote.

At the end of May 1930, both McGurn and Capone indulged their love of another sport – horse racing – namely the American Derby being held at Washington Park, Illinois. On that day, in addition to the usual entourage, Temo Zilla Fitzsimmons accompanied them and was delighted when the members of the party insisted on introducing her around as their guest of honour, adding that her every whim be catered to. She in turn, made a point of telling anyone who would listen that all that was written in the newspapers about Al Capone or any of his friends, was completely erroneous, fictitious material designed to malign a successful individual. Whether Capone and McGurn's affection truly was based on respect for her husband, is a question on which only they know the answer, though if one wishes to be cynical, one could argue that they were merely buying capacious and invaluable public relations.

An example of a less legitimate relationship, concerns the story of Chicago White Sox pitcher, Arthur 'Art the Great' Shires. Shires was undoubtedly a great, if not the greatest pitcher that Chicago had ever seen. However, it soon became apparent that he was also a pretty good puncher, though he seemed to have trouble distinguishing who to punch and who to leave alone. Not content with giving Lena Blackburne, the Chicago White Sox skipper, a beating on two separate occasions, he turned his attention to the clubs travel secretary, Lou Barber, subsequently blacking both his eyes. Following this outburst, Shires was suspended from the club and fined the immense sum of $3,000.

In an effort to eradicate this debt, Shires turned to boxing promoter Joe Blackburn, who immediately set up a fight between Shires and a Cleveland import named Dan Daley. Shires KO'd Daley just inside 21 seconds and soon began to fancy himself as the next Heavyweight champion. His second fight was scheduled to be against a former Chicago Bears pro footballer, named George Trafton. However, the outcome seemed to be a foregone conclusion, when two days before the bout was due to take place, Trafton was visited by *'two men obviously packing guns who wanted to know who was going to win the fight'* When Trafton replied that he was, they responded with *"Well that's where you're wrong."* Just as he was beginning to feel himself being trapped into a fixed bout, he had another visitor, this time in the form of Jack McGurn. McGurn too wished to know who was going to win the fight, and when Trafton nervously announced that he was, McGurn replied *"Good."* Trafton then went on to tell McGurn of the other two men who had visited him earlier. According to Trafton, McGurn simply said *"Oh, don't you worry about them. You just go out there and win the fight. They'll be taken care of."* Naturally, McGurn's diplomacy skills at sorting out just this kind of predicament paid off, for the two hoodlums suddenly disappeared, never to be seen or heard from again. Trafton did win the fight, knocking out Shires in three rounds.

A few weeks later, McGurn and Capone took in a Cubs baseball game, being played at Wrigley Field. On that occasion their guest of honour was a man named Roland V. Libonati, a State Senator who would later go on to become a US Congressman. There is reason to suspect that this relationship was far from benign, for when a photograph of his smiling conversation with Jack McGurn appeared in the Chicago Tribune, without any prompting Libonati publicly stated that he had merely been asked over to speak to Capone's son. This was of course a reasonable explanation, or rather it would have been, were it not for the fact that Capone's son was not present that particular day. It may well have been the case that the conversation between Libonati and McGurn was regarding the latter's recent and pressing legal troubles. After all, what better ally could one have to call on should a character witness be needed? Notwithstanding this fact however, all the meeting and greeting in the world could not completely detract McGurn and Capone's attention from the remaining serious business of setting a rattrap.

The Outfit's information network was, it could be said, the very best in the country, with its success due in no small part to the alliances which had been formed with the various other major gangs throughout the nation. There was the Circus Gang in St. Louis, the all Jewish Purple Gang in Detroit, New York's Egan Rats and the Four Points, not to mention the collusion of corrupt police officers in each of the major American cities. So organized was this labyrinth of confederates that virtually any information could be secretly sent across the country within a matter of minutes. As soon as it emerged that Jack Zuta had fled Chicago, the word went out, and probably before he had even reached his destination, hoodlums in their hundreds were on the lookout. For a while it seemed that Zuta was far wilier than anyone had given him credit, for there was no sign of him for weeks, no clue that he even remained on the planet. Then, on July 27, 1930, there was a breakthrough. A call came through to the Lexington Hotel from an informer in Wisconsin. Jack Zuta had been spotted at the Lake View Hotel on Upper Nemahbin Lake in Delafield, a vacation resort located about twenty five miles west of Milwaukee. Further information gleaned from the underground spy, disclosed that Zuta had resided at several resorts in that area throughout the past month, on each occasion registering as J. H.

Goodman from Aurora, Illinois.

The Outfit's reaction was swift, so swift in fact that the following day a group of nine men rented a cottage on the shores of Lake Nemahbin, not far from the Lake View Hotel. From the descriptions given by other vacationing residents, it is generally believed that the men were Jack McGurn, Philip D'Andrea, Louis Campagna, Danny Stanton, a huge gorilla of a man and a newcomer to the force, Frankie Rio and Frank Diamond, who despite being known Outfit members were not considered to be part of the hit crew, Frank Maritote, Capone's brother-in-law, Tony Accardo and Ted Newberry, who had defected from the North Siders in the aftermath of the St. Valentines Day Massacre. Witnesses also stated that the men remained at the lake for four days, and that on each of the days their attention seemed to be focused on the nearby Lake View Hotel. Needless to say, none of the witnesses was aware of the tourist's deadly mission.

The evening of Friday, August 1, 1930, found Zuta standing in the dance hall of the Lake View Hotel. A nickelodeon stood in the far left hand corner of the room and witnesses stated that Zuta walked over and began to feed money into it. The first song which sounded from the machine was a popular show time tune, entitled '*Good for You But So Bad for Me.*' At about the same time, the nine men entered the dance hall, unnoticed by Zuta who had his back turned to the door. Three of the men guarded the front entrance, three crossed the floor and stationed themselves at the rear exit, whilst the remaining three men walked up to Zuta. The gang leader, whose description of being around five feet ten inches, one-hundred and sixty pounds with jet black hair, led police to believe was Jack McGurn, asked Zuta to turn around. The minute he did so, a bullet hit him full in the mouth, the force sending him tumbling backwards over the nickelodeon, as the other dance hall members dived under tables or behind the bar for cover. As he hit the floor, the three gunmen walked calmly behind the nickelodeon, stood over Zuta whose audible agony was slowly being choked by the copious amounts of blood running into his mouth, before firing a total of sixteen further shots into his body. He took two bullets in each arm, four in the chest, seven in the legs and groin and the final shot, the intended *coup de grace,* in the middle of his forehead. Without so much as break in their stride, the nine men left as calmly and as quickly as they had arrived, leaving the lifeless and bloody heap that was Jack Zuta, exactly where he had fallen. It seems ironic that the man who was noted for his ability to get anything and everything had failed to get himself off the hook or indeed, out of reach of the omnipresent Outfit.

The investigating officers, indeed police forces nationwide, were in no doubt as to who had ordered the killing and as to whose men had carried out the final act. The main clue, aside from the witness descriptions, was the fact that Zuta had been shot first in the mouth. His crime had been to talk too much, leading knowledgeable officers to believe that this initial shot was a typical gangland punishment tactic, in that even if he survived, he would in all likelihood never speak again. As with nearly all the gangland murders ever committed, the perpetrators were never identified, let alone brought to justice, although in Zuta's case, it soon became apparent that it was of great political interest that the killers be left alone.

In the ensuing investigation, Special Investigator Pat Roche managed to track down four safe deposit boxes owned by Zuta. In Greek mythology, Pandora's Box contained all the elements capable of leading to the destruction of mankind, and upon opening the deposit boxes owned by Zuta, Roche discovered that they too held the same kind of power. Years of gangland secrecy were over, the boxes finally revealing their Arcanum in the form a cache of corruption memorabilia, dating back to 1921. There were memos, letters and records, all of which implicated police, newspapermen, judges and politicians who were in receipt of monies, not only from the North Siders, but also from the Outfit or directly from Capone. One of the letters, written by the Chief of Police, William O' Freeman, implored Zuta to ask Capone whether it would be possible to have a loan of four C's ($400) for a couple of months. There were cheque book stubs, totalling $8,950 that had been paid to two judges, two State Senators, a city editor, two police officers, the Assistant Manager of the Board of Education and the Chief Deputy Coroner. There was also a balance sheet from Zuta's days as accountant for the old North Siders. The sheet denoted that it represented the income of the group for the week of November 6-12, 1927. The total on the bottom of the sheet was $429,150, with roughly a quarter of that amount, $110,000 going directly to the Chicago Police Department.

Roche handed the finds over to Judge John A. Swanson, a known staunch reformist and pious prohibition enforcer and asked him to immediately present this evidence to a Grand Jury. Swanson stated that he would do no such thing until, he said *"all the connections . . . had been traced."* When Roche intimated that the public may look upon that as a cover up, Swanson reportedly replied that *"they will just have to take it that way then."* Following this ominous statement, the records which if released would surely destroy the entire political fabric of Chicago, disappeared without trace, leaving only the word of Roche against that of Swanson's as to whether they had ever existed at all. To this day, not a single scrap of paper from the five hundred letters, memos or records has ever been recovered.

The murder of Jack Zuta failed to make any impression upon Joe Aiello, who was still proving himself to be the new bugbear of the Outfit. One would have imagined that he would have been at least a little anxious over the fact that, not only had the rat been discovered, but that it was also a sure bet that the connection between the rat and himself had been made. Nevertheless, he continued to take over where Bugs Moran had left off, making every possible effort to get Capone, or indeed anyone connected with the Outfit, no matter how remotely. Thus far, almost every single one of their efforts had failed, the one near miss coming at the time when nine of the Outfit's hit squad were in Wisconsin taking care of Jack Zuta. Inexplicably, one of Aiello's men managed to get past Capone's security cordon at the Lexington and into Capone's suite. At the time, Capone was sitting, as usual in his high backed leather chair facing the window, so that the back of the chair was facing the door. Aiello's assassin fired four shots at the back of the chair, before he was eventually overpowered and exterminated by the remaining Outfit bulldogs. Fortunately, the bullets failed to have any effect, as the chair was equipped with a bullet proofed, armour plated back, an addition which had ironically been given as a gift by Frankie Yale.

When the nine strong hit squad arrived back in the Windy City and subsequently heard of the incredible near miss, Jack McGurn was animatedly enraged. His rage did not stem from the assassination attempt itself, but from the fact that the remaining security had failed. McGurn, as it has been proven, took his job as head of security extremely seriously, and was now both angered and embarrassed that his men had failed to do their job and had placed his close friend in danger. Indeed, so intense was his anger, that it took Philip D'Andrea and Louis Campagna to restrain him from a direct physical assault on those members involved. Once the furore had died down however, McGurn met with Capone to discuss the course of action which should be taken against the Aiello's. Needless to say not a great deal of discussion was needed, for both men along with the entire Outfit, were in uniform agreement that Aiello had to go. Whilst they were discussing Aiello's fate however, the enemy himself was putting his own dramatic course of action into effect.

Joe Aiello's latest plan was as ludicrous as it was dangerous. An underground spy had recently conveyed information to the effect that Capone had a favourite restaurant, namely the Bella Napoli, owned by Joe Esposito. The spy also revealed that Capone ate there at least once a week, and that more often than not, he ordered the fish soup. This information had a somewhat formulaic effect on the mind of Aiello, who immediately dispatched an emissary with a message for the head chef of the Bella Napoli. The message was that Joe Aiello would personally guarantee him a cash payment of $35,000, if he would mix prussic acid into Capone's next order of soup, adding that the money would enable him to leave Chicago for good in order to escape the obvious repercussions of such an act. The chef sent word back that Aiello had a deal, on the condition that he was paid up front. Believing that the demise of Capone was now a foregone conclusion, Aiello readily agreed, and the very next day, the messenger returned to the restaurant bearing the $35,000 in cash. Aiello believed that all he now needed to do, was to sit and wait until word reached the street that Capone was dead. However, things were not set to go according to plan, for the admittedly naive but otherwise intelligent chef suddenly had a change of heart. He realized that with such an amount of money in hand, he could quite easily flee Chicago without fulfilling his side of the bargain, and no one, except the Aiello's and himself, would be any the wiser. Yet for some unknown reason, he decided to go to the Lexington, to inform Capone of the plan and to admit his own involvement.

On arrival at the hotel however, he was informed that Capone was holding a press conference in his suite and that he would not be receiving visitors that day. The chef implored the guard to allow him to speak to someone, stressing that it was a matter of great importance regarding security. It seemed that no sooner had the word *'security'* left his lips, than he was greeted by Jack McGurn, who informed him that anything he had to say, he could say to him. The chef proceeded to relate a rather prolix account of the Aiello offer, including his own potential involvement. Initially, McGurn thought that this was nothing more than a well orchestrated joke, after all, who would agree to kill Al Capone and then go to admit the deed to the man himself. However, McGurn took the chef far more seriously when he was shown the money, for he knew that there were very few other explanations as to where a chef could obtain $35,000. By now the chef had reduced himself to little more than a blubbering wreck, a fact which in all probability helped save his life. McGurn took pity on him, telling him that he could keep the money and his life on the condition that he leave Chicago within the next twenty four hours and never return. Readily, the chef agreed, leaving the hotel more like a scolded infant than a man, whilst McGurn went to inform Capone of the latest plot on his life and to request authority to prepare for war.

Battle preparations had barely begun, when the Outfit received word of Joe Aiello's latest plan. Having heard of the chef's recalcitrance, Aiello now realized that it was his own life which was in imminent danger, thus perpetuating a somewhat desperate move. The Outfit's own underground spies related that Aiello had placed a message on the gangland grapevine – the most alacritous way to place word onto the street – that he was willing to pay $50,000 to anyone who could kill Capone *and* secure his own ascendancy as Outfit leader. Many native Chicagoans, whose trade was based on freelance criminality, realized that no matter what the amount, anyone who took up the offer would undoubtedly be signing their own death warrant. Even the criminal rookies realized that it was ludicrous to even consider that Capone would not hear of the plan almost as soon as, if not before everyone else. Even so, there always have been, and undoubtedly always will be, that certain percentage of the human race which appears to be predisposed to the lure of money, no matter what must be done in return.

Between August and October of 1930, no less than four such foolhardy individuals travelled from their home towns, to try their hand at disposing of the undisputed Chicago ruler. They were Tony Torchio, from New York,

James Russo from St. Louis, Vincent Spicuzza, also from St. Louis, Sam Valente from Cleveland, plus a Chicago born barman-come hit man, named Dominic Cinderello, but whom everyone knew as Cinderella. Not a single one of them counted on the Outfit being quite so organized, indeed, the Outfit knew that each imported hit man was in town before they had even stepped off the train. Needless to say, of the four out of town hit men who came to Chicago, none returned home alive. One of them, Tony Torchio, having no surviving family members, was buried in Chicago's Mount Carmel Cemetery with only the presiding priest in attendance. It is highly likely that Jack McGurn had a hand in the elimination of each one of these potential threats, yet the only instance in which his involvement can be proved, if only with moral certainty, is in the case of Cinderella.

Cinderella was one of the most high profile of Chicago's freelancers, a man of whom it could be said was rather schizophrenic in his nature, having two separate personalities and flipping from one to the other with little or no warning. The primary persona was a rather effeminate exhibitionist, the life and soul of any party, indeed he was so outgoing that strangers would often invite him to their carouses simply to get the evening going. Not the kind of person to hide his light under a bushel as it were, Cinderella turned the light onto himself so that everyone would be aware of him. Paradoxically, his alter ego was decidedly more sinister, a man who could match any of history's most vicious Black Handers for ruthlessness. Should any gang leader put a *'buckwheat'* order, which is to order a person's immediate death by the slowest and most painful means possible, Cinderella was an ideal choice to carry out the awful deed. It is therefore not at all surprising that the Outfit now viewed Cinderella as their most potent threat.

On the evening of September 15, 1930, Jack McGurn and Orchell De Grazio were leaving Sonny's Bar on North State Street. Having been drinking in the bar for a few hours, they decided that enough was enough and that they would head back to the Lexington. A few yards down the street, they were met by an affable, if rather naive barman named Philip De Luca, who was employed in one of the multitude of Outfit owned speakeasies. The three men entered into a brief conversation, during the course of which De Luca chuckled and said that he would bet McGurn and De Grazio $10 that they could not guess who he had locked, in a drunken slumber, in the speak where he worked. McGurn and De Grazio replied that they weren't in the mood for guessing games, and handed him the $10 in order to find out the snoozer's identity. When he blurted out that the drunk was none other than Cinderella, McGurn and De Grazio saw their chance. They inquired as to whether De Luca had the keys to get back into the bar, to which he replied that he had, at which point they told him to hand them over. The awful reality of the consequences of his flippant comment hit De Luca with the force of a juggernaut, yet he was now left with no choice but to hand over the keys. He later told police that when he inquired as to what they were going to do, McGurn smiled and replied *"We're just going to put a pillow under his head and give him a blanket so he don't get cold."* The next morning, the body of Cinderella, his torso blown apart by three shotgun blasts, was found sprawled across the floor of the speakeasy. Significantly, in his left hand he held an Indian Head nickel, possibly a cruel McGurn joke that may have been intended to signify that his life was only worth a nickel.

In the ensuing investigation, Jack McGurn and Orchell De Grazio were arrested. During the interrogation, they were told that Philip De Luca had spilled his guts and told the officers about the conversation he'd had with the two men on the night Cinderella was killed. McGurn and De Grazio claimed that they had been merely joking with De Luca, that everyone knew he was naive and that they just wanted to wind him up a bit. Besides which, the mere fact that they had told De Luca that they were going to go to the bar, was hardly conclusive proof that they did indeed go there. With no possibility of De Luca testifying at a trial, no murder weapon and more importantly, no motive that was obvious to the police, the two were released without charge. A significant part of this tale is the fact that the Chicago police were now faced with a murder in which an Indian head nickel was again a clue, just as they had been seven years earlier. Yet despite McGurn now being implicated in this most recent slaying, the police department failed to make any connection.

Just as they had done when the Weiss-Drucci-Moran led North Siders had begun to get too close for comfort, the Outfit were now slowly eliminating each potential threat with their usual marked degree of accuracy. It therefore appears rather bizarre that Joe Aiello did not believe his own life to be in any more danger than usual, or if he did, he certainly did not allow his enemies to gain that impression. He still came and went as he pleased, going about his business with no security detail in tow. Such was the case on Thursday, October 23, 1930, at 8.30pm. A taxi drew to a halt outside 405 Kolmar Avenue, Chicago, the home of Pasquale Prestogiacoma, known simply to his friends as Patsy Presto. One such friend was Joe Aiello, indeed it was he who had summoned the taxi to the house. 405 Kolmar, was a large, brown brick building, with a series of steps leading from the street up to the front door. The taxi driver, James Ruane, exited the cab and sounded his horn, before standing by his vehicle with the passenger door opened ready to admit his fare. A few moments later Aiello, accompanied by Patsy Presto, stepped from the building into the cold night air. As both men descended the buildings front steps, heading towards the taxi, from across the street came the sudden and distinctive rattle of machine gun fire. Instantly, Presto ran back up the steps and ducked inside his doorway, escaping the fusillade unscathed, while Ruane crouched low behind his taxi, and in doing so also managed to escape without a scratch. Aiello, who had reacted too late, was hit thirteen times before he remarkably managed to stagger into a nearby alleyway in an attempt to escape. No sooner had he entered what he believed to be relative safety, than another machine gun opened up, puncturing his body with a further seventeen pieces of hot lead. With blood pouring from each one of the thirty bullet holes, Aiello fell in a crumpled heap against the wall of the alley. Since the time of Hymie Weiss, when McGurn's warnings continued to go unheeded, Capone had learnt his lesson of dealing ruthlessly and efficiently with his enemies. Indeed, it seemed that everyone except Aiello himself, knew just how this latest war for supremacy would end.

As with all the murder investigations that had gone before, the police knew exactly who the perpetrators of this particular crime were, yet they were at a total loss as to how to go about proving it. As always, no one had seen anything and remarkably, as Aiello had been hit by Tommy Gun bullets, no one had heard anything. When these witnesses were asked what they were doing at the time of the attack, Chicago Amnesia suddenly descended, forcing each one in turn to lose their memory. Once again, with no witnesses, no apparent motive and no murder weapon, no arrests were ever made.

Following the murder of their brother, Sam and Pete Aiello fled Chicago, in favour of the sanctuary of Springfield, Illinois. Their safety however, was less than secured, for Jack McGurn knew all too well the dangers of a sibling's vengeance. He believed that the Outfit would be ill advised to allow the remaining brothers to stay alive and so, with the blessing of Capone, a hit squad was dispatched to the neighbouring town. The hit was unsurprisingly successful, with Sam and Pete Aiello, joining their brother Joe on November 10. Unlike the North Siders who had fell before them, the Aiello's were not laid to rest in Chicago's Mount Carmel Cemetery. Rather their family decided that Acacia Park Cemetery and Mausoleum on the outskirts of Chicago, should be the final resting place of the very last of the North Siders.

With the latest threat to the Outfit's domination of Chicago thoroughly eliminated, a feeling of calm was to envelope the streets of gangland. The peace was however, set to be cut short, for another battle was preparing to be fought, although this one would be fought in the courts rather than on the streets. Jack McGurn and Louise Rolfe were preparing themselves for what could ultimately be the fight of their lives, with their appeal against their Mann Act convictions set to be heard by the Circuit Court of Appeals. However, in terms of importance as far as the stability of the Outfit was concerned, the threat posed to Capone by the United States Attorney George E. Q. Johnson, was the most potent that he would ever face. Had Johnson been a gangster, the threat could have easily been eliminated by Capone's favourite and most trusted bodyguard, Jack McGurn. Yet although McGurn could do what he could to tip the scales in Capone's favour, this was ultimately one fight which Capone would have to face alone.

CHAPTER TWENTY-ONE

VINDICATION

From the moment news of the impending trial reached the media, right up until the day itself, Capone held regular press conferences in his suite at the Lexington Hotel, making one statement after another about the outcome of his fight with the judiciary. Each statement tended to be along the same lines, in that he was of course a little nervous about the impending trial, but that he had faith that justice would be done and that he would be acquitted of all charges. Standing rigidly by his side throughout the duration of each meeting with the media, was Jack McGurn. He was there at the request of Capone himself, for he enjoyed the company of his premier hit man. He had confided many times in those whom he considered close friends, that being around McGurn made him feel secure, safe, and powerful. One wonders at how the most powerful man in Chicago could ever feel more powerful in the company of an underling, yet as Philip D'Andrea observed years later when asked about the trial, *"McGurn had killed so many men and had gotten away with it on each occasion, so Capone could see no reason why he should not get off the hook when it came to a trifling tax charge."* McGurn was good for Capone, and vice versa. They gave each other strength, fed from one another, and so long as they worked in conjunction with each other, they perceived themselves to be invincible.

The Outfit, or rather Capone, had more than one reason to feel confident in the outcome of the trial. As has been previously stated, having so many influential people on the payroll can, at times, yield priceless dividends. In this case, Capone's contacts within the justice system had been instrumental in providing the Outfit with the names and addresses of those twelve individuals destined to sit on the jury; the fact that the jury was selected just one day before the trial was due to begin, proves just how exigently the Outfit could obtain information. Undoubtedly, the list in question did not remain in Capone's back pocket, for each potential juror was paid a visit by a *'dark and sinister looking man, who wished to have a quiet word.'* For the most part, threats were not necessary, for the mere mention of the fact that they were about to sit in judgment on Al Capone, were the only words needed in order for the message to come through loud and clear.

However, the Outfit was not unary in holding influential contacts within the judicial system. George Emmerson Q. Johnson also wielded his own power, and it was not long before the information concerning the leaked jury list came to his attention. Without hesitation, Johnson consulted the man who was to be the presiding judge, James H. Wilkerson, on what could be done about the matter. Wilkerson, never a man of many words, simply declared that matters should be placed within his hands, and that come the day of the trial, everything would have been dealt with. Johnson wondered at how anything significant could be achieved within a matter of a few hours, yet Wilkerson assured him that by the time Capone arrived in court the following day, the stumbling block would have been removed.

The day of the trial eventually arrived, and Capone, flanked as usual by Jack McGurn and Philip D'Andrea, arrived at the Federal Court Building where he had appeared sixty-eight days earlier. Should any member of the jury be unsure as to the level of danger their lives would be in should they reach the incorrect decision, D'Andrea entered the courtroom carrying a .38 calibre pistol, concealed under his jacket. At a pre designated moment, once the proceedings had commenced, D'Andrea had been instructed to briefly open his jacket, revealing the pistol to the jury. Yet before the prosecution even had a chance to make their opening statement, Judge Wilkerson demonstrated that Capone was not about to have it all his own way, and proved to George Johnson that, as promised, he had matters firmly in hand.

In a startling manoeuvre, Wilkerson instructed the bailiff to go to Judge Barnes' courtroom next door and bring back his entire jury panel. He was then to escort Wilkerson's jury panel to Judge Barnes, thus eliminating any possibility of jury tampering, at least that was the theory. It was a fact that, should the Outfit wish to get to this new jury panel, they could very well do so, for there was little that the government could do to protect them, save from sequestering each one of them for the duration of the trial. As always in high profile and sensitive situations, the media played their part to perfection, ensuring that each new jury member's name appeared in the following day's papers. Once the switch had been made, reporters stated that Capone's confident smile hardened into a mask, as though he were trying, with all his might, to comprehend why he was suddenly not in control of these proceedings. McGurn and D'Andrea, stunned at the judicial coup, simply glared at the new panel, as if attempting to telepathically convey their most violent and malevolent thoughts. With no intimidated jury, a judge who would obviously stand for no nonsense in his courtroom, and a prosecution determined that, come hell or high water, they would get their man, there was little that the Outfit could do except to allow events to take their true and natural course.

For McGurn, aside from accompanying his boss to court every day and taking care of the regular security duties, his time was spent in consultation with his attorneys over his own legal battle. Following the conviction, Ferre C. Watkins had stepped aside, to allow an eminent attorney named Ben Feldman, a man with a thorough knowledge of the Mann Act, to partner Charles O'Rundall. A few years later, the FBI, via informants and retired gangsters, obtained statements which appear to give a good indication as to McGurn's state of mind at this time. He was reported to have confided in a close friend, (name withheld under the Privacy Act,) that he was not so much concerned for himself, than for Louise. Reportedly, he said that should all the appeals fail, despite the fact that he would much rather not, he would be able to handle going to prison, reasoning that if he could handle himself on the outside, he could certainly do so on the inside. He was less sure however, about Louise, who for the most part, had been shielded from the real world. This seems a bizarre statement to make of someone who had spent a number of years consorting with gangsters, and who had indeed married one. Yet McGurn was always notably meticulous, just as he had been with Helena, never to allow her to perceive the true nature of his business. Of course she knew of the clubs, the nightlife, the parties, and the seemingly endless glitz and glamour, but she knew nothing of the other side, the altogether more sickening side, complete with its beatings, intimidations and murders. In fact, had anyone asked Louise whether she believed that Jack had committed murder, or was capable of murder, she very probably would have answered in all honesty, absolutely not.

It appears that this was the main factor that the government, or anyone else for that matter, failed to comprehend. They naturally assumed that McGurn, for all his murders, corruption, threats and intimidation, must have had some kind of perverted hold over Louise in order for her to remain with him. It was totally incomprehensible to them that she could have ever stayed with him of her own free will. However, if we take the notion that everything in this life has an equal and exact opposite, then by that rule, there must be a complete opposite to the murderous side of Jack McGurn, a side not too dissimilar to Vincenzo Gibaldi. This side, a side full of adoring affection, lavishness in the extreme bestowed upon friends and strangers alike, a side which prevented him from raising his voice, let alone his hand to someone he cared deeply for, was the only side that Louise had known, indeed that Helena had known until recently. Therefore, considering the fact that Louise had never had cause to see her husband's violent nature, does it remain so incomprehensible that she could, of her own free will, fall in love with him?

★ ★ ★

One of the facets most prevalent in human nature, is that of morbid curiosity. For example, one need only take note of the sheer number of rubber-neckers who stop or slow down around the scene of a traffic accident. By the same token, it is a fact that TV ratings soar dramatically when real life death and destruction are broadcast. The same saturnine rule holds true when it comes to high profile, celebrity trials. Undoubtedly, there are those who merely wish to capitalize on the chance to see a luminary member of society at close quarters, though for the most part, it is purely a case of secretly wishing to see a high flier take a fall. This angle becomes even more perverse when the observer is heralded as a celebrity himself. So it was in the trial of Al Capone, when, after eight days of testimony, the courtroom was blessed by the appearance of Edward G. Robinson, the actor who had portrayed Capone in the hit film, 'Little Caesar,' earlier in the year. The notion of art imitating life had never been more true.

"Gentlemen of the jury. The government in this case asks you not to take a single fact, yet to take the entire picture as it has been painted for you. We ask that

you take every fact and circumstance and consider it. I am going to ask you to think about the thousands of men and women who earn just a little above $1,500 and who pay taxes to the government. It is not public clamor that brings this defendant to the bar of justice. I am asking you to treat this case as if it were John Brown. This is a case that future generations will remember, for the simple reason that it will establish this: whether a man can be above the law. Whether a man can conduct his affairs so that he can escape entirely the burdens of government and that is the record, gentlemen of the jury, that your verdict will write in this case. When you do all this, you will discover that every page of this record cries out, for all to hear, the guilt of this defendant."

October 17, 1931, and the United States Attorney, George E.Q. Johnson's final summation resounded around the white walls of the court-room. The speech was then followed by the summing up of Judge Wilkerson, in which, albeit not blatantly, he placed himself firmly on the side of the prosecution. He pointed out to the jury the ways in which they could convict Capone, and these words, it can be said, were altogether more heavily weighted than those he used to inform as to how to acquit. In fact, should the same trial take place today, it would certainly be deemed illegal purely on the basis of the judge's instructions.

After an hour of listening to their final directions, the jury retired to consider their verdict. The prosecution hoped for an early decision, for it is a well documented fact that the longer a jury remains out, the greater the likelihood of an acquittal. As the hours passed, it became apparent that the decision would not be a speedy one, and eventually the court was closed for the evening, with both prosecution and defence counsel retiring to nearby hotels, whilst Capone retired to his suite at the Lexington. Throughout these final hours, McGurn was requested to remain with Capone, as though he believed that he may somehow double as a good luck charm. Capone was naturally in a sombre mood, whilst McGurn, though it would have been regarded as normal behaviour to attempt to assure his boss that every-thing would be all right, said nothing. He knew from experience, that in such situations, one speaks when spoken to.

10.51pm, eight hours and ten minutes after retiring to consider their verdict, the foreman of the jury, via a message to the bailiff of the court, informed Judge Wilkerson that a verdict had been reached. Capone, his defence counsel, and the counsel for the prosecution, were summoned from their respective quarters. As always, McGurn accompanied Capone, elbowing aside the throng of journalists and curiosity seekers, as they made their way up the steps of the Federal Court Building to hear the final reckoning.

Once inside the courtroom, Judge Wilkerson asked the foreman of the jury if they had reached a unanimous verdict, to which he replied in the affirmative. The foreman was then asked what that decision was. *"On the charge of failure to pay federal income taxes for the year 1924, we find the defendant not guilty. On the charge of attempting to evade and defeat income taxes for the year 1925, we find the defendant guilty. On the charge of attempting to evade and defeat income taxes for the year 1926, we find the defendant guilty. On the charge of attempting to evade and defeat income taxes for the year 1927, we find the defendant guilty. On the charges of failure to file for income tax for the years 1928, and 1929, we find the defendant guilty."*

Judge Wilkerson then asked each and every member of the jury whether this was their final verdict. Again they replied in the affirmative. Capone had been convicted of three felonies, that is crimes carrying a sentence of more than one year, and two misdemeanours, crimes with a sentence of one year or less. Given the lateness of the hour, Judge Wilkerson adjourned the proceedings until October 24, at which time he would deliver sentencing.

The guilty verdict delivered a hammer blow to the world of Jack McGurn. He knew, indeed everyone knew, that there was no way in which Capone could escape a prison sentence. The only unknown factor was exactly how long the sentence would be, and on that issue, every member of society had their own view. The government would of course, be pressing for the harshest penalty of thirty-three years, though they accepted that a term of perhaps four to five years would be the best they could expect. The Outfit meanwhile, held onto the belief that their illustrious leader would not be away for more than two years; the worst they were expecting was three. The ordinary citizens of Chicago also wanted to see the harshest penalty handed down, for over the past few years, the pendulum of public opinion had swung back towards the government. No longer did they view Capone and those like him, as public benefactors at war with the regime, but rather for what they truly were: smartly dressed hoodlums.

The problem for McGurn, was that whilst the various members of the Outfit accepted that Capone was going down and that there was nothing anybody could do to stop it, he needed Capone. His friend, boss, and mentor was also his protector; as long as he was around then McGurn was strictly off limits no matter what events may transpire. McGurn was not an unintelligent man, nor was he deaf, and over the years since he joined the Outfit, he had heard the rumblings of discontent, and witnessed the eyes filled with jealous hatred. He wondered what the future without Capone at the helm would hold, though one thing he knew for sure, was that Frank Nitti would inevitably take charge and that meant that the gangland waters would be less than calm. The time when Nitti was last in charge was now nothing more than a distant memory, yet he could well remember the sparks of friction which erupted between the two of them, and he knew that even now, the same effect was inevitable. The imbroglio also occasioned thoughts of rebellion, for any change in the power structure brings with it the threat of a possible take over, either by outside forces, or more disturbingly, from within ones own ranks. The only option available to McGurn at the present moment in time, was to wait and hope that should the demon of a *coup d'état* rear its ugly head, Nitti's powers of negotiation were less than honed, and that he would once again be forced to admit that the Outfit needed McGurn.

On October 24, 1931, Capone, accompanied by McGurn and Louis 'Little New York' Campagna (Philip D'Andrea had been arrested a few days earlier on account of his carrying a loaded weapon into a federal building) appeared in the court of Judge James H. Wilkerson, to hear the sentence that was to be handed down upon the gangland ruler. Once the bailiff had called order to the court, Wilkerson ordered that the defendant approach the bar before he orated his sentence. If the Outfit thought that the verdict was a bombshell, then what was about to come, held the force of an atomic blast. On the first felony charge, Wilkerson handed out a sentence of five years, together with a fine of $10,000. The same sentence was handed down for the following two felonies. On the first misdemeanour charge, the sentence was that of one year and a $10,000 fine. The same held true for the second misdemeanour. None of this was unexpected, for everyone had believed that the ruling would be a series of concurrent sentences. However, that was precisely what Wilkerson did not have mind. He declared that on the first two felony charges, the sentences would run concurrently, whilst the sentences on the remaining charges would be consecutive and cumulative. This meant that the supreme Chicagoan ruler had been sentenced to a total of seventeen years, of which he was demarcated to serve eleven. Ten of those would be served in a federal penitentiary. In addition to his incarceration, he had been ordered to pay the grand total of $80,000 in fines and court costs. The entire courtroom was in a state of shock, indeed, one suspects that had the four walls of the building collapsed and the roof had caved in, scarcely anyone would have noticed.

Leavenworth penitentiary is a maximum security penal institution located in Leavenworth County, Kansas. Its nickname, 'The Big Top,' stems from the placement, in 1926, of a large dome atop the central rotunda. The penitentiary began its life in 1895, when an act of Congress decreed that a military prison should be constructed on the site. Leavenworth already had its own prison, though serious overcrowding called for a new and bigger institution. To save on labour costs, the inmates from the existing prison were marched the three and a half miles to the proposed site, working ten hours a day constructing their new 'home.' The first residents entered the building in 1906, and since that time, the penitentiary had boasted the highest security levels in the entire United States. Up until the new institution came into existence, the system had seen a dramatic rise in the number of inmates attempting to tunnel to freedom. In order to combat this problem, the new penitentiary was surrounded by outer walls measuring forty feet high, and descending a further forty feet below ground. Maximum security meant that the inmates housed there were regarded as the greatest threat to society, and as such, in 1931, Leavenworth was regarded as the most vicious and hostile prison in the country. This reputation exists even today, due mainly to the serious overcrowding within the facility, with one-thousand, seven hundred and seventy-nine inmates squeezed into a building designed to hold one-thousand, one hundred and ninety-seven.

It was to this invidious community that Judge Wilkerson ordered Al Capone to be sent as soon as was practically possible. He added that it would be ideal that he be transferred there immediately, though he undoubtedly knew that such an action would never take place, if for no other reason than the dramatic arguments which would subsequently be presented by his counsel. Eventually, his defence team managed to persuade Judge Wilkerson that Leavenworth would be *the* worst place that Capone could be sent to, for the simple reason that over the past few years, various low and middle profile Outfit members had been sequestered there, and as such, should Capone be sent to join them, he would no doubt be free to issue orders to them upon their release. Reluctantly, Wilkerson backed down, declaring that Capone be sent to the Cook County Jail until arrangements could be made for his transferral to federal prison.

★   ★   ★

Much has been said about gangster chic, of the need for some members of society to ingratiate themselves with gangsters in order to feel important, or indeed, to obtain the superficial high that is derived from the sense of dealing with a certain amount of danger. This aspect however, becomes rather more complicated when one is dealing with close family members. Such was the case of Josephine Gibaldi, the mother of Jack McGurn. She viewed her son as a hero, a Sicilian son in the deepest traditional sense of the word. Whilst she never revealed it directly, she knew that it was her son who had wreaked vengeance on those men who had brutally murdered her beloved husband, just as the Old World codes dictated. When he had obtained his first employment, he had dutifully turned over half of it to his mother, just as he would have been required to do in Sicily. To Josephine Gibaldi, her eldest son was the embodiment of the Old World, transplanted into the new life she had longed him to have. McGurn reciprocated his mother's feelings, for he had seen how hard his family had struggled, heard of how they put everything they had, including their lives, on the line, simply to get to the New World in order that their children could grow up with a great deal more than they had done. In spite of what he had now become, McGurn still took great care of his mother. Though he did not give her money directly, he made sure that she wanted for nothing, that no longer did she have to go without. Josephine remained, by her own desires, within the confines of Little Sicily, feeling that it was her sanctuary away from the New World evils, though admittedly, she now lived like a queen. There was a certain sense of a continuation of the old Sicilian way of life, whereby the men would go out into the world, earning money and taking care of any arrangements that may need to be made for the good of the family, whilst the women were kept secluded in their homes, sheltered from the decadent attitudes of the outside world. This indeed suited Josephine, for she believed that the outside world never bothered to worry about all the troubles in her life, so why then should she have cause to worry about theirs? It also suited McGurn, for he knew at all times where his mother was, that she was safe, and that should anything at all happen to her, the combined Little Sicily and gangland grapevines would ensure that he knew within minutes.

When one takes this devoted affection between mother and son into account, it is hardly difficult to imagine the rage which built up in McGurn, when he discovered that the FBI had called at his mother's house. They had called upon Josephine for the same reason they had called on his estranged wife, Helena. Because of the fact that the Mann Act case regarding McGurn was subject to appeal, the prosecution desired further background information, in the hope that any further incriminating evidence may come to light. The FBI found Josephine to be not quite so forthcoming as they had hoped. Indeed, they had imagined that with such a disgrace for a son, she would be quite prepared to tell all she knew, just so that he could be out of her hair for a while. Not for the first time in their history, the esteemed FBI could not have been more wrong. The intense matriarchal defences were on full alert the moment that agents W. A. McSwain and D. O. Smith identified themselves and announced the purpose of their visit. It would not be true to say that Josephine was impolite in her dealing with the agents, for she could hardly have been more accommodating, yet it is not only gangland which holds the law of *omerta*, that is silence, dear to their hearts. Josephine talked at length to the agents, about her homeland, her experiences in America, her views on the social ills of the day, everything except the one topic that they had actually come to discuss. She spoke not a single word that gave any clue as to the background of her son, except that she knew he had owned a gun ever since his father was killed. After two hours, and gallons of coffee, the agents finally realized that they were as likely to extract information from Josephine, as they were blood from a stone. Thanking her for her hospitality, the agents left, no wiser than when they had arrived.

One thing which can be said about the Federal Bureau of Investigation, is that they are an extremely thorough organization. Upon reading the permanent file held on Jack McGurn, one comes across information that engenders wonderment as to how in the world such details were obtained. This meticulous attitude caused the agents who had interviewed Josephine, to call on her neighbours, the numerous inhabitants of Little Sicily. To their dismay, they received the same response. Not a single member was willing to talk to the agents, in fact, some were so full of contempt that it was all they could do to be polite. One woman was slightly more forthcoming than the others, though she said nothing which gave away anything incriminating. She told the agents that Jack McGurn, or Vincenzo as she knew him, was a wonderful man and a doting son. She gushed that he would do anything for anyone, and that they only need look at the way his mother lived, to see what a good provider he was. He also helped the community, anyone who needed help had only to ask and it was done. To Little Sicily, she said, Vincenzo was a modern day Robin Hood. When asked what she thought of the things which had recently been reported in the press about McGurn, she replied that it was an *infamita*, the worst kind of disgrace, to speak badly of such a kind and generous man.

Life in the Outfit without Capone was proving to be not as bad as McGurn had imagined. Capone's conviction was under appeal, in fact his defence counsel had not only appealed that the conviction be overturned, but that a retrial should also take place. Pending the outcome of the appeal, Capone was held in the Cook County Jail, Illinois, where the then head of the jail, Warden C. Moneypenny, ensured that he was afforded every privilege. In addition to this, the fact that the jail was in such close proximity to his old stomping ground, meant that Capone was in fact still the head of the Outfit. Whilst Frank Nitti had been announced as leader, it was accepted that this was strictly for appearances only; every decision, movement and day to day business still went through Capone. Despite the fact that Nitti despised McGurn, he was rendered impotent by the fact that Capone still idolized him almost as much as McGurn's own mother did. Members of the upper echelons of the Outfit were allowed virtual daily access to Capone, meaning that orders could still be personally meted out. When Christmas came around, Warden Moneypenny allowed Capone to have a Christmas Day celebration in his cell. It was as though his suite at the Lexington had been transplanted into the Cook County jail, with tiny lights and decorations adorning the walls, even a small Christmas tree complete with the traditional angel sitting atop it. Christmas dinner was sent in from outside caterers, and those sitting down to the meal included Frank Nitti, Jack McGurn, Louise Rolfe, plus Mae, Ralph and Sonny Capone, Al's wife, brother and son respectively. In spite of the government's best efforts to bring the combine to a halt, Outfit life went on as normal.

The year 1932, was set to be an important year in the lives of both McGurn and Capone. Late in 1931, the Circuit Court of Appeals had refused Capone's request for an acquittal and a retrial. Upon hearing the decision, he had instructed his counsel to appeal to the highest court possible, the United States Supreme Court. The Circuit Court of Appeals also upheld the convictions of Jack McGurn and Louise Rolfe. They too were set to apply to the United States Supreme Court, though the law dictated that they should be sent to prison whilst awaiting the verdict. However, their counsel presented the argument that the two parties had been presented with numerous opportunities to jump bail whilst awaiting their hearing at the Court of Appeals, and that by their appearance at the said hearing, they had obviously not been inclined to capitalize on those opportunities. It would therefore be completely erroneous to deny bail at such a late stage in the proceedings. The court agreed, subsequently releasing them on the same $15,000 and $3,000 bonds, pending the Supreme Court judgment. Jack and Louise were under no illusions as to the gravity of the matter in hand. They knew that should their Supreme Court appeal fail, it would be the end of the line, resulting in McGurn being sent to prison – Leavenworth in all probability – whilst Louise would be housed at the Cook County Jail. Capone too was under no delusions. He also knew that should his appeal fail, though he doubted it would, he would have to knuckle down to the fact that his eleven year sentence had effectively begun.

The same year was set to be an unforgettable one in the lives of many

Americans, for 1932, heralded *the* crime of the century. Up until then, it was believed that the St. Valentine's Day Massacre was the most nefarious crime which most people would witness in their lifetime, yet what was about to come was even more horrific than that hideous event. On the evening of March 1, Charles Lindbergh's twenty month old son, Charles Jr. was kidnapped from his New Jersey home. A ransom note, demanding $50,000 for the safe return of *'the eaglet,'* as the newspapers had begun calling the child, was discovered. New Jersey State Police, working in conjunction with the FBI, in addition to hundreds of volunteers began scouring the country, desperate for any news as to the whereabouts of the infant. Even Capone stepped forward, and offered to use his underworld influence to discover what had happened to the child, and also to find out the identity of his kidnapper. In return, all he wanted was a reduced sentence and two weeks out of prison to put the word on the street. Lindbergh said yes; the government gave an unequivocal no. He then offered to pass orders to his underlings to put the word out, and to do everything in their power to find the child. Once again, the government's answer was unconditionally negative. Then on May 12, two months and eleven days after the baby had disappeared, the badly decomposed body of a child was discovered four miles from the Lindbergh estate. Less than twenty four hours later, the body was identified as *'the eaglet.'* The nation was horrified, gangland was appalled, and once again public opinion swung in favour of the gangsters. The American citizens, moreover the Chicagoans, conceded that in spite of all the horrific deeds committed by gangsters, they would never do anything as despicable as to murder a child. The hoodlums concurred, adding that children were sacred, to be protected, and that anyone who merely harmed a child deserved to die. Not only that, but the gangsters had put their services into the public domain in order to help find the baby. Yet it was society's view that the powers that be had, to the people who in retrospect could perhaps have brought about the infants safe return, emphatically refused. Rather than putting the government on a pedestal for their unequivocal refusal to negotiate with designated public enemies, their declination merely gave rise to conspiracy theories that the government did not wish that the baby be found. Today, this aspect is still the topic of great discussion, and will undoubtedly continue to be so for a great many years to come.

Towards the middle of May, 1932, rumours began to be circulated as to the preferential treatment which Capone was being afforded by Warden Moneypenny. Following a short investigation, the United States Attorney, George E. Q. Johnson, declared that Capone should be moved, with immediate effect, to a high level security, federal penitentiary. The government concurred, and on May 16, Capone was shipped – under great protestations – to the federal penitentiary at Atlanta, Georgia. This was a blow not only to himself, but also to McGurn, who now realized that with his mentor so far from the action, Nitti would certainly assume overall control. Notwithstanding this fact, McGurn curiously did not feel as disheartened as he had believed he would in such a circumstance. He believed that knowledge was power, and as such, his previous experience of Outfit life with Nitti at the helm, had prepared him for what was to come. He knew how Nitti worked, knew his strengths, and moreover his weaknesses, after all, it was he who had been forced to come crawling back to McGurn. The one oversight on McGurn's part however, was that it was not just he who believed that knowledge was power. Nitti too held the same philosophy, having also learned from the mistakes which he had made the last time around. No longer would he be so tactless towards potential enemies, for he had seen that in order to be successful, one had to be firm but fair. A ruthless attitude only served to cause dissent, which he had discovered almost to his cost. Nitti had plans, plans which crucially did not involve McGurn.

Oblivious to the contrivances of Nitti, McGurn nevertheless decided that the time had come to dispense with the Lexington. He and Louise had lived the hotel life for long enough, and it was now time that they found a home of their own. The news delighted Louise, as for some months now she had grown tired of their luxurious, yet all too familiar hotel suite. Within days, the house hunting process began. The couple were looking for somewhere and something specific, for McGurn wished that Louise be kept in the manner in which she had become accustomed, which was undoubtedly unashamed extravagance. Over the course of two months, Jack and Louise viewed over a dozen separate properties all over Chicago, ranging from the modest, to the so over the top it had disappeared over the other side. Eventually they found what they believed was the perfect house for them in Oak Park. Located nine miles west of downtown Chicago, Oak Park was, and indeed still is, a seriously affluent neighbourhood. Every prairie style house had been designed by the esteemed master builder and architect, Frank Lloyd Wright, whilst the local residents were extremely proud of the fact that the area was the birthplace and current home of the great writer and poet, Ernest Hemingway.

The house they chose was at 1224 Kenilworth Avenue in central Oak Park, the crème de la crème of the Chicago property market. The house was dominated by a brilliant white facade, whilst the interior held four bedrooms, lounge, kitchen, dining room, and two bathrooms. It was the height of luxury, and McGurn wished that it be decorated and furnished in the same opulent style. Louise was subsequently dispatched on a mammoth shopping spree, in order to purchase all the furniture and fittings they required to make their new home into the dream they envisaged. It would hardly be surprising if McGurn felt more than a touch of *deja vu*, for the scene was almost a carbon copy to that played out when he was married to Helena. Louise had no price limit, a *carte blanche* on what she could spend...and spend she did. Within the next few weeks the house was besieged by delivery men and decorators, with luxurious elegance the only style on the agenda. Before long, the vision which Jack and Louise had of their dream home was realized.

Despite the true nature of McGurn's employment, the couple fitted in extremely well within the neighbourhood. The existing residents, whilst knowing the name Jack McGurn, did not make the connection between the hoodlum and the well dressed businessman named Vincent D'Oro who had recently moved into the area. They did not recognize him from any of the numerous newspaper photographs, and as such, knew nothing of his true activities. Louise too, blossomed in the new environment, making friends, accepting numerous luncheon invitations, hosting sessions of afternoon tea, and generally absorbing the trappings of the well-to-do lifestyle. In spite of their troubles, past, present and most probably future, their life was undeniably good.

The case of Jack McGurn and Louise Rolfe regarding their convictions on Mann Act charges, was heard by the United States Supreme Court on November 1, 1932. For both of them, this was a momentous occasion, for they knew that should the decision go against them, they would then be left with no recourse. This was the end of the line. Despite the fact that they hoped and prayed with every fibre of the bodies that the decision would be in their favour, they nevertheless steeled themselves for the possibility that they could very well be spending the next two years of their lives apart, with Louise in jail and McGurn in prison. (The difference between prison and jail, is that jail is where sentences of one year or less are to be served, whilst prison sentences are of one year or more.) The perverse fact was, that if the court upheld the decision, then Jack McGurn, known gangster, killer, black-mailer and right hand man to the most famous gangster in history, would be actually serving a prison sentence for a crime he did not commit. For the first time for many years, McGurn was frightened, not for himself, but for Louise. As he had previously confided to friends, he knew that he would be able to cope with life on the inside, yet he was not as sure about his wife. She had after all, been relatively sheltered from the horrors of this life, and now McGurn felt that the awful reality would be too much for her to bear. One wonders whether he needed to be so concerned however, for as Louise had shown during her interrogation following the St. Valentine's Day Massacre, she was quite capable of handling herself. She may very well have looked as fragile as a flower, yet her mentality was far stronger than either McGurn, or indeed her ex-husband would have credited. Nevertheless, once their case had been heard, the impending judgment, like the sword of Damocles, hung perilously over their heads.

November 7, 1932, six days after the initial Supreme Court hearing, Mr. Justice Stone announced the court's decision. The following excerpt is taken from the full, four page decision released by the US Supreme Court.

"The only question which we need consider here is whether, within the principles announced in this case, the evidence was sufficient to support a conviction. It is not to be supposed that the consent of an unmarried person to adultery with a married person, where the latter alone is guilty of the substantiative offence, would render the former an abettor or conspirator. Or that the acquiescence of a woman under the age of consent would make her a co-conspirator to commit statutory rape upon herself. The principle determinative of this case is the same. On the evidence before us, the woman petitioner has not violated the Mann Act and we hold, is not guilty of a conspiracy to do so. As there is no proof that the man conspired with anyone else to bring about the transportation of the woman,

the convictions of both parties must be . . . reversed."

The decision was a total vindication of McGurn and Rolfe, and a complete embarrassment for the US Attorney's office. The Supreme Court had determined that a woman cannot be guilty of conspiracy to violate the Mann Act simply because she agrees to her own transportation. They had also determined that in order for a man to be convicted on Mann Act charges, he had to have conspired with a third party, that is, a person other than the woman in question.

The media coverage surrounding the case was immense, and gave way, depending upon the State in which the newspaper was published, to a variety of wide ranging views. The most damning editorial, as far as the government was concerned, was that which appeared in the New York Times. *"Jack Gebardi, better known as Machine Gun Jack McGurn, Chicago gangster, was arrested on Mann Act charges by Federal officials conducting a drive against gangsters. McGurn's 'crime' was that he took a young unmarried woman on a trip through several states. He had married the girl before the federal officials had got around to arresting him, but the Mann Act was stretched and twisted to fit his case in the lower courts and he was convicted. The lower courts actually convicted McGurn and the girl on a charge of conspiring to violate the Mann Act by crossing state lines for allegedly immoral purposes. If a grotesque conviction like that could stand, why not convict a chauffeur for obeying his employers orders to take the employer and a young woman across state lines or across the Hudson River on a ferryboat? Anyway, the Supreme Court set aside McGurn's conviction. Thus, another foolishly framed statute requiring the Federal government to butt into private affairs is construed into comparative harmlessness by the United States Supreme Court."*

Public opinion concurred in the backlash, for they suddenly realized that had the conviction been upheld, then any one of them could have been prosecuted simply because they took a trip with their sweetheart. Eventually, the condemnatory wave of public disgust demanded the ultimate penalty for such a damning vindication, and called for the immediate resignation of the United States Attorney, George E. Q. Johnson and the Assistant US Attorney, Daniel Anderson. Whilst Johnson was embarrassed, he saw no reason why he should climb down from his lofty position. In the end, it was Anderson who capitulated, announcing his resignation on

December 30, 1932.

Never, in the history of the war between gangland and the judiciary, had a gangster been vindicated to such an overwhelming degree. Unlike McGurn's trial for carrying a concealed weapon, the theory that Capone could have had a hand in his acquittal, does not hold water in this case. Al Capone had been spirited away to Atlanta, and now wielded a fraction of the power that he had in his glorious, halcyon heyday. With no other Outfit member holding enough power to reach to the United States Supreme Court, there was no doubt that McGurn had been acquitted purely on the point of law relevant to his case. The United States government had set out to redress the balance, having been humiliated by its failed attempt to prosecute McGurn over the Massacre of 1929. Now, once again it was the subject of immense embarrassment and vilification, though this time the catalyst was its own Supreme Court. The government's best efforts had been summarily halted by a known gangster and there was nothing they could do about it.

CHAPTER TWENTY-TWO

NOBODY CARES

In 1933, the people of America were beginning to accept the fact that prohibition was now entering its thirteenth year and that this, combined with the ever deepening economic depression, was throwing the nation into a tailspin. The government had so far failed to realize the error of its ways, blind to the fact that their *'noble experiment'* was, in every respect, a comprehensive failure. Before the Volstead Act came into effect, the vast majority of the populace consumed beer as their alcoholic beverage of choice. Following the onset of prohibition however, people began to realize that they had to drink much more of the now watered down beer in order to feel drunk. With beer retailing at 25c a glass, whilst whiskey and bourbon sold for 40c a shot, it did not take a genius to work out that it was easier and cheaper to get drunk on whiskey or bourbon, than it was on beer. As a result, many people began turning to the stronger alcohol, and as their systems became increasingly tolerant of the level of alcohol in their bloodstream, they began to drink more and more to achieve desired effect. The overwhelming result was that rather than curbing or halting society's drinking habits, the governmental stance actually encouraged people to drink more, a factor which gave way to its own dramatic consequences indeed, in 1929, public drunkenness reached an all time high. The same was true of violent crimes as law abiding citizens, emboldened and purblind with *'Dutch Courage,'* looked purposefully for confrontations. Prohibition also raised the number of alcohol related homicides to a level never seen before, one which has not been beaten to this day. In 1925, the homicide rate reached its peak, with twenty bootlegging related murders in a single day.

Finally, on February 20, 1933, public vituperation triumphed, and in an attempt to rectify the anomaly, the government brought forth the

Twenty-First Amendment to the constitution, thus repealing the prohibition act. Whilst the amendment had yet to be ratified, so far as the government was concerned, that was merely a formality.

Away from the congressional negotiations, the Outfit was busy getting used to life without Capone. He had been incarcerated now for over a year, and with the failure of his final Supreme Court appeal, there was now no chance that he would return to gangland life in less than six years. With the permanent absence of Capone now a certainty, the numerous Outfit members were coming to terms with regarding Frank Nitti as their over-lord. As with all hierarchal changes, there were a relative few who disliked the modification and had decided to make their own move for power, only to find that whilst the leadership may have changed, the rule of loyalty remained the same. Nitti ensured that the recalcitrant minority were swiftly and severely dealt with in order to set an example to any other members who harboured ideas above their station.

Nitti also set about putting into practice a few major alterations, one of which was to once again demote Jack McGurn from head of security, to look out duty in the lobby of the Lexington. Aside from the embarrassment caused by the move, McGurn did not mind so much, for he reasoned that Nitti had made the same move the last time around, only to be forced to backtrack on his decision. Eventually, he believed, a situation would arise which required his tactical genius, and if he bided his time, he would be swiftly reinstated. However, as McGurn would later discover, Nitti had grown in stature and experience from the man he once was, and that to underestimate his capabilities was a fatal mistake.

For all his gangland menace, Frank Nitti was set to become the least of Jack McGurn's problems. Incensed by the humiliation caused by the failure of their trial, the governmental authorities, both locally and nationally, were out to make McGurn's life intolerable. Whilst they accepted that they were lacking sufficient evidence to bring about any further trial, they were quite prepared to make full use of two new laws which had recently come into force. The first was essentially an updated version of the old vagrancy law, which stated that if any person failed to show that they had a legal source of income, they could then be arrested as a vagrant and fined. The new law went a step further however, stating that as it had been declared that there was no legal source of income, once the offender was fined, should they attempt to pay the fine, they would then be brought back before a judge to explain where they had acquired the money. Should the explanation be deemed unsatisfactory, the *'vagrant'* could then be jailed for contempt of court.

The second law was far more controversial, and which would, over the following years, be the subject of numerous appeals. The law basically said that any person could be arrested on a public nuisance charge if, in the society where they resided, they had an unsavoury or violent reputation. Eventually an appeal was heard before the United States Supreme Court, which ruled that the law violated a person's human and constitutional rights, on account of the fact that one may have an unsavoury reputation, yet that reputation may very well be totally erroneous. However, no such appeal had yet been made, and the local Chicagoan authorities were preparing to exploit them to their full advantage.

The first incident came about on September 4, 1933. For many years, Jack McGurn had been a lover of golf and had, just as with any sport he turned his hand to, become so proficient that he was often urged to turn professional. (McGurn had in fact, been claiming to be a professional golfer for around seven years, for whenever he chose to use the alias Vincent Gebardi, he would often claim that golf was his profession in order to protect his family from the unsavoury rumours and stories that would inevitably be linked to his name) On this particular day, he was taking part in the Western Open Golf Championship, at Olympia Fields. Mingling amongst the crowd of spectators was his wife, Louise, who loved to watch her husband on the links. Unbeknown to either Jack or Louise however, they were both being observed by two Chicago federal agents. As Jack stepped up to take his shot on the fourteenth hole, the agents swooped down and arrested him on the new and updated vagrancy charge. Rather than resisting arrest, McGurn politely and calmly explained that he would appreciate it if he could be allowed to finish his round, after which, he would quite happily accompany the officers. The agents saw no harm in this, though they did insist on accompanying him the rest of the way. Distracted by the sudden and uninvited interruption, McGurn finished the course with an over par score of eighty-six.

McGurn was then taken to the Chicago police headquarters, where he was formally charged, before being brought before Judge K. I. Franchauser – the presiding judge in his earlier trial of carrying a concealed weapon. This time however, McGurn's lawyers were able to work their magic. They knew of the aspect of the law which stated that, should he attempt to pay the fine, he would have to prove where he obtained the money. They therefore arranged an elaborate charade which would serve to exonerate their client. Louise was called into court along with her friend, whose name is withheld under the Privacy Act. Louise handed over the money with which Jack could pay his $100 fine. As Louise was not officially employed, she was asked where she had obtained the money, to which she replied that she had obtained it from her friend, who was with her in court. The friend was then called forward and asked whether she held any form of legal employment, to which she replied that she did. When asked to state the nature of her employment, she replied that she was a hostess, working at The Green Mill. To the agents' intense chagrin, Judge Franchauser had no option but to accept the fine and release McGurn.

Following this incident, McGurn decided to take the advice of certain aficionados in the world of golf, and it was not long until a Vincent Gebardi enrolled as a golf professional at the Maywood Country Club, Cook County, Chicago. Indeed, it is highly likely that by this time, he was attempting to go straight, for having seen that his professional and personal life with Capone was indefinitely over, he had set out on the long road back to being the reticent young man from Little Sicily.

The second legal manoeuvre involved the new law concerning a person's reputation. On September 10, 1933, McGurn was walking with Louise in the Loop, when a passing patrol car doubled back at the end of the street and pulled up along side the couple. Two patrolmen stepped out, announcing that McGurn was under arrest on a charge of being '*a public nuisance determined by his unsavoury reputation.*' The whole episode had been staged, for September 10, was a Saturday, meaning that a judge would not be available until Monday morning. McGurn was forced to stay in the police cells until such time that he could be brought before a judge to plead his case. It was set never to go that far, for the police knew that in all probability, the presiding judge would throw out the charge. Therefore, as late as possible on Sunday evening, McGurn was suddenly released. The police had managed to inconvenience him for as long as possible, meaning that in their eyes at least, they had achieved their goal.

Frank Nitti meanwhile, was busy putting his plans for the Outfit into action, with each cold and calculated move being orchestrated for maximum effect. He had long since decided that McGurn did not fit in with any of his plans, though he was not about to let that be known immediately. Such a bold and unequivocal move would very likely set about a chain reaction, whereby other influential members would begin getting restless at the thought that the same may happen to them. Concerning McGurn, Nitti's first move had been his subtle demotion, an occurrence that went virtually unheeded. His next move was set to be slightly more dramatic. At the close of 1933, Nitti gave McGurn a Christmas present, in the form of an announcement, informing him that he was no longer needed in any aspect of the security detail. If at such time a further suitable position became available, McGurn would be given first refusal, yet up until that time he was free to spend his time taking care of his *'little club.'* That final part of the announcement, according to later reports, was laced with as much contempt as was humanly possible, for Nitti had recently taken over the previously North Side controlled club, The Rendezvous. This establishment was now double the size of The Green Mill, and so the words *'little club'* were designed to give more than an implied indication of insignificance.

McGurn took the news very badly. Had this happened around four years earlier there would have been little problem, however with the imminent ratification of the Twenty-First Amendment, allowing citizens to drink openly and freely, clubs and speakeasies were losing business hand over fist. This was not unexpected, for theirs had been a supply and demand business, and they could no longer supply that which was no longer demanded. Lady Luck was still on his side however, for The Green Mill had developed such a reputation as a chic and star studded nightspot, that people still continued to go there, though in decidedly fewer numbers than before. Although McGurn still maintained an income, albeit not a legal one, it was now nowhere near the level to which he and Louise had become accustomed and eventually, the time came when they could not afford to keep up their extravagant lifestyle. Before long, couple was forced to move from their palatial home at 1224 to 1130 Kenilworth Avenue.

Despite the fact that the new home was on the same stretch of road, number 1130 was located in a decidedly less affluent part of the neighbourhood, more on the outskirts of Oak Park than in the centre. Numerous stories have grown up around McGurn, often stating that at this point Louise abandoned him, that she was not interested in him now that he was no longer the high flier he once was. Whilst many people believe that the more a fact is accepted, the more truth it inevitably holds, the fact remains that this version of events is decidedly false. Louise did not leave Jack, a fact proven by statements which she made to federal agents, in which she reiterates over and over again her love for Jack, and that like any other devotedly married couple, no matter what life may choose to throw at them, they would face all obstacles together. She goes on to say that she took her wedding vows seriously, and that she would remain at her husband's side as long as he wanted her to be there. This is further proof, should any be needed, that no matter how the relationship may have begun, or whatever outsiders believed their relationship to be, Jack and Louise were head over heels in love with each other, a fact which if the true story of Jack McGurn is to be told, must be established.

McGurn was, at this point in time, in a difficult situation, for whilst he was attempting to go straight, gangland rules meant that he could not simply walk away from the Outfit life. Nevertheless, he was indeed troubled by the treatment that he was receiving from Frank Nitti. He found it difficult to pinpoint where the problem actually lay, for the two men had never been the closest of friends since McGurn was signed up to the Outfit. This question troubled him so much, that he decided to take a trip to Atlanta in order to see Capone, the man whom he still regarded as his boss. The trip was made in January, 1934, though the exact date has long since been irretrievably buried within the annals of criminal history. McGurn found Capone in relatively good spirits, quite surprising when one considers that he was being forced to become accustomed to life on the inside. McGurn talked to his mentor at length, and although Capone was overwhelmingly sympathetic, his hands were tied. Had he been incarcerated in Chicago, then it may have been different, but the distance, combined with the added security that had been placed around him, meant that there was very little he could do. McGurn came away from the meeting with a sense of anxiety, though not necessarily about his situation with Nitti. He had always known Capone as an astute man, fully aware of his surroundings, conscious of everything, oblivious to nothing. Yet on this particular occasion, there were times when Capone seemed distant, distracted, maybe even a little confused. Despite the fact that not a single person was aware of it – not even Capone himself – these were the first symptoms of the Syphilitic paresis to which his brain was succumbing, a condition caused by the untreated Syphilis contracted when he was just a teenager. As McGurn bade Capone farewell, both men were blissfully unaware that this was the last time they would ever see each other.

The second instalment of Nitti's plan regarding Jack McGurn, came into effect around the middle of 1934. Without warning, McGurn was called into the Lexington Suite 202, whereupon he was informed that he was being relieved of The Green Mill. McGurn was astounded, for normally such a move would only be made when there had been a transgression of the rules in one form or another. He requested an explanation over what he had supposedly done wrong, to which the answer was nothing. Nitti explained that the Outfit was moving its operations to Florida, and as such, all excess baggage was being offloaded, baggage which unfortunately for McGurn, included The Green Mill. McGurn told Nitti that he had not been informed of the impending move south, and that he would need time to put his affairs in Chicago in order before he could go anywhere. It was at this point when Nitti chose to inform him that he was not to be included in the trip to Florida, and that he was to remain in Chicago. McGurn was now certain that he had committed some kind of malfeasance, and he questioned Nitti over and over again as to what exactly he had done. Time and again the answer was that he had done nothing wrong, that the move was a simple case of *'housecleaning.'*

However, Nitti was faced with a problem, for gangland rules state that unless an inter-gang crime had been committed, a member could not be left without a source of income. This was a fact to which McGurn now drew Nitti's attention. If he was stripping him of the club ownership, he was bound by the rules to either provide him with another source of income, or prove that some inter-gang malpractice had taken place. As Nitti could not simply conjure up an excuse from thin air, he was obliged to supply an alternative income, though the form of which was not what McGurn had in mind. McGurn was hoping that he would be given another club, at the very least a partnership in one, yet all he was offered was a twenty percent stake in a handbook, or horse race betting establishment. That was the deal in its entirety. Take it or leave it. McGurn was left with very few options, for should he choose to reject the offer, Nitti was then under no obligation to propose anything else. Grudgingly, and against his better judgment, McGurn accepted.

Later that day, as McGurn sat in his semi-palatial home in Oak Park, he found it increasingly difficult to comprehend exactly how this situation in which he now found himself, had come about. No matter how he twisted the events, or from whatever angle he viewed his professional life, he could not pinpoint the precise moment when the obvious hatred which Nitti felt for him, had begun to manifest itself; indeed, until relatively recently, the two men had had little cause to have to deal very much with each other. As McGurn considered the situation, he began to believe that Nitti must be suffering from some kind of paranoia, and that he was convinced that he had to get rid of McGurn before he got rid of him. Studies of various records reveal that McGurn was indeed correct in his conviction, though the paranoia belief was a little less accurate. Nitti had no valid reason whatsoever for loathing McGurn with such venom, in fact the only reason which immediately becomes apparent, is that of bad chemistry accented with more than a hint of jealousy. Nitti believed that McGurn had set out to intentionally undermine what had been his close relationship with Capone, and it was on this point that he had been dwelling for the past three years. Whilst this was certainly a foolish belief, McGurn could nevertheless regard himself as extremely fortunate, for a great number of hoodlums would still be alive, had it not been for the presence of the green-eyed monster.

Over the next few weeks, it became apparent that McGurn was taking his demotion rather badly. Until Frank Nitti had sought his revenge, McGurn had been the owner of one of the most prestigious clubs in Chicago, a glamorous gangster who clad himself in tailor made suits and custom made shoes, a man who regularly played host to the big name stars of the day, who in turn revelled at the prospect of performing before such an infamous audience. Now however, he owned a twenty percent stake in a handbook, and his days were spent chalking betting odds on a blackboard, whilst breathing the cheap cigar smoke that emanated from the throng of gambling junkies, who studied the form of each horse, hoping to double their money just so they could blow it all on the next race. To him, this was not a life, merely an existence. He had made the transition from Vincenzo Gibaldi to 'Machine Gun' Jack McGurn with startling ease and efficiency, however, the return journey was one which he now felt ill equipped to make.

McGurn's mood deteriorated further, when he was forced to sell one of his Packard's in order to supplement the household coffers. Louise had offered to go back to work, for as she pointed out, she sometimes made good money in the chorus lines, and she was sure that she could still do the work. However, McGurn flatly refused, countering that it was one thing for her to do that kind of work in his club, but it was another thing entirely to have her flaunting herself in front of another club owner who would know damned well who her husband was. Besides which, he had certain skills and talents that he was sure would not go unused in gangland.

In order to cope with the stresses and strains of no longer being regarded as a high flier, McGurn immersed himself in various sporting activities. Whilst he still loved to play a round or two on the links, the superior courses were private, open to members only, and whose membership tariffs were now out of his reach. As a substitute, he turned to bowling, and like all the other sports he had sampled over the years, discovered that he was relatively good at the game. He soon established the Avenue Recreation Rooms at 805 Milwaukee Avenue, as his favourite place to play. A two storey establishment, the bowling lanes were located on the upper floor and were owned by William Alloisi, a man who would later describe Jack McGurn as *'a very likeable fellow.'* McGurn became a frequent visitor to the Recreation Rooms, and over the course of time, he and Alloisi would become good friends.

Over a period of a few weeks, McGurn's proficiency was noticed by a group of regulars who had formed a league, and they inquired of McGurn as to whether he would be interested in joining them. They went on to say that they usually played on Friday evenings, starting at around 11pm and ending at around 2am. Apparently, McGurn was delighted with the offer and accepted immediately; perhaps he was attracted by the prospect of once again being involved with a group, a bowling *'outfit'* for want of a better phrase. Certainly, his newfound membership improved his mood no end, for he once again felt that he was involved, that he belonged. As a result, Friday's became his habitual bowling night, and although the play ended at around 2am, the actual evening would only officially end somewhere around 6am. It may be recalled that the downfall of Orazzio Tropea was aided by his being a creature of habit, and in just the same way, it would prove deleterious to McGurn to allow his movements to become so predictable.

★   ★   ★

Every professional man, at some point or another in his professional life, harbours a pet project, a dream with which every fibre of their being yearns to see through to fruition. For the then Attorney General, Homer S. Cummings, the project which formed the make up of his dreams was that of creating a maximum security prison, the likes of which the world had never before seen. (In fact the world had seen something akin to his vision. Named *Devils Island* and located on the most southern of the *Iles de Salut*, off French Guiana in the Caribbean Sea, it was home to a penal colony which had housed mainly political prisoners since 1852.) He dreamed that the prison would be inescapable, and that it would harbour the most dangerous and despicable criminals ever to walk the face of the earth. He had already designated the perfect location, an island situated in the San Francisco Bay, named by its Indian founders as *Isla de Alcatraces*, or *Island of the Pelicans*. Over the years, the title had been Americanized to the name we all know today: *Alcatraz*.

The building which sat atop the island had previously been a military prison, though it had long since been abandoned and allowed to fall into a state of disrepair. What made the location so formidable, was the fact that it was completely surrounded by water, water which was home to sharks and vicious undercurrents that made a swim to the mainland a virtual impossibility. Cummings had channelled funds into restoring the garrison to its former glory, and in July of 1934, the prison which would come to be known as *'The Rock,'* was ready for its first inhabitants. One such soul, Cummings decided, should be the fallen Chicago gang leader, Al Capone.

As promised, in 1935, Frank Nitti moved the headquarters of the Outfit to Florida. The southbound group consisted of Nitti himself, Jake Guzik, Harry Guzik, Jake's brother, and a new rising star within the Outfit, Paul Ricca. The rest of the members remained in Chicago, taking care of the day to day running of the numerous businesses and outlets. The exact reason why Nitti decided to move south remains a mystery, the solution to which is known only by Nitti himself. One theory is that Nitti was under investigation for federal income tax evasion, and therefore considered a move from Chicago to be a wise decision. This however, leaves the question as to why he chose to take Jake and Harry Guzik, plus Paul Ricca, along with him. The answer is relatively simple, in that he did not wish to leave either of the Guzik brothers in charge, believing that they may possibly mount a takeover bid in his absence. Yet he could not ask them alone to accompany him, for that may reveal his doubts about their loyalty, which was why Paul Ricca was also invited along for the ride. Nevertheless, without the benefit of documentary evidence, or indeed an interview with the man himself, this widely accepted fact remains a mere theory.

Before Nitti departed for Florida, he had one more surprise in store for Jack McGurn. Since taking over the Outfit, he had watched the infamous 'Machine Gun' twisting in the wind, being forced to comply with his every decision, no matter how incredulous. McGurn, for his part, was completely oblivious to the trap which Nitti was setting up around him, a trap which would be sprung at any moment. Even as he was called into Nitti's Lexington suite, McGurn was still unaware of the bombshell that was about to hit his world. There was no prolix, indeed Nitti's entire statement was made in an extremely non-pleonastic way. McGurn was out, not just out of the move to Florida, but out of the Outfit entirely. Needless to say, McGurn was stunned by the statement, so much so, that it seemed an age until he managed to inquire as to why. Once again, the answer was straight forward and simple. He was no longer a good enough earner. The set-up suddenly became clear, a tactical manoeuvre of which McGurn himself would have been proud. Subtly and systematically, Nitti had whittled down McGurn's earning capacity to the point where he could legitimately exclude him from all Outfit operations. By first stripping McGurn of his title of head of security, then replacing his ownership of The Green Mill with a twenty percent stake in a hand book, Nitti had made sure that the money now being kicked back to him by McGurn was considerably less than McGurn's salary. As he now explained to McGurn, it was no longer viable to Outfit business to keep him in employment. Before McGurn could present his rebuttal, he was told that he could leave which, in Outfit terms, was a direct order.

Over the duration of time, many stories have grown up around this point in McGurn's life. Whilst many are inconsequential to say the least, the most prominent tale which continually rears its head, regards narcotics. It is said that, having been left without a significant form of income, McGurn was forced to begin dealing in drugs, a business strictly prohibited within the confines of gangland. However, within the numerous files held on Jack McGurn by various agencies, including the FBI, there is no evidence whatsoever to support such a story. Indeed, the only evidence regarding any business ventures at this point in time, refers to the sole illegality of his stake in the hand book. It is therefore to be assumed that such stories regarding narcotics are purely the product of a decade's long game of Chinese Whispers.

McGurn's greatest hope had been that Frank Nitti would be forced to come crawling back, begging for his assistance for the good of the Outfit and himself. This notion had demonstrably been far from what would actually take place, and in a bizarre turn of events, it was McGurn who was forced to do the crawling. During the course of his career, McGurn had made countless enemies, and though many of them had long since been annihilated, a few still remained to harbour their grudges. Whether or not any of them should actually have been regarded as dangerous is difficult to call, as it largely depends on a man's strength of character as to his handling of a problem. Nevertheless, at the close of 1935, McGurn began to receive anonymous threats. Louise would later claim that Jack never took the threats seriously and that neither did she for that matter, for she could not think of a single person who would have any cause to harm her husband. It is possible that McGurn simply played down the threats for the sake of Louise, for further analysis of the records reveal that he did in fact take the threats very seriously indeed. This is demonstrated by a trip he took to Florida in December, 1935, whereupon he met with Nitti, Jake and Harry Guzik, and Paul Ricca. He asked that, should it be proved that his life was in danger, could they offer him protection either in the form of bodyguards, or by putting word on the street that he was off limits. Nitti reminded McGurn that he was now no longer an Outfit member, and therefore, the Outfit were no more obliged to protect his life than they were any other member of the public. Besides which, Nitti harboured nothing but contempt for McGurn, and so it is possible that he actually relished the chance to inform him that both of his requests would be denied.

★ ★ ★

Friday February 14, 1936, and Jack and Louise were planning to spend St. Valentine's Day in each others company. Louise prepared a romantic champagne lunch for them, whilst Jack showered her with chocolates and roses. To round off the day, following their lunch, the couple retired to bed, where they made love before falling asleep in each others arms. Whilst it had been an incredibly romantic day, a day when they both knew just how special they were to each other, they would have undoubtedly made more of it had they known that this was the last day they would ever spend together. Yet life has an unfortunate habit of reminding all of us that it is anything but predictable.

Jack awoke at around 10pm, and bathed, before dressing in white shirt, grey trousers, red braces, black shoes, grey jacket and a heavy black overcoat; despite their financial straits, McGurn always maintained that image was everything. Gently, he woke Louise and reminded her that Friday was his bowling night, and that he was about to leave for the Avenue Recreation Rooms. Sleepily, she kissed him goodbye, blissfully unaware that she was kissing him goodbye forever.

Since the repeal of prohibition, many businesses had been forced to try out new sales techniques, not only to entice new customers onto the premises, but also in an attempt to prevent their existing customers from going elsewhere. Such was the case with the Avenue Recreation Rooms which had, since the ratification of the Twenty-First Amendment, tried out a great many angles with which to boost trade. One such angle was in place on the night of February 14, as William Alloisi had declared this particular evening *'Soft Drinks Night'* when no alcohol whatsoever would be served. A few years ago, such a declaration would have resulted in desertion *en masse*, yet in the current climate, a soft drinks night was indeed a welcome breath of fresh air.

The second floor bowling alley of the Avenue Recreation Rooms was, in essence, a large, brightly lit hall, with a small narrow entrance at the top of a large set of stairs. A long drinks bar stretched along the far left hand wall, with the numerous bowling lanes situated opposite to the right, whilst bench seats and small tables were dotted around the spacious floor. McGurn entered shortly after 11pm, before walking to the bar and ordering nothing more intoxicating than a glass of water. Leaning on the bar for a few moments, he sipped his water as he scanned the room for signs of the rest of the team. People milled about here and there, some watching their friends display their skills, whilst others sipped their drinks and waited for their turn. However, there was as yet no sign of his friends, and so presuming that they must be running a little late, McGurn decided to get in some practice on his own.

He had only been bowling for a few minutes however, when the first two members of the bowling team arrived. The trio exchanged pleasantries, talked about nothing more important than the terrible weather, before they too embarked on a few practice runs. As the minutes ticked by, the trio began to wonder where their friends could be; they all knew that 11pm was the meeting time and it was now almost 11.45pm. Although the three men were quite content with playing each other, the fact that they could not begin their usual league play, was something that was seriously messing up their routine. Nevertheless, there was little else to do except to continue with their practice, for they reasoned that the others must have simply been held up somewhere.

At around midnight, the small door of the Avenue Recreation Rooms once again swung open. Framed in the doorway was the image of three men, each of whom appeared to be holding some kind of object. As they stepped into the full light of the hall, it became apparent that the objects were in fact revolvers. It was William Alloisi who saw them first. Initially, he wondered why the three men held such a curious look, but when he caught sight of their weapons, the reason became all too obvious. He desperately wanted to shout a warning to his patrons, who were still milling around and playing their games, innocently oblivious to the lethal peril which they were undoubtedly in. Alloisi feared that his bowling hall would be rapidly trans-formed into a scene of carnage, yet the bravery which he so badly needed, deserted him and he merely stood behind the bar, petrified with fear. His eyes followed the three men as they now stepped further into the hall; his heart beat hard in his chest as the lead man suddenly waved his revolver in the air and shouted *"Everybody stand where they are…this is a stick-up!"* In the years of prohibition, scenes such as this were all too familiar to native Chicagoans indeed, they had almost been considered an everyday normality. Now in 1936, however, the words took everyone by surprise, so that almost *en bloc,* the entire room – including McGurn – flinched, and then stood statue like, awaiting the gunmen's next instructions.

To some of the braver patrons, that is those who dared to steal a fleeting glance at the gunman triumvirate, it became apparent that robbery was not what these three men had in mind; their expressions were too severe, their eyes too focused for this to be an ordinary stick-up. The room was deathly quiet, though everyone felt deafened by the panicked beating of their own hearts.

Suddenly, everything seemed to dissolve into slow motion, and as the trio walked stealthily across the room, each footstep squeaked on the polished floor, piercing the petrified, anxious silence. The three men stopped close to fifteen feet from where McGurn and his companions were standing, all of whom had their backs to the armed intruders. Slowly and purposefully, the lead man raised his gun and levelled it squarely at the head of McGurn…and then the whole room seemed to explode. Six shots rang out from the revolver, the noise reverberating around the walls, seemingly amplified by the whitewashed brickwork. McGurn caught the first two bullets, with the first hitting him just below the right ear, whilst the second buried itself deep into the nape of his neck. His back arched involuntarily, as though his body were autonomously bracing itself against the searing pain of the hot ammunition. The shots continued to ring out, although these slugs were rendered harmless, caught as they were by the nearby masonry. McGurn's knees buckled underneath him, and he slumped to the floor in a fashion not too dissimilar from that of his own bloodstained victims. As shockingly horrific as the scene was, sheer terror prevented the petrified onlookers from making any verbal reaction; instead they remained in their statue like positions, though the panicked look which passed between them eloquently betrayed the dread that any one of them could be next. With the subtlest of signals, the three gunmen took their leave, but not before one of them had hastily thrown a card near to McGurn's bleeding body. As the triumvirate disappeared out of the doorway, the room returned to normal speed, with the eye witness statues finally able to gasp in horror at the sight which none of them would ever be able to forget. Though the entire hall was coming back to life, the same could not be said for McGurn; Lady Luck, the guardian angel who had unfailingly accompanied him throughout his life, had finally taken her leave and deserted him. The man who had master-minded the most infamous mass slaying in gangland history, the close friend and trusted confidante of the notorious Al Capone, the atypical para-digm of a *'good boy gone bad,'* the notorious 'Machine Gun' Jack McGurn, was dead.

One of the witnesses stooped over the body to read the card that the gunman had thrown. It was a comic Valentine card, and bore a cartoon drawing of a man and woman in their underwear, standing outside a house which had a *'For Sale'* sign attached to it. Next to the house was a pile of furniture, with another sign which read *'House Contents For Sale.'* Underneath was a poignantly tragic Valentine message which read:

> You've lost your job
> You've lost your dough
> Your jewels and cars and handsome houses
> But things could still be worse you know
> At least you haven't lost your trousers.

Within minutes, the police were on the scene, though it did not take them long to figure out what had happened. Usually in a murder inquiry, there is the long drawn out process of identifying the body, though in this instance, that was hardly a problem. McGurn's infamy preceded him, and he was instantly recognizable to the investigating officers. Their first line of thought was that he had been gunned down by his own people, in revenge for some misdemeanour or other. The fact that this could potentially mean that a member of the Outfit may be arrested, meant that Chicago's Police Chief Collins took charge of the investigation. His first action was to dispatch two deputies to the McGurn household on Kenilworth Avenue, so that Louise may be informed of the death of her husband. Whilst they were there, they were to also undertake a sensitive line of questioning, in order to glean any information about who may wish to kill Jack.

The patrol car pulled to the curb outside 1130 Kenilworth Avenue, and the two deputies stepped out and walked towards the front door. To their surprise, it was immediately opened by a sobbing Louise, who announced that she knew why they were there, and that her husband was dead. One of the deputies inquired – rather suspiciously – as to how she knew, when no one except the persons present at the time of the killing, was aware that anything untoward had occurred. Louise replied that around 12.05am, she had been woken by the telephone ringing. When she answered, an anonymous voice asked if it was Louise, and when she replied that it was, the voice said that something terrible had happened to Jack. She said that after that, she knew he was dead. The deputies asked her if she recognized the voice on the other end of the phone, to which she replied that she did not. They then asked if she knew of anyone who would have cause to kill Jack, or any reason which would occasion that kind of order being given. Again the answer was negative. After asking whether she wanted someone to come to stay with her, the two deputies left, with no more information as to the killers identity, and more importantly, no explanation as to why McGurn had been killed in the first place.

The next phase of the investigation centred around the suspicion which hung over the Outfit, especially Frank Nitti. Street gossip meant that it was no secret that Nitti hated McGurn with a vengeance, and therefore, with no other leads, he now became the prime suspect. To the disappointment of the entire police force however, Nitti had a watertight alibi, for not only was he in Florida, but he had also been attending a dinner engagement at the time

McGurn was killed. Of course, no alibi in the world could eliminate the possibility that he gave the order for the killing, yet it would be equally difficult to prove such an accusation.

The investigation was, as always in cases of gangland murders, hampered by uncooperative witnesses. Of all the people that were present at the bowling alley at the time of the killing, only one person claimed to have seen the gunmen, though he admitted that he would be unable to recognize them if he saw them again. With no motive, no suspect, no murder weapon and no witnesses, the investigation began to wind down. This was not to say that the police had placed all their efforts behind finding the killers in the first instance, for as the majority of them were concerned, a dead hoodlum was one less problem for them to deal with. Finally, on March 4, 1936, Frank S. Walsh and James J. Whalen, Cook County Coroner and Deputy Coroner respectively, issued death certificate #6850, which stated that Vincent Gibaldi, aged 32 years, was shot by three unknown men on February 15, 1936, at 12.02am. The cause of death was given as *"multiple (two) bullet wounds of the head."*

Later that morning, it seemed that not a single newspaper, either in Chicago or the rest of the United States, failed to carry the story. The Washington Star for example, carried the headline:

"GANG TRIO SLAY AL CAPONE AID"
MCGURN, FIGURE IN 1929 ST.
VALENTINE DAY MASSACRE,
SHOT IN BOWLING ALLEY.

The story went on to read:

Dapper "Machine Gun" Jack McGurn, former Capone gangster, received a comic valentine and two shots in the back of the head, killing him in much the same fashion as seven George 'Bugs' Moran gangsters died seven years ago in the bloody St. Valentine Day Massacre, for which he was later indicted. The gangster's death came with the same dramatic suddenness as did the massacre of the Moran men. While McGurn and two unidentified companions sat in a second floor bowling alley at 805

Milwaukee Avenue, on the North West side awaiting their turn, three men entered the place and ordered "Stick em up. Stand where you are." McGurn, his back to the men, stood erect. Without another word, the trio opened fire. One shot struck McGurn just behind the right ear and the other in the lower part of the neck. The police called McGurn a cold blooded killer and one of Scarface Al Capone's chief Tommy Gun operators. The deliberate killing came just an hour too late to fall exactly on the seventh anniversary of the massacre of which he was accused.

Every headline and story followed along in the same fashion, with not a single paper failing to mention the infamous massacre. In each instance, the reports carried more of a tone of morbid curiosity, rather than one of shock and horror. Some newspapers attempted to hype the story, by claiming that the killing heralded the beginning of more gang wars, and that the streets of Chicago would once again reverberate with the sound of machine gun fire, as bodies fell in their hundreds onto the sidewalks. The fact was, that there was as much a chance of that happening, as there was of Al Capone receiving a presidential pardon. As with all news, the next day it was old news, and the reporters were soon on the lookout for other happenings with which to fill their pages.

On February 18, 1936, the coffin containing the body of Vincenzo Gibaldi, a.k.a. 'Machine Gun' Jack McGurn, was taken from the Rago Brothers Funeral Home at 624 North Western Avenue, and loaded into the hearse which would take him on his final journey. There was none of the pomp and circumstance which surrounded the funerals of so many of his victims. The only mourners present were the close friends of the family, and the immediate family members. Louise was inconsolable in her grief at the loss of her beloved husband of just four years. His mother Josephine, weak with the pain of losing her eldest son, steadied herself on the arm of a friend. The hearse travelled south along North Western Avenue, heading towards the old Capone territory of the South Side, until it reached the junction of Roosevelt Road. Turning onto Roosevelt, the mourners headed towards the now infamous Mount Carmel Cemetery. The Catholic Church broke with tradition and allowed the body to be buried in consecrated ground, though their reasons are known only to themselves. It seems rather ironic that McGurn should be buried in this location, joining those who had earlier died at his hands. As the casket was lowered into the cemetery's consecrated ground, the presiding priest prayed that god would have mercy on his soul, whilst his wife and mother wept uncontrollably in the finality of their last goodbye. In a telling testament to the confusion surrounding the pronunciation of his surname, his gravestone reads:

BELOVED SON
VINCENT GEBARDI
1902 – 1936

It is also interesting to note, that the gravestone shows his date of birth as 1902. This somewhat contradicts the coroner's report, which indicates the year of his birth to be 1903, however, it is highly likely that his younger brother Anthony, who gave the details to the coroner, was unsure as to the exact year that his brother was born. Of course, had his mother felt strong enough to deal with the coroner herself, she would more than likely have given all the correct details, as she seems to have done for the gravestone. Therefore, whilst the coroner's report states that Vincenzo was thirty-two years old at the time of his death, the ship manifest and various other records, including the FBI's permanent file on Jack McGurn, shows his age as thirty-three years and seven months.

Whilst many theories abound as to the identity of the killers of Jack McGurn, there are two which not only return time after time, but which also makes the most sense. The first theory is that the killing was ordered by Frank Nitti, and carried out by members of the Outfit. Whilst this is entirely possible, given the intense hatred which Nitti felt for McGurn, the killing did not bear any hallmarks of a gangland hit. For example, all three gunmen crossed the floor to be within range of McGurn. In a normal gangland slaying, at least one of the gunmen would have stayed near to the doorway in order to ensure that no one leaves or enters the building, just as they did in the killing of Jack Zuta. Also, the gunmen stopped around fifteen feet from McGurn. Had it been Outfit orchestrated, the gunmen would have had no problem in firing from point blank range, thus making certain that the job was done, and done correctly. In addition to that fact, had the gunmen been professional hit men, it is almost certain that McGurn would have caught more than two shots out of a possible six. The final fact which appears to indicate the likelihood of a non professional hit, is the fact that he was shot in the back of the head. When one looks at the case of Dion O'Banion, or indeed Jack Zuta, where the killing had been ordered out of hatred and necessity, it was deemed essential that the victim faced his killers, so that he could take the vision of who had committed the act against him to the grave. Not only that, but when a victim is facing the gunman, there is every chance that one of the shots will hit him in the face, thus making it impossible for the family to order an open coffin at the wake, something which amongst Italians and Sicilians, is considered the final insult.

The second theory is that McGurn was killed for revenge. It may be recalled that Frank and Pete Gusenburg, two of the victims of the St. Valentine's Day Massacre, had a younger brother, with whom they were to meet on the day they were killed. The idea that it could have been he who killed McGurn, is of course entirely possible, however there is one fact which appears to cast aspersions upon this theory. Whilst many sources lay claim to the fact that McGurn was murdered on St. Valentine's Day, the time of death given on the death certificate is 12.02am. Therefore, McGurn was actually murdered on February 15. However, paradoxically, it is this very fact which gives rise to the plausibility of this theory, indeed it is romantic to believe that the younger Gusenburg brother was acting quixoti-cally in exacting revenge, not only for the death of his siblings, but also for the death of his friends who had died with them. Thus he would wait seven years, one year for each of the victims. His brothers and friends had died on St. Valentine's Day, therefore Jack McGurn, the mastermind behind the killings should also die on that day. Yet, when one is not an experienced killer, the fear factor plays an enormous role within the psyche. Just as McGurn himself had done all those years ago, when he planned the demise of his father's murderers, the idea that he may miscalculate certain aspects of the plan plagued his thoughts. In this respect, could it be that the young brother miscalculated the time, meaning that his victim would actually die a day later than planned? Was it also the fear factor which forced him to shoot McGurn in the back of the head, rather than have him turn around so that he could look into the eyes of his brothers' killer? Or, was it that his brothers had their backs to their killers on that fateful day, meaning that he intended that McGurn would never face his killer?

In the case of Jack McGurn, in spite of all the theories, one factor is one-hundred percent certain. Someone knows who pulled the trigger, indeed, maybe they know that it was they themselves who made the ultimate decision that a man would die. There is now a bizarre and perverse bond between these two people: both have gotten away with murder. Additionally, one tragic aspect remains. So long as men choose to live and die by the gun, the perpetual cycle of violence will never be broken, meaning that there will always be a heartbroken family left to ask why, left to pick up the pieces of their shattered lives.

There is a certain sense of justice in the way in which Jack McGurn met his death. For a man who had led such an intriguingly violent life, it would have seemed rather inappropriate had he died peacefully in his sleep. In spite of the fact that the legend of 'Machine Gun' Jack McGurn lives on in the annals of criminal history, the fact remains that nobody really cared to discover his killer's identity, and it is doubtful that anybody ever will.

CHAPTER TWENTY-THREE

WHAT HAPPENED TO THE PLAYERS?

The torrid tale of Chicago's gangland did not end with the murder of Jack McGurn. Despite the fact that he himself had departed, there were others – whose names have previously been mentioned – who were left behind. It could therefore be considered somewhat of an anticlimax not to make further reference to the fates which befell these fortunate, or as is often the case, unfortunate souls.

FRANK NITTI

In the wake of McGurn's death, Nitti continued to run the Outfit for a further seven years, though his road of power did not run smoothly. In 1937, the Federal government, buoyed by the success it had gained with the prosecution, not only of Capone, but of many more notorious gangsters, indicted Nitti for federal income tax evasion. The case went back and forth from the courts, until the prosecution finally admitted that it had a substantial lack of concrete evidence, forcing the case to be dropped.

At the beginning of 1943, the Federal government, armed with volume upon volume of new evidence, re-indicted Nitti for income tax evasion. They also simultaneously indicted every single one of the remaining Outfit members on the same charge, though admittedly, Nitti was the biggest fish. Seizing the opportunity, the Outfit members met with the government and offered Nitti as the sacrificial lamb, proposing to tell all they knew about any crime he had ever committed, in return for the dropping of the charges against all the other members. The government, seeing that this was a once in a lifetime opportunity, accepted the deal.

Realizing his isolation from friend and foe alike, Frank Nitti was left with a difficult decision. He could either stay and face the music, have his day in court and fight on until the bitter end, or outwit both the government and the Outfit in one fell swoop, and remove himself from the equation. He chose the latter, and on March 19, 1943, Frank Nitti went into the basement of his Chicago home and shot himself with his own revolver, making him the only high profile gangster of the Capone era to commit suicide.

Frank Nitti was buried in Mount Carmel Cemetery, ironically, just a few meters from his nemesis, Jack McGurn.

GEORGE 'BUGS' MORAN

In the aftermath of the St. Valentine's Day Massacre, one may remember Moran's speech to the waiting media, in which he declared that he was through with the rackets, and was effectively announcing his retirement. The risks, he said, now far outweighed the benefits, and he was tired of being forced to look over his shoulder every time he stepped out of his front door. When one considers the source, this address was thoroughly admirable, and appeared to show that Moran did indeed have some gumption after all. However, this was not entirely the case, for although Moran did leave the rackets, and Chicago for that matter, he nevertheless reverted back to the bank robberies of his earlier days. Despite the fact that the rewards from bank hold-ups were far diminished from the wealth he accrued during his prohibition days, this was what Moran did best. To him, a bank heist was as easy as taking candy from a baby.

Moran would have been wise to take into account the law enforcement's opinion of his new found occupation. Whereas it was relatively simple to persuade the correct people to look the other way while you unloaded a shipment of illegal hooch, it was virtually impossible to persuade anyone to turn a blind eye to a bank hold-up. Indeed, the same was true of public opinion, for as far as they were concerned, there was nothing really wrong about beer barons, after all, it was merely supply and demand. Bank hold-ups however, were in their eyes, inherently wrong, a crime for which there was simply no excuse or justification whatsoever.

Eventually, in 1956, the FBI caught up with Moran in Missouri, charging him in connection with a bank robbery that he had committed years earlier. He was tried, convicted, and finally sentenced to ten years imprisonment, time which was to be served at Leavenworth penitentiary.

He was however, set to serve less than a year of his sentence, for later that year he was diagnosed with lung cancer. In spite of a fierce battle against the disease, Moran finally lost the fight in February, 1957. The one time arch enemy of Al Capone was laid to rest in a wooden casket in the prison grounds. Ceremonial observance was not required for a serving felon, and to this day, there stands not so much as a marker to designate his final resting place.

CLAUDE MADDOX

After being McGurn's accessory in the St. Valentine's Day Massacre, before and after the fact, Claude Maddox left St. Louis for his native New York. There he teamed up with various cohorts of Charles 'Lucky' Luciano, who carried out murders at his behest, although they were hardly beholden to Luciano in particular. Instead, their services were offered to anyone who could afford the asking price. Maddox and his band of professional killers were eventually dubbed by the media as *Murder Inc.* Over a period of time, the various members of Murder Inc. were either murdered themselves, or incarcerated for the rest of their lives, until finally there remained just four members, one of which was Maddox.

Realizing that he may be pushing his luck a little too far, Maddox took early retirement, and all but disappeared from the face of the planet. Very little is known about him after this point in time, for his name is recorded in neither the FBI files, nor local police files. In fact, the only occasion after this point when his name does resurface, is on December 28, 1968, when the coroner recorded his death. Whilst rumours abounded that he had died of strychnine poisoning, the pathologist, after discovering no evidence of toxic substances in his system, determined that he had died of a heart attack. Claude Maddox, real name John Moore, was buried in St. Charles Cemetery, New York. His name is recorded in history as one of the few noteworthy gangsters of the Capone era to die of natural causes.

PHILIP D'ANDREA

Upon completing a short sentence for contempt of court, with reference to his carrying a loaded revolver into the trial of Capone, D'Andrea was released from the Cook County Jail, before promptly returning to his Outfit duties. Nitti promoted him to the position previously held by McGurn, that of principal bodyguard and hit man. He remained with the Outfit until 1950, when he was summoned to appear before the Special Investigating Committee on Organized Crime, headed by Senator Estes Kefauver. The committee failed to extract any information of worth from him, as each question was followed by the standard reply that he *'respectfully declined to answer that question on the grounds that he may incriminate himself.'* Perhaps shaken by his subpoenaed appearance before the committee, D'Andrea announced his retirement from the Outfit. On June 5, 1955, he suffered a massive heart attack at his Cicero home. He died almost instantly.

GEORGE EMMERSON Q. JOHNSON

So impressed was the then president of the United States, Herbert Hoover, by George Johnson's successful prosecution of Al Capone, that he recommended him personally for a seat in the Senate. Johnson dutifully obliged the President, and on August 3, 1932, he became Senator elect for the state of Illinois, subject to formal election by the serving senate members. This of course, was merely a formality, and on December 7, 1932, he was officially elected to the Senate and began to look forward with relish to furthering his already illustrious career. His felicity was set to be short lived however, for soon after, the Senate declared that they had not received official confirmation of the appointment, and on March 3, 1933, his service was terminated.

Johnson returned to Chicago, where he opened his own legal practice, specializing in the many and varied aspects of the income tax laws. He remained as head of the practice until his retirement in 1949. George Emmerson Q. Johnson, the man who had succeeded in quelling Capone, died of natural causes on September 19, 1949.

JUDGE JAMES H. WILKERSON

September, 1949, also witnessed the loss of another potent Capone foe, with the death of Judge Wilkerson from natural causes. In the wake of the Capone trial, Judge Wilkerson applied for a confirmation to serve on the bench of the Circuit Court of Appeals. Despite a denial of this request, he nevertheless continued in service at the Federal Court of Chicago, with his indomitable career spanning a further eighteen years.

AL CAPONE

Soon after his transferral to Alcatraz, it was noticed that he was suffering bouts of confusion, often mixed with paranoia. Although it is widely accepted within psychological circles that paranoia erupts in ones mid thirties, and that at the time his paranoia became noticeable, Capone was thirty five, in his case the condition was caused by a medical problem, rather than a psychological one. During his late teens, he began frequenting prostitutes, a practice which continued on into his marriage, only ending upon his incarceration. It is accepted that during one of his first visits to a house of ill repute, he was exposed to the disease known as Syphilis. He was however, not diagnosed as being Syphilitic, until he underwent a thorough medical examination at Alcatraz. This may seem rather bizarre, that a man can live for sixteen years without knowing that he is carrying, what was then a serious disease. Yet Syphilis is a rather silent ailment, in that it only very occasionally produces symptoms, and can only be diagnosed with a blood test. This, combined with the fact that Capone had a pathological fear of anything piercing his skin, were the reasons why it went undiagnosed for so many years.

Unfortunately for Capone, by the time it was determined that it was Syphilis which was the cause of his paranoia and confusion, it was too late. The disease was in what is known as its *'tertiary'* stage, which is when the bacteria or *'spirochetes'* begin to attack the brain itself, thus causing slow dementia, and reducing the immune system to almost nil. Once at this point, the disease is incurable.

Capone was released from Alcatraz on January 6, 1939, to be transferred to a Federal Correctional Institution known as Terminal Island, near Los Angeles. Judge Wilkerson had ordered that the final part of his sentence should be served at Chicago's Cook County Jail, yet Capone was physically and mentally in such a bad way, that it was decided that the long haul to Chicago would be detrimental to his health. Upon arrival at Terminal Island, he was placed under the care of Dr. Hess, who performed a spinal puncture upon Capone, whereupon he concluded that there was nothing that could be done for this patient, save from alleviating the disturbing symptoms. Capone spent ten months at Terminal Island, until he was finally released back into the community on November 25, 1939.

His family took him back to Florida, where he lived out the rest of his days in a perpetual haze. Then on Monday, January 20, 1947, three days after celebrating his forty-eighth birthday, Capone contracted pneumonia. Over the next few days his condition gradually worsened, as his body grew increasingly weak, unable to fight off even the slightest infection. Finally, on Saturday, January 25, 1947, at 7.15am, Capone could fight no more and he died peacefully in his sleep. It appears somewhat ironic that it should be sickness, and not the gun of a rival gangster, which ended his daily battle for survival.

Capone's body was, like so many of his allies and enemies, buried in Chicago's Mount Olivet Cemetery on February 4, 1947, before being transferred, at a later date, to the now famous Mount Carmel Cemetery. Despite the best governmental efforts, it was disease which succeeded in ridding the world of Capone. Nevertheless, it appears to be somewhat of a fitting tribute, that Al Capone, the man who created the inextricable link between the *'Windy City'* and the prohibition era, should return like the prodigal son, to remain in Chicago forever.

LOUISE ROLFE

Soon after the death of Jack McGurn, an automobile owned by Louise, was involved in a fatal road accident. She however, escaped unhurt and uncharged, as a friend had been at the wheel that day. She remained in Chicago, where she remarried a further two times, with each marriage enduring a minimal amount of time. In 1940, the Chicago police arrested and charged her with possession of a revolver, which had been used by her third husband in a bank hold-up. Louise was later released, and the charge dropped, due to the fact that the police could not prove beyond doubt that she had knowledge of the incident. She was arrested again in Michigan in 1943, at which time she was charged and subsequently convicted, of harbouring an army deserter, who happened to be her fourth husband. It seemed that Louise then disappeared for forty years, until 1983, when she resurfaced in San Francisco. She died in 1988, with her body lying in an unknown cemetery in northern California.

JOSEPHINE GIBALDI

Throughout her life, despite the fact that she undoubtedly knew that it was her beloved eldest son who had brought his controlled, yet vicious wrath, down upon those who had robbed his family of a father, she never once made any allusion to the fact. Nor did she make any suggestion which gave any inkling that she knew that his new found wealth was not made altogether legally, even though all the will in the world could not have blinded her to such an axiom. Indeed, whenever any mention was made of her son's reputation, she was swift and unwavering in the defence of his honour. Having been born and raised in Sicily, where society is confronted with the Mafia as a part of daily life, she was impervious to the fact that her son was placing himself on the wrong side of the law. To her, he was the perfect son, just as Angelo had been the perfect husband, both true Sicilians in every sense. In her eyes, Vincenzo could do no wrong and, until the day he died, she was immensely proud of him.

When Vincenzo, or 'Jack', was gunned down in the Avenue Recreation Rooms, Josephine was heartbroken. Her friends claimed that she never quite recovered from the shock of losing her son. Despite the best efforts of her family and friends, she remained grief stricken, and on November 20, 1939, she died. Despite the actual cause of death being given as chronic myocarditis, her family, and moreover her friends, maintained that she died of a broken heart. It seemed as though it was not only Vincenzo who was killed that day, for he took a part of his mother with him, a part which never returned. Josephine was laid to rest in Mount Carmel Cemetery, beside the son whom she loved so dearly. Her gravestone, written in the same fashion as that of Vincenzo, reads simply:

BELOVED MOTHER
JOSEPHINE GEBARDI
DE MORY
1887 – 1939

HELEN JOSEPHINE GIBALDI

Very little, if anything, is known about the daughter of Jack McGurn, with all information seemingly protected by the Privacy Act section of the Freedom of Information Act. Whilst this may seem somewhat of an anticlimax to the story, to Helen, it may be a blessing. Should she still be alive today, and there is every possibility that she may be, there would undoubtedly be many people wishing to track her down, to question her about her past, or her father. Similarly, there would undoubtedly be those unscrupulous members of law enforcement, who would make life intolerable, should they know her history. As Shakespeare wrote in *'The Merchant of Venice,'* *"The sins of the father are to be laid upon the children."* No matter what atrocities may have been perpetrated by Jack McGurn, the fact remains that he was her father and she was his daughter, and surely, that is something which must always be respected.

INDEX